유수연 토익 실전1000제
LC 문제집

커넥츠 영단기

유수연 토익 실전 1000제 LC 문제집

저자	유수연
연구 개발	함연식 조인희 김혜림 김서애 박가영
기획 총괄	공정아
기획 · 편집	정유상
마케팅 · 영업	손지한 김정현 양윤화 김은지 김보경
디자인 총괄	김지원
표지 디자인	이정화
내지 디자인	닷츠
펴낸날	초판 1쇄 2018년 5월 15일
	3쇄 2021년 7월 15일
펴낸이	윤성혁
펴낸곳	(주)에스티유니타스
홈페이지	eng.conects.com
고객센터	1600-1517
주소	서울시 강남구 영동대로 417 오토웨이타워 2F
등록번호	제2015-000186호

머리말

"우리는 오늘도 토익을 준비하고 있다."

취업을 준비하는 우리의 목표는 단기간에 효율적으로 토익 고득점을 만들어 최대한의 경쟁력을 갖추는 것입니다.

그러기 위해서는 우선 토익을 제대로 이해하는 것부터 시작해야 합니다.
우리가 접해 온 수능 영어나 토플은 상위 학습을 위한 지식의 습득을 목표로 하기 때문에 아카데믹한 성향이 강하며, 문장 해석 위주로 내용을 이해하는 것에 초점을 두었습니다. 하지만 토익은 아카데믹한 성향의 수험 영어와는 달리 커뮤니케이션 능력에 중점을 두어 일상생활 또는 국제 업무 등에 필요한 실용 영어 능력을 평가하는 시험입니다.

특히, 토익 LC는 무조건 열심히 듣는다고 고득점이 나오는 것은 아닙니다.
자주 나오는 상황이나 대화 또는 담화의 유형 등을 '눈과 머리'로 먼저 공부한 후 귀로 훈련을 해야 합니다. 아는 만큼 들리는 것이기 때문에 PART별 전략과 패턴들을 습득한 후에 듣기 훈련에 들어가는 것이 효과적입니다.
또한 실전 모의고사를 푼 후에는 항상 푼 문제를 철저히 분석하여 정답과 오답의 패턴을 파악하고 빈출 어휘, 주요 표현 등을 확인하는 과정이 필요합니다.

〈유수연 토익 실전 1000제 LC〉는 수험생 여러분이 단기간에 목표 점수를 달성할 수 있도록 최근 1년간 토익의 출제 경향과 난이도를 완벽히 분석하여 현 토익 트렌드를 정확히 반영한 실전 문제집입니다. 해설에는 토익 LC에 출제되는 정답과 오답 패턴을 수록하여 실전 문제이지만 수험생 여러분이 꼼꼼히 기본기를 다질 수 있도록 제작하였습니다.

경기 침체 속에 취업을 해야 하는 이 어려운 시기에, 여러분의 노력이 최대한의 결과를 가져오기를 희망하며, 단기간에 '토익'이라는 시험을 넘고 좀 더 경쟁력 있는 자신을 만들어 가기 바랍니다.

유수연 드림

유수연의 토익 LC
끝내기 라인업

토익 끝내기 5단계 라인업

기초/입문	기본/중급	실전 대비	최종 점검	시험 직후
영단기 토익 스타트 LC	영단기 토익 LC	유수연 토익 실전 1000제 LC	마라톤 특강	토익 총평 강의

토익 단기 고득점을 위해서는 분명한 공부 전략과 시험에 반드시 나오는 유형만을 짚어 주는 1등 강사에게 배워야 합니다.

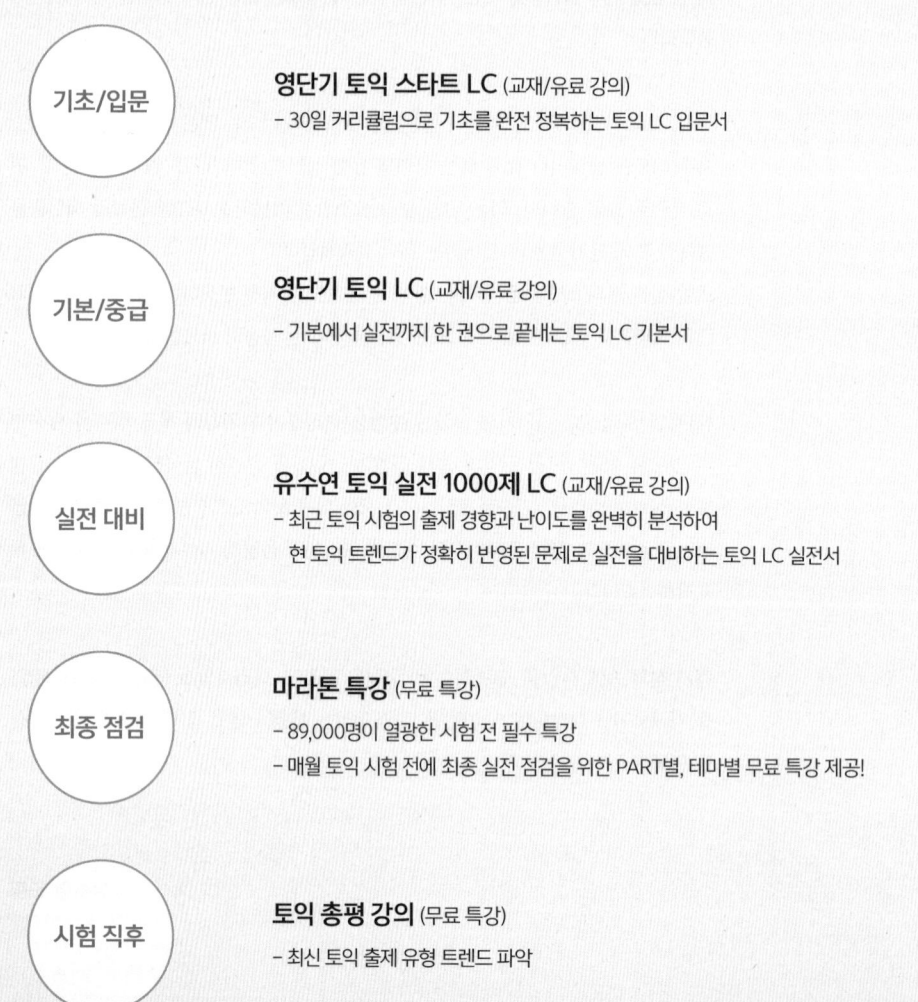

기초/입문

영단기 토익 스타트 LC (교재/유료 강의)
- 30일 커리큘럼으로 기초를 완전 정복하는 토익 LC 입문서

기본/중급

영단기 토익 LC (교재/유료 강의)
- 기본에서 실전까지 한 권으로 끝내는 토익 LC 기본서

실전 대비

유수연 토익 실전 1000제 LC (교재/유료 강의)
- 최근 토익 시험의 출제 경향과 난이도를 완벽히 분석하여
  현 토익 트렌드가 정확히 반영된 문제로 실전을 대비하는 토익 LC 실전서

최종 점검

마라톤 특강 (무료 특강)
- 89,000명이 열광한 시험 전 필수 특강
- 매월 토익 시험 전에 최종 실전 점검을 위한 PART별, 테마별 무료 특강 제공!

시험 직후

토익 총평 강의 (무료 특강)
- 최신 토익 출제 유형 트렌드 파악

유수연의 토익 LC
끝내기 비법 FAQ

Q1	신토익으로 바뀌면서 LC에서 가장 많이 달라진 부분은 무엇인가요?

| A | **1. PART별 문항 수의 변화**
PART 1 10문제 → 6문제
PART 2 30문제 → 25문제
PART 3 30문제 → 39문제
PART 4 30문제 → 30문제 | **2. PART 3, 4에 신유형 문제 추가**
PART 3, 4에서 '화자의 의도 파악 문제'가 각 2, 3문제,
'시각 자료 연계 문제'가 각 3, 2문제씩 출제되며,
PART 3에서 2명의 대화만 나오는 것이 아니라 3명의 대화가 1~2개 출제됩니다. |

Q2	신유형이 추가되면서 난이도의 변화도 있나요?

| A | 네, PART별 문항 수가 변화되고, 신유형 문제가 추가되어 실질적인 난이도가 높아졌습니다.
PART 2에서 직접적인 답변의 출제 빈도는 줄고, 우회성 답변의 출제 빈도가 높아졌습니다.
PART 3, 4의 '화자의 의도 파악 문제'는 대화/담화 속 해당 표현 앞뒤 내용의 정확한 이해가 필요합니다.
PART 3, 4의 '시각 자료 연계 문제'는 대화/담화에서 언급되는 내용과 문제지에 제시된 시각 자료를 연계하여 답을 찾아야 합니다. |

Q3	모의고사 문제를 풀 때 가장 중요한 것은 무엇인가요?

| A | 많은 분들이 실전 감각을 익히기 위해 모의고사로 마무리 학습을 하거나 정기적으로 주 1회 모의고사를 풉니다. 하지만 단순히 모의고사를 많이 푼다고 실전 감각이 생기는 것은 아닙니다. 실전 감각을 익힌다는 것은 실제 시험에서 자신이 아는 것을 최대한 점수로 연결시킬 수 있게 연습을 하는 것입니다. 그러기 위해서는 단 1회의 모의고사를 풀더라도 채점 후 철저한 스크립트 분석과 틀린 문제의 정확한 출제 의도 파악, 잘못된 문제 풀이 접근 방법을 개선하고자 하는 고민과 노력이 필요합니다. |

Q4	선생님이 추천하는 LC PART별 공부법은 무엇인가요?

| A | 모든 PART에서 가장 중요한 것은 스크립트 분석입니다. 문제를 푼 후에는 꼭 스크립트 분석을 하시기를 권합니다.
PART 1, 2는 소거 대상인 오답 어휘를 확인하고 해당 어휘의 정확한 의미와 쓰임을 알아 두시는 것이 중요합니다.
특히 PART 2는 질문의 의도를 알 수 있는 앞에 3~4단어에 표시하고 보기에서 답을 선택해 봅니다. 오답 보기도 그냥 넘어가지 말고, 출제자가 어떤 이유로 이 오답 보기를 출제했는지 5가지 오답 유형에서 확인하기 바랍니다.
PART 3, 4는 문제에서 키워드를 정확히 확인하고 문제의 의도가 무엇인지 적어 둡니다. 그리고 정답의 단서가 대화/담화의 상·중·하 어느 부분에서 언급되는지 표시합니다. 또한 대화/담화의 스크립트를 반복적으로 읽으면서 내용과 흐름을 파악해 두시기 바랍니다. 점수대가 낮은 초급자나 입문자의 경우 해석을 보면서 대화/담화의 내용과 흐름을 파악하는 것이 좋습니다.
마지막 한 가지! 몰랐던 단어나 표현들은 문장이나 구 단위로 소리 내어 읽으면서 암기합니다. |

유수연의 토익 LC PART별 실전 전략

출제 의도를 알아야 토익을 단기간에 끝낼 수 있다.

토익은 출제자의 의도를 정확히 파악해야 단기간에 원하는 점수를 얻을 수 있다. PART 1은 상황별 어휘 및 표현 구사력을 묻고, PART 2는 질문을 빠르게 파악하여 적절한 응답을 고를 수 있는지를 묻는다. 상대적으로 내용이 긴 PART 3, 4는 대화/담화의 상황을 이해하고 필요한 정보를 캐치할 수 있는지 묻는 것이다.

PART 1 기본 문제 풀이 전략

- STEP 1 사진 파악 음성이 나오기 전에 사진을 미리 보고 시선을 떼지 않는다.
- STEP 2 받아쓰기 음성을 들으면서 빠르게 핵심어 1~2단어를 받아쓴다.
- STEP 3 소거법 사진에서 보이지 않는 단어(동사, 명사)가 들리는 보기는 바로 소거한다.
- STEP 4 정답 확인 오답을 먼저 제거하고 남은 것을 정답으로 선택한다.

고난도 문제 풀이 전략

1. 유사한 동작을 묘사하더라도 마지막에 언급되는 명사를 확인하라.
2. 사람 유무에 관계없이 정답이 되는 수동태 진행형(be being p.p.)은 따로 있다.
3. 익숙하지 않은 사물이나 자연 현상을 묘사하는 표현을 확인하라.

PART 2 기본 문제 풀이 전략

- PART 2 문제의 80%는 앞의 3단어에서 답이 결정된다.
- 5가지 오답 유형 제거가 중요하다.
- 문제를 듣자마자 보기가 나오기 전에 15가지 출제 유형을 파악해야 한다.
- 중급자들은 받아쓰기를 위주로, 고득점자는 reaction을 위주로 공부해야 한다.

15가지 출제 유형과 5가지 오답 유형

15가지 출제 유형		5가지 오답 유형
의문사 의문문	1. Who 의문문	
	2. Where 의문문	
	3. When 의문문	
	4. Why 의문문	1. Yes/No 오류
	5. How 의문문	2. 다른 의문사(의도)에 대한 답변
	6. What/Which 의문문	3. 주어(대명사) 오류
일반 조동사 의문문	7. 간접 의문문	4. 유사 발음, 동일/연상 어휘 오류
	8. 조동사 의문문	5. 시제 오류
	9. 선택 의문문	
	10. 권유/제안/요청 의문문	
	11. 부가/부정 의문문	

평서문	12. 평서문	
우회성 답변	13. I don't know	
	14. 반문	
	15. 간접 상황	

PART 3, 4 기본 문제 풀이 전략

- STEP 1 문제의 키워드를 반드시 확인하라.
- STEP 2 키워드를 통해 문제의 의도를 확인하고 대화/담화의 흐름을 예측하라.
- STEP 3 문제의 정답 단서는 문제가 제시된 순서대로 언급된다.

PART 3, 4 불변의 원칙

1. 정답은 대화/담화의 진행 순서대로 등장한다.
2. 질문은 정해진 유형에서 벗어나지 않는다.
3. 대화/담화에서는 구체적인 내용으로 언급되지만 정답은 포괄적인 표현으로 제시된다.
4. man(남자) 질문은 남자의 대사에서 답이 나온다. / 담화의 전개 방식은 패턴화되어 있다.

빈출 문제 유형

- 유형1 기본 정보
  - 대화/담화 상황에 대한 기본적인 정보를 묻는 문제로, 처음 2줄에 정답의 단서가 있는 문제
  - 주제/목적/장소/직업/업종 문제
- 유형2 구체적 정보
  - 대화/담화에서 언급되는 구체적인 내용을 묻는 문제로, 지문 중간에 정답의 단서가 있는 문제
- 유형3 미래 정보
  - 대화/담화 이후에 발생할 내용을 묻는 문제로 마지막 2줄에 정답의 단서가 있는 문제
  - 권유/제안, 요구/요청, next, 미래 시점 문제

신유형 문제 풀이 전략

화자의 의도 파악 문제 풀이 전략	시각 자료 연계 문제 풀이 전략
1. 제시된 문장과 같은 뜻의 보기는 제거한다.	1. 대화/담화에서 직접적으로 언급된 보기는 정답이 아니다.
2. 포괄적으로 상황을 설명한 것이 정답이다.	2. 일정표는 일정의 변경, 취소 등을 확인하라.
3. 대화/담화에서 문제에 제시된 표현이 언급되는 곳 앞뒤에 있는 연결어를 주의한다.	3. 지도 관련 시각 자료는 장소 전치사가 문제 풀이의 핵심이다.
	4. 그래프는 서수, 최상급, 수량에 대한 언급에서 정답을 파악할 수 있다.
	5. 브로셔, 쿠폰, 영수증은 잘못된 정보를 찾는 문제가 주로 나온다.

토익 시험 정보의 모든 것

TOEIC 시험이란?

TEST OF ENGLISH FOR INTERNATIONAL COMMUNICATION의 약자로, 모국어가 영어가 아닌 사람이 일상적인 생활 또는 업무에서 의사소통이 가능한지를 평가하는 시험입니다.

시험 구성

듣기(LC) 4개 PART 100문제와 읽기(RC) 3개 PART 100문제로 총 7개 PART에 걸쳐 200문제가 출제됩니다. 200문제 모두 선택지 중에서 정답을 찾는 객관식 문제로 출제됩니다.

구성	PART 구성	출제 내용	문항수	시간	점수
LC (Listening Comprehension)	PART 1	사진 묘사 (사진 보고 문제 풀기)	6	45분 내외	495점
	PART 2	질문-대답 (질문 듣고 답변 고르기)	25		
	PART 3	짧은 대화 (두 사람 혹은 세 사람의 대화를 듣고 질문에 답하기)	39		
	PART 4	설명문 (전화 메시지, 연설문, 안내 방송, 일기 예보 등을 듣고 질문에 답하기)	30		
RC (Reading Comprehension)	PART 5	문장 빈칸 채우기 (하나의 문장 안에 있는 빈칸에 알맞은 말(문법 & 어휘) 고르기)	30	75분	495점
	PART 6	지문 빈칸 채우기 (짧은 지문 안에 있는 빈칸에 알맞은 말(문법&어휘&문장) 고르기)	16		
	PART 7	싱글 지문 (1개의 지문을 읽고 질문에 답하기)	29		
		더블 지문 (2개의 지문을 읽고 질문에 답하기)	10		
		트리플 지문 (3개의 지문을 읽고 질문에 답하기)	15		
총계			200	약 120분	990점

출제 범위 및 주제

일상생활 및 업무에 대한 영어 의사소통 능력을 평가하기 때문에 특정 분야의 전문 지식 또는 이와 관련된 어휘는 출제하지 않습니다. 국제 업무 환경에 맞게 다양한 국가의 지명과 성명이 등장하며, 듣기 평가에서는 미국, 영국, 호주 발음이 고르게 섞여 출제됩니다. 다음의 주제를 참고해 봅시다.

기업 일반	이사회, 편지, 공지, 전화, 팩스, 이메일, 사무실 장비 및 가구, 사무실 규정, 계약, 협상, 합병 및 인수, 판매, 보증, 사업 계획, 회의, 노사 관계
공식 연회	식사 및 연회, 장소 예약
엔터테인먼트	영화, 공연, 전시
재무	은행 업무, 투자, 세금, 회계, 청구
의료	건강 보험, 병원 방문 및 예약
부동산	건설 및 보수 내역, 부동산 구매 및 임대, 기타 설비
제조	제품 조립, 공장 경영, 품질 관리
인사	모집, 고용, 퇴임, 승진, 급여, 일자리 지원, 구인 광고, 연금, 시상
구매	쇼핑, 주문, 배송, 송장
기술	전자 장비, 기술 지원, 컴퓨터, 연구실과 관련 장비
여행	교통 관련 일정, 교통 관련 각종 공지, 렌터카, 호텔 예약, 연착 및 취소

1. 토익 접수 방법

- 토익 시험의 인터넷 접수 기간을 한국 TOEIC 위원회 사이트(www.toeic.co.kr)에서 확인합니다.
- 사이트에서 인터넷 접수를 선택하고 시험일, 고사장, 수험 정보 등의 정보를 입력합니다.
- 시험 접수 시 최근 6개월 이내 사진(JPG 형식)이 필요하오니 미리 준비합니다.

 약 시험 D-30부터는 특별 추가 접수에 해당하여 5천원 정도의 추가 비용이 발생합니다. 미리 시험을 접수하는 것이 좋습니다.

2. 시험 당일 꼭! 챙겨야 할 준비물

- 규정 신분증

  성인의 경우, 주민등록증, 운전면허증, 기간 만료 전 여권, 공무원증 등이 인정됩니다. 중고등학생에 한하여 학생증(국내 학생증만 허용)도 신분증으로 인정됩니다.

- 연필 (볼펜, 사인펜은 No!)

  연필 끝을 뭉뚝하게 만들어 준비하면 답안 마킹을 더 쉽게 할 수 있습니다.

- 지우개
- 아날로그 손목시계 (전자식 시계는 No!)

3. 입실 전 유의 사항

- 시험 시간이 오전일 경우, 오전 9:20까지, 시험 시간이 오후일 경우 오후 2:20까지 입실합니다.

 오전 시험은 오전 9:50 이후, 오후 시험은 오후 2:50 이후로는 절대 입실할 수 없으니 꼭 시간을 지켜 미리 입실합니다.

시험 시간 직전에는 독해 문제를 풀기보다는 듣기 연습을 충분히 하여 귀를 훈련시키는 게 더 효과적입니다.

4. 시험 진행 안내

오전 시험	오후 시험	시험 진행
9:30~9:45 (15분)	2:30~2:45 (15분)	답안지 작성 오리엔테이션
9:45~9:50 (5분)	2:45~2:50 (5분)	쉬는 시간
9:50~10:05 (15분)	2:50~3:05 (15분)	신분증 확인
10:05~10:10 (5분)	3:05~3:10 (5분)	문제지 배부, 파본 확인
10:10~10:55 (45분)	3:10~3:55 (45분)	듣기 평가 (LC)
10:55~12:10 (75분)	3:55~5:10 (75분)	독해 평가 (RC)

5. 성적 확인 및 성적표 발급 방법 알아보기

- 시험일로부터 10일 후 낮 12시에 한국 TOEIC 위원회 사이트(www.toeic.co.kr)에서 성적 확인이 가능합니다.

  (토요일 시행 시험 등 일부 회차 시험은 11일 후에 발표될 수 있습니다.)

- 성적표 수령은 온라인 출력이나 우편 수령을 택할 수 있습니다.
- 온라인 출력 선택 시, 성적 유효 기간 내 홈페이지에서 출력이 가능합니다.
- 우편 수령 선택 시, 성적 발표 후 접수 시 기입한 주소로 성적표가 우편 발송됩니다. (약 7~10일 소요)
- 온라인 출력과 우편 수령은 1회 발급만 무료이며, 이후에는 유료로 발급됩니다.

유수연 토익 실전 1000제 LC
문제집 사용법

STEP 1

토익
준비 운동하기

토익을 파악하고
전략을 세우자!

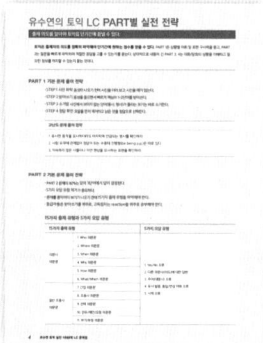

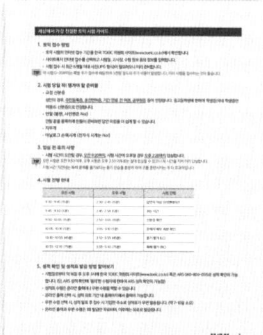

**유수연의 토익 LC
끝내기 비법 FAQ**

토익을 준비하는 수험생들이 자주
하는 질문을 모아 유수연 선생님
만의 핵심 노하우로 상세하게 답
변하였습니다.

**유수연의 토익 LC
PART별 실전 전략**

유수연 선생님의 토익 LC PART
별 기본 문제 풀이 전략을 수록하
였습니다.

**세상에서 가장 친절한
토익 시험 가이드**

토익 접수 방법부터 시험 당일
팁까지 유용한 정보를 수록하
였습니다.

STEP 2

LC 실전
TEST 풀기

토익 출제 경향을
철저히 반영한
새로운 문제!

＋

**시험장 환경에
최대한 가까워지는
구성으로 실전 감각
기르기**

토익 LC 실전 TEST 10회분

〈유수연 토익 실전 1000제 LC 문제집〉은 최신 출제
경향을 철저히 분석하여 제대로 정밀하게 반영하였습니
다. 문제의 배치까지 실제 토익 문제지와 동일하게 구현
하였으므로, 토익 시험에 응시하기 전 실전 TEST 10회
분을 정복하면 진정한 토익 고수가 될 수 있습니다.

ANSWER SHEETS

실제 토익 시험에서는 별도의 마킹 시간이 주어지지 않으므로
녹음 파일의 재생 시간 내에 마킹까지 모두 끝내야 합니다. 반쪽
짜리가 아닌 전체 ANSWER SHEET도 함께 수록하여 문제지와
함께 펼쳐 두고 마킹을 해 보는 연습을 할 수 있습니다.

MP3 다운로드

MP3에 편리하게 접근할 수 있도록 각 TEST 소개 페이지에
QR코드를 실었습니다. MP3는 실제 토익 시험과 동일하게 미국,
영국, 호주 성우가 녹음하였으며, QR코드에는 'TEST, 고속,
고사장 소음, 복습' 총 4가지 버전이 수록되어 있어 다양하게
학습할 수 있습니다.

STEP 3

채점 및 복습하기

자신의 실력을 확인하고 점검하자!

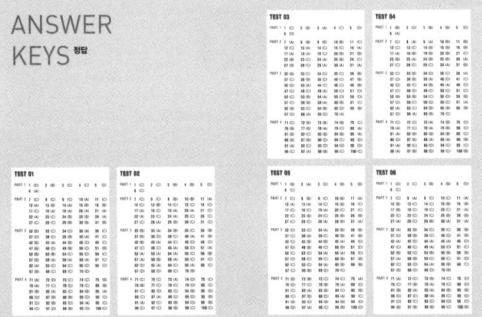

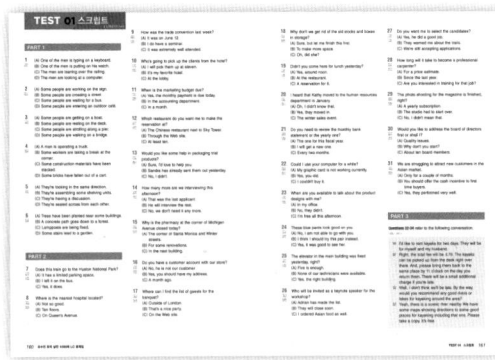

정답표/점수 환산표/점수 향상표

각 TEST를 마친 후 교재 뒤에 수록된 정답표를 통해 채점을 한 뒤, 점수 환산표에서 자신의 점수를 확인하세요. 각 TEST가 끝날 때마다 점수 향상표에 점수를 기록함으로써 자신의 실력을 파악하고 학습 계획을 세울 수 있습니다.

LC 스크립트 전문 수록

1000문제의 녹음 스크립트를 교재 후반에 실었습니다. 문제를 풀면서 잘 안 들렸던 부분이나 놓친 부분을 확인할 수 있고, 틀린 문제의 경우 어느 부분에서 정보를 놓쳤는지를 스크립트를 통해 꼼꼼히 확인하고 다시 반복해서 듣는 연습을 통해 LC 실력을 향상시킬 수 있습니다.

STEP 4

부가 자료 활용하기

토익 고득점으로 가는 가장 빠른 지름길!

꿀팁 추가 자료! 유수연 新토익 공식집과 예습/복습/필기노트 제공 (PDF)
유수연 토익 유료 온라인 강의 수강 시 제공합니다.
(*강좌별로 제공되는 자료는 상이할 수 있습니다.)

토익커들이 열광하는 유수연의 독한 마라톤 특강 (무료)
매월 토익 시험 전, 최종 실전 점검을 위한 PART별, 테마별 무료 특강을 제공합니다.

정확한 분석과 예측이 가능한 토익 총평 강의 (무료)
매월 토익 시험 후, 정확한 분석을 통해 최신 토익 트렌드를 파악할 수 있습니다.

유수연 토익 실전 1000제 LC
해설집 미리보기 [별매]

PART 1 / 2

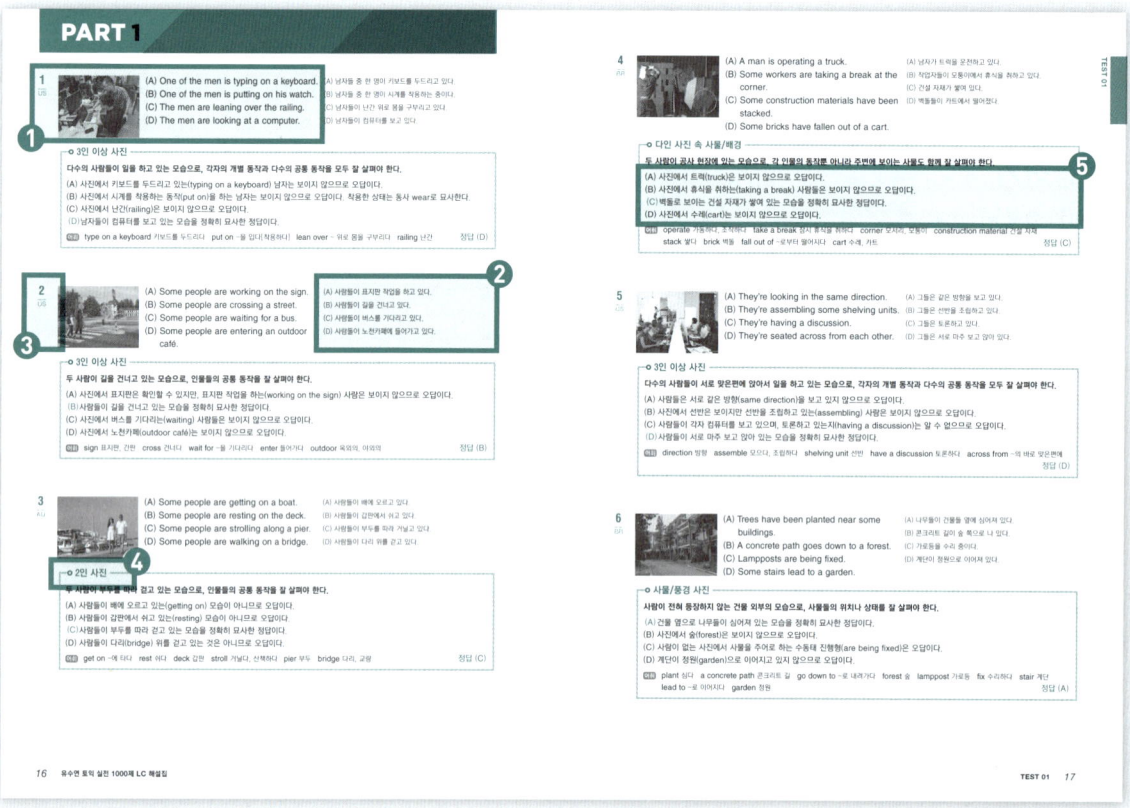

❶ 문제
문제를 그대로 수록하여 문제집을 옆에 같이 펼쳐 놓지 않아도 복습이 가능합니다. 정답은 스크립트에 표시를 하지 않고 문제에서 최대한 먼 곳에 따로 배치하여, 해설을 보기 전에 문제를 다시 한 번 풀어 보며 복습해 볼 수 있도록 하였습니다.

❷ 해석
정확한 한글 해석을 달아서 궁금한 표현은 바로 의미를 확인하고 문장 구조를 파악할 수 있습니다.

❸ 국가별 발음 표시
실제 토익 시험과 동일하게 미국, 영국, 호주 성우가 녹음하였습니다. 문제마다 어떤 나라의 영어 발음인지 확인할 수 있도록 표시하였으므로, 잘 들리지 않았던 부분이 국가별 상이한 발음 때문인지 파악할 수 있습니다. (미국: US 영국: BR 호주: AU)

❹ 문제 유형
실전에 자주 출제되는 문제 유형, 또는 자신이 취약한 유형이 무엇인지 파악할 수 있도록 모든 문제에 문제 유형을 표기하였습니다. 문제 유형은 『영단기 新토익 LC』의 문제 유형 분류를 따르고 있으므로, 취약 유형을 더 깊이 학습하고 싶을 때 쉽게 찾아볼 수 있도록 하였습니다.

❺ 해설
문제에 대한 기본적인 설명을 제시한 뒤, 해설을 알기 쉽게 풀어 썼습니다. 정답의 이유, 전형적인 정답 유형, 오답의 함정 등 자세한 설명을 담았습니다.

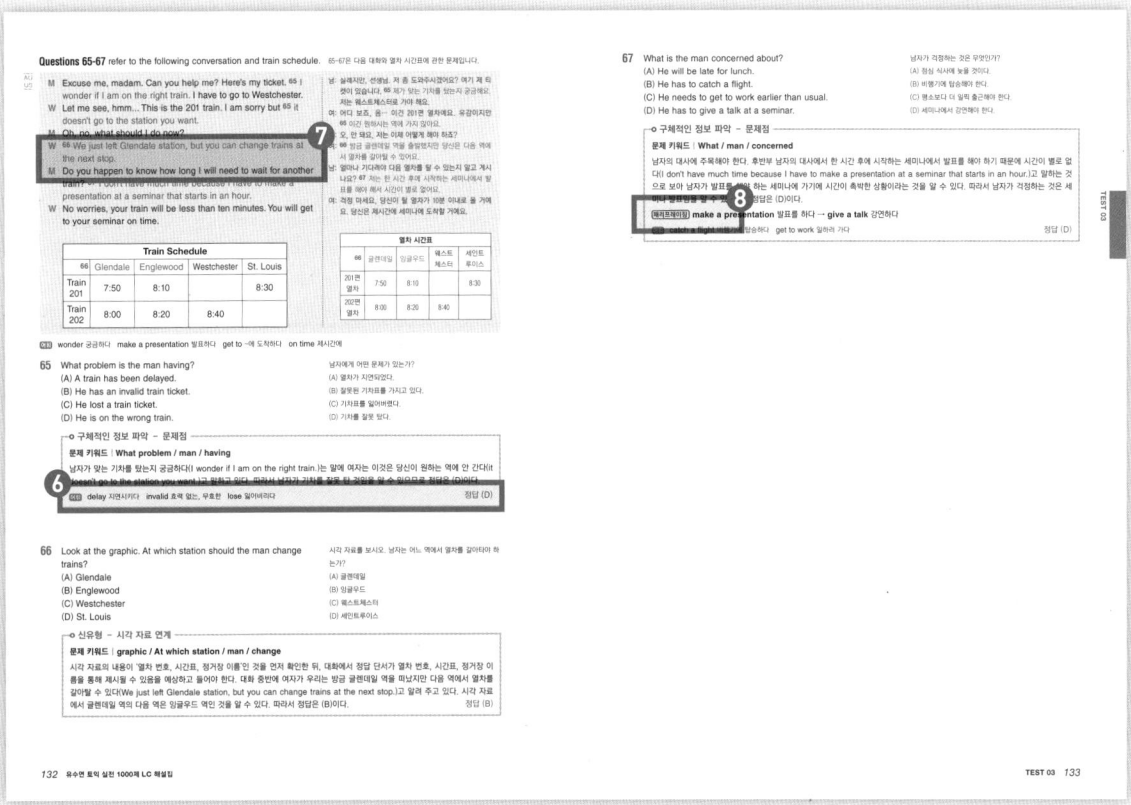

---

❻ 어휘

문제에 나온 중요 단어나 구를 별도로 정리하여 뜻을 모르는 단어를 사전으로 찾아보는 수고를 덜 수 있도록 하였습니다.

---

❼ 정답의 단서 표시

지문에서 정답을 선택하는 데 단서가 되는 부분을 해당 문제 번호와 함께 표시하였습니다. 단서를 통해 문제별로 해당 내용이 나올 위치를 예측하는 연습을 할 수 있습니다.

---

❽ 패러프레이징

대화/담화에서 언급된 정답의 단서가 정답에서 비슷한 표현으로 바꿔서 제시된 경우, 이를 따로 정리하여 한눈에 확인할 수 있도록 하였습니다.

목차 및
학습 플래너

페이지	TEST	공부한 날	TEST 소요 시간	점수	스크립트 페이지	복습 여부
14	**TEST 01**	☐ 월 ☐ 일	녹음 파일의 재생 시간 내에 마킹까지 끝냈나요? ○ l ×	맞은 개수 _____ 환산 점수 _____	160	○ l ×
28	**TEST 02**	☐ 월 ☐ 일	녹음 파일의 재생 시간 내에 마킹까지 끝냈나요? ○ l ×	맞은 개수 _____ 환산 점수 _____	166	○ l ×
42	**TEST 03**	☐ 월 ☐ 일	녹음 파일의 재생 시간 내에 마킹까지 끝냈나요? ○ l ×	맞은 개수 _____ 환산 점수 _____	173	○ l ×
56	**TEST 04**	☐ 월 ☐ 일	녹음 파일의 재생 시간 내에 마킹까지 끝냈나요? ○ l ×	맞은 개수 _____ 환산 점수 _____	179	○ l ×
70	**TEST 05**	☐ 월 ☐ 일	녹음 파일의 재생 시간 내에 마킹까지 끝냈나요? ○ l ×	맞은 개수 _____ 환산 점수 _____	185	○ l ×

*환산 점수는 p. 159의 '점수 환산표'를 참고하세요.

페이지	TEST	공부한 날	TEST 소요 시간	점수	스크립트 페이지	복습 여부
84	**TEST 06**	☐월 ☐일	녹음 파일의 재생 시간 내에 마킹까지 끝냈나요? ○ I ×	맞은 개수 _____ 환산 점수 _____	191	○ I ×
98	**TEST 07**	☐월 ☐일	녹음 파일의 재생 시간 내에 마킹까지 끝냈나요? ○ I ×	맞은 개수 _____ 환산 점수 _____	198	○ I ×
112	**TEST 08**	☐월 ☐일	녹음 파일의 재생 시간 내에 마킹까지 끝냈나요? ○ I ×	맞은 개수 _____ 환산 점수 _____	204	○ I ×
126	**TEST 09**	☐월 ☐일	녹음 파일의 재생 시간 내에 마킹까지 끝냈나요? ○ I ×	맞은 개수 _____ 환산 점수 _____	211	○ I ×
140	**TEST 10**	☐월 ☐일	녹음 파일의 재생 시간 내에 마킹까지 끝냈나요? ○ I ×	맞은 개수 _____ 환산 점수 _____	217	○ I ×

*환산 점수는 p. 159의 '점수 환산표'를 참고하세요.

TEST 01

PART 1
PART 2
PART 3
PART 4

토익 Listening Comprehension은 약 45분 동안 진행됩니다.
반드시 녹음 파일의 재생 시간 내에
모든 문제 풀이를 완료하세요.

LISTENING TEST

In the Listening test, you will be asked to demonstrate how well you understand spoken English. The entire Listening test will last approximately 45 minutes. There are four parts, and directions are given for each part. You must mark your answers on the separate answer sheet. Do not write your answers in your test book.

PART 1

Directions: For each question in this part, you will hear four statements about a picture in your test book. When you hear the statements, you must select the one statement that best describes what you see in the picture. Then find the number of the question on your answer sheet and mark your answer. The statements will not be printed in your test book and will be spoken only one time.

Statement (C), "They are sitting at a table," is the best description of the picture, so you should select answer (C) and mark it on your answer sheet.

1.

2.

GO ON TO THE NEXT PAGE

3.

4.

5.

6.

GO ON TO THE NEXT PAGE

PART 2

Directions: You will hear a question or statement and three responses spoken in English. They will not be printed in your test book and will be spoken only one time. Select the best response to the question or statement and mark the letter (A), (B), or (C) on your answer sheet.

7. Mark your answer on your answer sheet.

8. Mark your answer on your answer sheet.

9. Mark your answer on your answer sheet.

10. Mark your answer on your answer sheet.

11. Mark your answer on your answer sheet.

12. Mark your answer on your answer sheet.

13. Mark your answer on your answer sheet.

14. Mark your answer on your answer sheet.

15. Mark your answer on your answer sheet.

16. Mark your answer on your answer sheet.

17. Mark your answer on your answer sheet.

18. Mark your answer on your answer sheet.

19. Mark your answer on your answer sheet.

20. Mark your answer on your answer sheet.

21. Mark your answer on your answer sheet.

22. Mark your answer on your answer sheet.

23. Mark your answer on your answer sheet.

24. Mark your answer on your answer sheet.

25. Mark your answer on your answer sheet.

26. Mark your answer on your answer sheet.

27. Mark your answer on your answer sheet.

28. Mark your answer on your answer sheet.

29. Mark your answer on your answer sheet.

30. Mark your answer on your answer sheet.

31. Mark your answer on your answer sheet.

PART 3

Directions: You will hear some conversations between two or more people. You will be asked to answer three questions about what the speakers say in each conversation. Select the best response to each question and mark the letter (A), (B), (C), or (D) on your answer sheet. The conversations will not be printed in your test book and will be spoken only one time.

32. What does the woman want to do?

(A) Apply for membership
(B) Rent some leisure equipment
(C) Book a flight ticket
(D) Purchase a map

33. What will happen if the woman is late?

(A) An additional product will be shipped.
(B) A reservation will be canceled.
(C) An extra charge will be added.
(D) An employee will work overtime.

34. What does the man provide to the woman?

(A) A complimentary T-shirt
(B) Some discount vouchers
(C) Some refreshments
(D) A map of the area

35. Why is the woman trying to see Baker?

(A) To submit a form
(B) To conduct an interview
(C) To make a presentation
(D) To ask for some directions

36. Why is Baker not in the office?

(A) He is away on holiday.
(B) He called in sick.
(C) He is meeting a client.
(D) He went to a branch office.

37. What will the woman most likely do next?

(A) Leave for the day
(B) Set up an appointment
(C) Print out some documents
(D) Attend an interview

38. What kind of business do the speakers work for?

(A) A public library
(B) A culinary school
(C) A broadcasting station
(D) A local supermarket

39. According to the woman, what will Erica Riley most likely do?

(A) Purchase some new equipment
(B) Show how to cook a dish
(C) Close a deal with a local business
(D) Autograph her new publications

40. What does the woman say she will do tomorrow?

(A) Review a list
(B) Meet with a chef
(C) Go shopping for some food
(D) Put up a sign for a show

41. What kind of company do the speakers most likely work for?

(A) A delivery service
(B) A repair center
(C) A manufacturing plant
(D) A real estate agency

42. What do the women mention about the problem?

(A) Additional workers are needed.
(B) Equipment is not fast enough.
(C) Some materials are not delivered on time.
(D) Workspace is too small.

43. What does the man suggest doing?

(A) Scheduling a time for a repair
(B) Asking for an inspection
(C) Ordering a new machine
(D) Renewing a warranty

GO ON TO THE NEXT PAGE

44. What is the conversation mainly about?

(A) Conducting research
(B) Developing a marketing strategy
(C) Hiring an advertising agency
(D) Reducing a budget

45. What does the man mention about the product?

(A) It is cheaper than others.
(B) It is no longer available.
(C) It can be purchased only at a store.
(D) It is involved with another company.

46. What does the woman suggest?

(A) Soliciting customer feedback
(B) Offering a free warranty
(C) Providing a discount
(D) Changing a warranty period

47. What is the purpose of the woman's call?

(A) To submit an order
(B) To request some assistance
(C) To advertise a product
(D) To install a software program

48. What does the woman mean when she says, "I'm out of the office at the moment"?

(A) She started her work earlier than usual.
(B) She wants to delay a meeting.
(C) She wants someone to come to her office.
(D) She is not able to give some information.

49. What does the man offer to do for the woman?

(A) Revise a report
(B) Forward instructions by e-mail
(C) Fill out a request form
(D) Reinstall some software

50. Why did the man receive a prize?

(A) For developing a new product
(B) For establishing a good relationship with coworkers
(C) For selling the most products
(D) For working late for a project

51. What will the man do this weekend?

(A) Attend a trade fair
(B) Leave for vacation
(C) Go to another branch
(D) Meet with players

52. According to the man, what will he do with the prize?

(A) Get a refund for it
(B) Give it to someone
(C) Keep it at home
(D) Show it to his friends

53. What has the man been involved in doing?

(A) Scheduling an annual event
(B) Developing a mobile application
(C) Updating client information
(D) Revising a user manual

54. What does the man mean when he says, "someone from the software team might be able to tell you that"?

(A) He is well aware of an issue.
(B) A change will be made.
(C) He is not sure about the answer.
(D) A new project will start soon.

55. What is the woman worried about?

(A) Working overtime
(B) Acquiring wrong data
(C) Organizing a new team
(D) Finishing a project in time

56. Who most likely is the man?

(A) A maintenance worker
(B) A car mechanic
(C) A medical professional
(D) A shop assistant

57. Why does the man want to rent an office on the first floor?

(A) It is located near restaurants and cafés.
(B) It makes it easier for visitors to access his clinic.
(C) It provides a larger space than other offices.
(D) It is much cheaper than offices on other floors.

58. What advantage does the woman mention?

(A) A complex has its own parking area.
(B) A rental fee is not expensive.
(C) Some offices are under renovation.
(D) A complex is conveniently located.

59. Why is the man visiting Horton Marketing?

(A) To discuss a job opportunity
(B) To win a building contract
(C) To sell some products
(D) To make them register for an event

60. According to the man, what are his specialties?

(A) Designing Web pages
(B) Reducing costs
(C) Developing products
(D) Extending a client base

61. Why does the man mention he is quite impressed with Horton?

(A) It is so innovative.
(B) It is an international organization.
(C) It thinks its employees are important.
(D) It provides great employee benefits.

July Travel Itinerary	
Friday, 10th	London
Monday, 13th	Manchester
Tuesday, 14th	Amsterdam
Wednesday, 15th	Firenze

62. What is the woman's team scheduled to do?

(A) Attend a professional conference
(B) Demonstrate a new product
(C) Promote some machines
(D) Develop a new design

63. According to the woman, why do consumers prefer a new design?

(A) It is lightweight.
(B) It is easy to use.
(C) It looks modern.
(D) It is more durable.

64. Look at the graphic. When will the woman's team likely go to Paris?

(A) On Friday
(B) On Tuesday
(C) On Wednesday
(D) On Thursday

GO ON TO THE NEXT PAGE

```
I. Trial Setup          □
II. Regular Setup       □
III. Custom Setup       □
IV. Advanced Setup      □
```

**Outline of
Business Plan**

Section 1 ...... Overview of Business
Section 2 ...... Analysis of Industry
Section 3 ...... Product and Service
Section 4 ...... Sales and Marketing
Section 5 ...... Projection of Budget

65. What does the woman say she wanted to do?

(A) Forward a document to a colleague
(B) Update a Web page
(C) Open some files on her computer
(D) Buy some software programs

66. Look at the graphic. Which option does the man suggest the woman try?

(A) Trial Setup
(B) Regular Setup
(C) Custom Setup
(D) Advanced Setup

67. What will the woman most likely do next?

(A) Print out some documents
(B) Set up a software program
(C) Go to a conference
(D) Prepare a presentation

68. What type of business is the woman trying to start?

(A) A café
(B) A bakery
(C) A hotel
(D) A clothing store

69. According to the woman, what did she learn from her last business?

(A) How to apply for a loan
(B) Where to begin an advertising campaign
(C) How to attract potential customers
(D) Where to start a new business

70. Look at the graphic. Which section of the business plan does the man say needs to be revised?

(A) Section 1
(B) Section 3
(C) Section 4
(D) Section 5

PART 4

Directions: You will hear some talks given by a single speaker. You will be asked to answer three questions about what the speaker says in each talk. Select the best response to each question and mark the letter (A), (B), (C), or (D) on your answer sheet. The talks will not be printed in your test book and will be spoken only one time.

71. Where most likely are the listeners?

(A) At an award banquet
(B) At a wedding reception
(C) At a graduation ceremony
(D) At a fund-raising party

72. What kind of business does the speaker say Ms. Horton runs?

(A) A supermarket
(B) A shoe store
(C) A financial institute
(D) A restaurant

73. How has Ms. Horton helped students carry on their studies?

(A) She has invited many professionals to a school.
(B) She has established some educational institutions.
(C) She has started a scholarship program.
(D) She has given many lectures.

74. What type of business will the listeners work for?

(A) An advertising company
(B) An architectural firm
(C) A market research agency
(D) A food supplier

75. What does the speaker ask the listeners to do before the training?

(A) Revise a handbook
(B) Complete a form
(C) Meet with coworkers
(D) Look around a facility

76. According to the speaker, what is available by the window?

(A) Some refreshments
(B) Information packets
(C) Extra chairs
(D) Company brochures

77. Where most likely are the listeners?

(A) At a hotel
(B) In a local supermarket
(C) At a museum of history
(D) In a sports stadium

78. What does the speaker encourage the listeners to do before they leave?

(A) Obtain a pamphlet
(B) Enjoy some refreshments
(C) Answer a questionnaire
(D) Come by a souvenir store

79. Why does the speaker say, "you can meet some of our restoration specialists"?

(A) To encourage visitors to sign up for another event
(B) To show where to solve a problem
(C) To suggest visitors to obtain more information
(D) To explain why a wing is not accessible

80. Who most likely is leaving the message?

(A) A building inspector
(B) An apartment resident
(C) A city official
(D) A bank teller

81. According to the speaker, what will most likely happen on Wednesday?

(A) An agreement will be signed.
(B) Some family members will come.
(C) A new tenant will move in.
(D) Some construction projects will start.

82. What does the speaker ask the listener to do?

(A) Change a schedule
(B) Arrive early
(C) Pay a visit regularly
(D) Revise a policy

GO ON TO THE NEXT PAGE

83. According to the speaker, what will the listeners need to do by Thursday?

(A) Conduct a survey
(B) Revise a report
(C) Turn in a time sheet
(D) Register for an event

84. What is mentioned as great news to the listeners?

(A) Some employees will be able to take extra time off.
(B) Revenues have risen dramatically.
(C) An employee was promoted to a higher position.
(D) New products will be released soon.

85. Why does the speaker say, "some important clients from Washington are visiting us for a week"?

(A) To make an excuse about a delay
(B) To request more assistance
(C) To explain a new project
(D) To address an important issue

86. What is the broadcast mainly about?

(A) A public park
(B) A new computer system
(C) A package tour
(D) A transportation card

87. What is the reason some commuters are happy with a change?

(A) It is much cheaper.
(B) It is more convenient.
(C) It is far safer.
(D) It is more reliable.

88. According to the speaker, what will happen in July?

(A) Some stations in the town will be closed.
(B) A service will be available in more areas.
(C) Some buildings will be under renovation.
(D) A new system will be introduced.

89. What type of event are the listeners attending?

(A) A social gathering
(B) A board meeting
(C) A financial consultation
(D) A professional seminar

90. According to the speaker, what is a frequent problem for the firm?

(A) Staff members who need more training
(B) Equipment that should be replaced
(C) Misunderstandings of other cultures
(D) Projects requiring more funds

91. What will the listeners do next?

(A) Submit a form
(B) Contact some clients
(C) Fill out a document
(D) Take a look at a brochure

92. What kind of business do the listeners work for?

(A) An electronics manufacturer
(B) A construction company
(C) A travel agency
(D) An online advertising agency

93. According to the speaker, how can the listeners improve efficiency?

(A) By hiring experienced staff
(B) By contracting with a local company
(C) By replacing old equipment
(D) By holding online meetings

94. What does the speaker imply when she says, "Please check your computer is turned on"?

(A) She will now give a demonstration.
(B) She wants to see if a replacement is needed.
(C) She will suggest ways to save energy.
(D) She will use a different computer.

Los Angeles → Grand Canyon

Departure Time : 8:30 A.M.
Arrival Time : 6:00 P.M.
Seat Number : 23A
Platform : 12

Satellite TV Package Options		
Options	Accessible Channels	Monthly Fee
1	National	£10.50
2	National + Movies	£12.95
3	National + Movies + Sports	£17.95
4	National + Movies + Drama	£20.95

95. According to the announcement, what is the main reason of the delay?

(A) System failure
(B) Track maintenance work
(C) Severe weather conditions
(D) Schedule changes

96. Look at the graphic. According to the announcement, which part of information will be updated?

(A) Los Angeles
(B) 8:30 A.M.
(C) 6:00 P.M.
(D) 23A

97. What will be provided to the listeners for free?

(A) Guidebooks
(B) Questionnaires
(C) Full refunds
(D) Vouchers for food

98. Where most likely are the listeners?

(A) At an executive meeting
(B) At a training session
(C) At an opening ceremony
(D) At a trade fair

99. Look at the graphic. What option is described as the best?

(A) Option 1
(B) Option 2
(C) Option 3
(D) Option 4

100. According to the speaker, what incentive will the listeners receive?

(A) Some product samples
(B) Free movie tickets
(C) A monetary prize
(D) Additional time off

This is the end of the Listening test.

정답 p. 156 / 점수 환산표 p. 159 / 스크립트 p. 160

TEST

02

PART 1
PART 2
PART 3
PART 4

토익 Listening Comprehension은 약 45분 동안 진행됩니다.
반드시 녹음 파일의 재생 시간 내에
모든 문제 풀이를 완료하세요.

LISTENING TEST

In the Listening test, you will be asked to demonstrate how well you understand spoken English. The entire Listening test will last approximately 45 minutes. There are four parts, and directions are given for each part. You must mark your answers on the separate answer sheet. Do not write your answers in your test book.

PART 1

Directions: For each question in this part, you will hear four statements about a picture in your test book. When you hear the statements, you must select the one statement that best describes what you see in the picture. Then find the number of the question on your answer sheet and mark your answer. The statements will not be printed in your test book and will be spoken only one time.

Statement (C), "They are sitting at a table," is the best description of the picture, so you should select answer (C) and mark it on your answer sheet.

1.

2.

GO ON TO THE NEXT PAGE

3.

4.

5.

6.

GO ON TO THE NEXT PAGE

PART 2

Directions: You will hear a question or statement and three responses spoken in English. They will not be printed in your test book and will be spoken only one time. Select the best response to the question or statement and mark the letter (A), (B), or (C) on your answer sheet.

7.   Mark your answer on your answer sheet.

8.   Mark your answer on your answer sheet.

9.   Mark your answer on your answer sheet.

10. Mark your answer on your answer sheet.

11. Mark your answer on your answer sheet.

12. Mark your answer on your answer sheet.

13. Mark your answer on your answer sheet.

14. Mark your answer on your answer sheet.

15. Mark your answer on your answer sheet.

16. Mark your answer on your answer sheet.

17. Mark your answer on your answer sheet.

18. Mark your answer on your answer sheet.

19. Mark your answer on your answer sheet.

20. Mark your answer on your answer sheet.

21. Mark your answer on your answer sheet.

22. Mark your answer on your answer sheet.

23. Mark your answer on your answer sheet.

24. Mark your answer on your answer sheet.

25. Mark your answer on your answer sheet.

26. Mark your answer on your answer sheet.

27. Mark your answer on your answer sheet.

28. Mark your answer on your answer sheet.

29. Mark your answer on your answer sheet.

30. Mark your answer on your answer sheet.

31. Mark your answer on your answer sheet.

PART 3

Directions: You will hear some conversations between two or more people. You will be asked to answer three questions about what the speakers say in each conversation. Select the best response to each question and mark the letter (A), (B), (C), or (D) on your answer sheet. The conversations will not be printed in your test book and will be spoken only one time.

32. Where is the conversation taking place?

(A) At a manufacturing plant
(B) At a camera shop
(C) At a photo studio
(D) At a repair center

33. According to the woman, what is the problem?

(A) An item is not working.
(B) A receipt has been misplaced.
(C) A shipment has not arrived.
(D) A product is sold out.

34. What does the man suggest the woman do?

(A) Fill out a survey
(B) Call a manufacturer
(C) Visit a Web site
(D) Consult an instruction manual

35. Who most likely is the woman?

(A) A local farmer
(B) A bus driver
(C) A restaurant employee
(D) An architect

36. How did the men know about the place?

(A) Through an old friend
(B) Through an article in a newspaper
(C) Through an advertisement on the Internet
(D) Through a cooking show

37. According to the woman, what will most likely happen next month?

(A) Some menu items will be unavailable.
(B) A new branch will open.
(C) Prices will be lowered.
(D) A new chef will be hired.

38. What kind of product does the woman want to buy?

(A) Storage cabinets
(B) Wooden counters
(C) Shopping carts
(D) Display shelves

39. According to the woman, what product feature is the most important?

(A) Adjustability
(B) Price
(C) Design
(D) Mobility

40. What does the man advise the woman about?

(A) Sizes
(B) Durability
(C) Current availability
(D) Shipping costs

41. What does the man say has caused a problem?

(A) Technical issues
(B) Severe weather conditions
(C) Errors in a reservation system
(D) High volume of tourist travel

42. What is the woman supposed to do tomorrow evening?

(A) Rent a vehicle
(B) Attend a meeting
(C) See a movie
(D) Prepare a presentation

43. Why does the man say, "we have a few seats left on the 2 P.M. flight"?

(A) To recommend another option
(B) To make a correction
(C) To turn down a request
(D) To transfer a phone call

GO ON TO THE NEXT PAGE

44. What type of business do the speakers most likely work for?

(A) A local nursery
(B) A sports equipment store
(C) An advertising firm
(D) A shoe manufacturing plant

45. What kind of product is being discussed by the speakers?

(A) Suitcases
(B) Workout equipment
(C) Textbooks
(D) Footwear

46. According to the man, what aspect of the product can attract customers?

(A) It is very affordable.
(B) It can be used all year round.
(C) It is available in various designs.
(D) It comes with a lifetime warranty.

47. Why is the man calling the woman?

(A) To give an invitation
(B) To complete a payment
(C) To talk about an order
(D) To ask for additional staff

48. What does the woman mean when she says, "the client requested to use the ingredient"?

(A) Someone has an allergy to some food.
(B) High quality food supplies are required.
(C) Making a change is impossible.
(D) The delivery of materials is running late.

49. What does the man offer to do?

(A) Contact some other businesses
(B) Update a request form
(C) Close a deal
(D) Arrange an event

50. What are the speakers mainly talking about?

(A) Finding a new supplier
(B) Hiring additional employees
(C) Renovating a store
(D) Moving a business to a new location

51. What will the woman do after lunch?

(A) Contact a landlord
(B) Pick up some products
(C) Review a lease agreement
(D) Reschedule a meeting

52. What will the man most likely do next?

(A) Put up some signs
(B) Install new equipment
(C) Take a measurement
(D) Sign a contract

53. Where most likely are the speakers?

(A) At a local outdoor market
(B) At a music concert hall
(C) At a small café
(D) At an orchard

54. Why does the man thank the woman?

(A) He was informed where to go.
(B) He received a discount on some items.
(C) He made a contract with the woman.
(D) He can purchase a ticket for a concert.

55. What will be taking place in the evening?

(A) An award banquet
(B) A cooking show
(C) A musical performance
(D) An annual parade

56. Why does the man thank the woman?

(A) Because of a great review

(B) Because of financial support

(C) Because of participation in an educational program

(D) Because of an advertisement for an exhibit

57. What information does the man try to check with the woman?

(A) Her current address

(B) Her full name

(C) Her ID number

(D) Her membership code

58. According to the man, what will happen in a week?

(A) The gallery will be under renovation.

(B) A gift will be delivered to the woman.

(C) A reporter will get in touch with the woman.

(D) A new exhibit will be open to the public.

59. What is the main reason of the women's trip to Kenton city?

(A) To meet with new clients

(B) To conduct a survey

(C) To see relatives

(D) To attend a conference

60. Why did Karen have some problems?

(A) She missed her flight by mistake.

(B) She has not been trained properly yet.

(C) She did not know well about some information.

(D) She was late for an important client meeting.

61. According to the man, why is a new manual being created?

(A) To update an old version

(B) To distribute them to clients

(C) To help employees

(D) To promote a new product line

Transaction No.	: 9854
Sending from	: Neil Obrien
Received by	: Sean Ortiz
Month/Date	: June 19
Total amount	: £295.00
Transfer fee	: £1.50

62. Look at the graphic. What detail does the man ask about?

(A) The transaction number

(B) The receiver

(C) The total amount

(D) The transfer fee

63. What is the man worried about?

(A) When the money will get to Washington

(B) How he can find another branch

(C) What information is needed to apply for membership

(D) Who can take care of his request

64. What does the man mention about a store?

(A) It will be relocated to a different location.

(B) It has many branches.

(C) It is located near his place.

(D) It is looking for a new employee.

GO ON TO THE NEXT PAGE

Daily Specials

Jacket potato with melted cheese	£4.50
Tuna and mayonnaise sandwich	£6.25
Beef hamburger	£7.00
Roasted chicken salads	£8.00

Drive Slowly Near Gate A	Security Camera Operates 24 hours B
Must NOT Block Gate C	All Visitors Come to the Security Office to Sign in D

65. What most likely is the woman's job?

(A) A server
(B) A delivery person
(C) A factory manager
(D) A food critic

66. What is the reason for making a change in today's specials?

(A) An employee made a mistake.
(B) There have been some customer complaints.
(C) An ingredient is not available.
(D) Some dishes are no longer popular.

67. Look at the graphic. What's the price of the new special?

(A) £4.50
(B) £6.25
(C) £7.00
(D) £8.00

68. Look at the graphic. Which sign does the woman refer to?

(A) Sign A
(B) Sign B
(C) Sign C
(D) Sign D

69. What is the reason of the woman's visit to the facility?

(A) To attend a demonstration
(B) To verify some experiment results
(C) To have a job interview
(D) To repair a vehicle

70. What does the man provide to the woman?

(A) A floor plan
(B) A parking permit
(C) A business card
(D) A request form

PART 4

Directions: You will hear some talks given by a single speaker. You will be asked to answer three questions about what the speaker says in each talk. Select the best response to each question and mark the letter (A), (B), (C), or (D) on your answer sheet. The talks will not be printed in your test book and will be spoken only one time.

71. Why is the speaker calling?
(A) To invite a client to lunch
(B) To set up an appointment
(C) To cancel a meeting
(D) To ask some information

72. What is the speaker doing tomorrow?
(A) Taking a day off
(B) Traveling on business
(C) Giving a tour of the factory
(D) Visiting the clients

73. What does the speaker suggest that the listener do?
(A) Talk to another colleague
(B) Join the project
(C) Borrow a projector
(D) Get a copy of a contract

74. Who most likely is the podcast intended for?
(A) Software developers
(B) Banking professionals
(C) Headhunters
(D) Business owners

75. What is the main topic of today's program?
(A) Managerial skills
(B) Corporate laws
(C) Accounting programs
(D) Public relations

76. What are listeners encouraged to do?
(A) Make a call for questions
(B) Make a financial contribution
(C) Submit a request form
(D) Register for an event

77. What most likely is being advertised?
(A) A sports game
(B) A moving service
(C) A sales event
(D) An opening celebration

78. What product does the business mainly sell?
(A) Sports shoes
(B) Camping gear
(C) Clothes
(D) Tools

79. What does the speaker say customers can do at an online store?
(A) Complete a questionnaire
(B) Pay for a purchase
(C) Apply for membership
(D) Obtain a coupon

80. What is the talk mainly about?
(A) A business event to arrange
(B) Recent changes to a company's policies
(C) Some newly installed software
(D) A coworker's promotion

81. What is Ethel Mason scheduled to do?
(A) Update employees on a project
(B) Reserve a function room
(C) Hold some training sessions
(D) Invite some special speakers

82. What does the speaker encourage the listeners to do?
(A) Back up some files
(B) Print out some instructions
(C) Collaborate with a coworker
(D) Register for a training course

GO ON TO THE NEXT PAGE

83. What kind of product is being discussed by the speaker?
    (A) Presentation equipment
    (B) Office supplies
    (C) Beverages
    (D) Home appliances

84. Why does the speaker say, "we decided to make some changes to our advertising strategy"?
    (A) Because of complaints about a product
    (B) Because of poor sales figures
    (C) Because of scheduling conflicts
    (D) Because of staff shortages

85. What does the speaker encourage the listeners to do?
    (A) Revise a document
    (B) Arrange an event
    (C) Come up with a solution
    (D) Watch a slide presentation

86. What is the main reason the talk is being given?
    (A) To hire some teachers
    (B) To advertise new accounting software
    (C) To welcome participants in an educational program
    (D) To announce a newly elected mayor

87. What does the speaker suggest the listeners do?
    (A) Check jobs posted online
    (B) Focus on just one field
    (C) Update their résumés regularly
    (D) Apply for as many jobs as they can

88. What will the listeners most likely do next?
    (A) See a film
    (B) Take a short break
    (C) Arrange a presentation
    (D) Look around a facility

89. What kind of industry does the speaker work in?
    (A) Accounting service
    (B) Computer engineering
    (C) Legal consulting
    (D) Company training

90. Why does the speaker say, "You can visit our Web site to find out more about it"?
    (A) To leave some comments
    (B) To give an example
    (C) To advertise a new service
    (D) To provide an alternative

91. What does the speaker say she will do this week?
    (A) Go on holiday
    (B) Meet with coordinators
    (C) Attend a conference
    (D) Update a contract

92. What is the speaker discussing?
    (A) Moving some artworks
    (B) Filming a documentary
    (C) Converting data
    (D) Learning at a university

93. What does the speaker say Ms. Moore is pleased about?
    (A) Adding new artworks
    (B) Providing easy access to materials
    (C) Increasing job opportunities
    (D) Offering better working conditions

94. What does the speaker imply when he says, "it was not an easy task"?
    (A) Special care was needed.
    (B) Some residents were against it.
    (C) It was difficult to persuade the investors.
    (D) It took longer than expected.

**Fitted Wardrobe
Installation Handbook**

Contents

Layout 1

Layout 2

Layout 3

Layout 4

95. What type of business do the listeners most likely work for?

(A) An appliance supplier
(B) A furniture manufacturer
(C) A local newspaper
(D) A printing shop

96. Look at the graphic. Which topic will be covered today?

(A) Brief Intro.
(B) Standard Procedures
(C) Personalized Designs
(D) Solutions for Problems

97. What does the speaker indicate about the session after lunch?

(A) New uniforms will be provided.
(B) It will be a little bit delayed.
(C) It will be held in a different area.
(D) ID cards will be issued.

98. What type of event is the speaker most likely talking about?

(A) A board meeting
(B) An annual conference
(C) An orientation for new employees
(D) A preview of a film

99. Why are many more people expected to come to the event?

(A) The venue is much larger than the previous one.
(B) New software is scheduled to be released.
(C) Some top professionals will make presentations.
(D) Free gifts will be given away to attendees.

100. Look at the graphic. Which layout will be used in room 303-A?

(A) Layout 1
(B) Layout 2
(C) Layout 3
(D) Layout 4

This is the end of the Listening test.

정답 p. 156 / 점수 환산표 p. 159 / 스크립트 p. 166

TEST

03

PART 1
PART 2
PART 3
PART 4

토익 Listening Comprehension은 약 45분 동안 진행됩니다.
반드시 녹음 파일의 재생 시간 내에
모든 문제 풀이를 완료하세요.

LISTENING TEST

In the Listening test, you will be asked to demonstrate how well you understand spoken English. The entire Listening test will last approximately 45 minutes. There are four parts, and directions are given for each part. You must mark your answers on the separate answer sheet. Do not write your answers in your test book.

PART 1

Directions: For each question in this part, you will hear four statements about a picture in your test book. When you hear the statements, you must select the one statement that best describes what you see in the picture. Then find the number of the question on your answer sheet and mark your answer. The statements will not be printed in your test book and will be spoken only one time.

Statement (C), "They are sitting at a table," is the best description of the picture, so you should select answer (C) and mark it on your answer sheet.

1.

2.

GO ON TO THE NEXT PAGE

3.

4.

5.

6.

GO ON TO THE NEXT PAGE

PART 2

Directions: You will hear a question or statement and three responses spoken in English. They will not be printed in your test book and will be spoken only one time. Select the best response to the question or statement and mark the letter (A), (B), or (C) on your answer sheet.

7. Mark your answer on your answer sheet.

8. Mark your answer on your answer sheet.

9. Mark your answer on your answer sheet.

10. Mark your answer on your answer sheet.

11. Mark your answer on your answer sheet.

12. Mark your answer on your answer sheet.

13. Mark your answer on your answer sheet.

14. Mark your answer on your answer sheet.

15. Mark your answer on your answer sheet.

16. Mark your answer on your answer sheet.

17. Mark your answer on your answer sheet.

18. Mark your answer on your answer sheet.

19. Mark your answer on your answer sheet.

20. Mark your answer on your answer sheet.

21. Mark your answer on your answer sheet.

22. Mark your answer on your answer sheet.

23. Mark your answer on your answer sheet.

24. Mark your answer on your answer sheet.

25. Mark your answer on your answer sheet.

26. Mark your answer on your answer sheet.

27. Mark your answer on your answer sheet.

28. Mark your answer on your answer sheet.

29. Mark your answer on your answer sheet.

30. Mark your answer on your answer sheet.

31. Mark your answer on your answer sheet.

PART 3

Directions: You will hear some conversations between two or more people. You will be asked to answer three questions about what the speakers say in each conversation. Select the best response to each question and mark the letter (A), (B), (C), or (D) on your answer sheet. The conversations will not be printed in your test book and will be spoken only one time.

32. What issue are the speakers talking about?

(A) Many current clients are unsatisfied.
(B) Some equipment is malfunctioning.
(C) Several products are not available.
(D) A few staff members often come to work late.

33. Where are the speakers most likely working?

(A) At an appliance store
(B) At a service center
(C) At a factory
(D) At a supermarket

34. What does the man ask the woman to do?

(A) Work additional hours
(B) Rearrange some products
(C) Relocate machines to another plant
(D) Check the availability of products

35. What are the speakers mainly talking about?

(A) An annual conference
(B) A job interview
(C) An employee seminar
(D) A new competitor

36. What does the woman say has been changed?

(A) The location of a conference
(B) The time of an event
(C) The list of visitors
(D) The budget for an annual banquet

37. What does the man say about Connie Ray?

(A) He is a fan of her books.
(B) She will retire soon.
(C) He once worked with her.
(D) She has her own company.

38. What is the purpose of the man's visit?

(A) To make a delivery
(B) To have an interview
(C) To inspect a building
(D) To see his acquaintance

39. What does the man need to do to get a visitor's badge?

(A) Provide contact information
(B) Fill out an application form
(C) Proceed to another office
(D) Present some identification

40. How can the man be exempt from the parking fee?

(A) By contacting an office
(B) By leaving the building early
(C) By having a stamp on a ticket
(D) By parking his car in a different location

41. Why does the man say, "I have to get ready for a presentation"?

(A) To extend a deadline
(B) To turn down an invitation
(C) To recommend an alternative
(D) To reschedule an appointment

42. According to the man, what needs to be done for his presentation?

(A) Reviewing some documents
(B) Arranging transportation
(C) Printing an itinerary
(D) Finding a shop to prepare materials

43. What does the woman suggest the man do?

(A) Consult with a hotel staff member
(B) Hold a regular meeting
(C) Reserve a room in advance
(D) Sign up for a training session

GO ON TO THE NEXT PAGE

44. Where most likely are the speakers?

(A) At a service center
(B) At a local clothing shop
(C) At a manufacturing plant
(D) At a car dealership

45. According to the man, what can the women do after the tour?

(A) Go to other facilities
(B) Watch an instructional video
(C) Put on work uniforms
(D) Hear from a manager

46. What does the man say happens on a regular basis?

(A) New uniforms are provided.
(B) Inspections are carried out.
(C) Finished goods are shipped out.
(D) Work shifts are changed.

47. What did the speakers do in February?

(A) They revised a policy.
(B) They conducted a customer survey.
(C) They finished renovating their store.
(D) They started their own business.

48. According to the man, what aspect of the business appeals to customers?

(A) The high quality service
(B) The various items
(C) The affordable prices
(D) The business hours

49. What does the man offer to do?

(A) Call a supplier
(B) Put up a new sign
(C) Rearrange products
(D) Contact a coworker

50. What has the woman not done yet?

(A) Made a reservation
(B) Met with clients
(C) Handed in a form
(D) Replied to an e-mail

51. What does the man mean when he says, "Oh, that's not a big issue"?

(A) He thinks the job is not important.
(B) He is willing to put off a trip.
(C) He is aware of what went wrong.
(D) He can take care of a problem.

52. Why does the woman need to know a link to a software?

(A) To manage her schedules
(B) To report her work hours
(C) To record expenses
(D) To keep track of inventory

53. What kind of business do the speakers work for?

(A) A history museum
(B) An advertising firm
(C) A local newspaper
(D) An appliance dealership

54. What does the man say happened last week?

(A) A deal was closed.
(B) A branch office was reopened.
(C) A facility was acquired.
(D) A new product was released.

55. What will Erma do next?

(A) Complete some forms
(B) Attend a training session
(C) Meet with other managers
(D) Look around the office

56. What type of industry do the speakers most likely work in?

(A) Real estate
(B) Architecture
(C) Accounting
(D) Web design

57. What suggestion does the woman make?

(A) Relocating to a larger office
(B) Rescheduling a meeting
(C) Employing an accountant
(D) Working overtime

58. What does the man mention he will do?

(A) Make a list of businesses
(B) Set up a meeting
(C) Hand in a document
(D) Pick up a coworker

59. What is scheduled to take place during the first weekend of June?

(A) System maintenance
(B) An executive visit
(C) Building renovation
(D) A job interview

60. According to the woman, what will all employees not be able to do?

(A) Enter an office building
(B) Access a network system
(C) Leave work early
(D) Park their cars

61. What will the man most likely do next?

(A) Shut off a computer
(B) Make a reservation
(C) Send an e-mail
(D) Revise a document

Frequent Error Code with Access Card	
ER1-----	Limited Access to Database
ER2-----	System Failure
ER3-----	Damaged Access Card
ER4-----	Defect of Network

62. What department does the man most likely work in?

(A) The facility maintenance
(B) The security team
(C) The research and development
(D) The sales division

63. Look at the graphic. Which error code does the woman notice?

(A) Limited Access to Database
(B) System Failure
(C) Damaged Access Card
(D) Defect of Network

64. Why does the woman need a new card as soon as possible?

(A) She is leaving for a business trip.
(B) She is trying to meet a deadline.
(C) She needs to pick up a client from the airport.
(D) She doesn't want to be late for a meeting.

GO ON TO THE NEXT PAGE

Train Schedule				
	Glendale	Englewood	Westchester	St. Louis
Train 201	7:50	8:10		8:30
Train 202	8:00	8:20	8:40	

65. What problem is the man having?

(A) A train has been delayed.
(B) He has an invalid train ticket.
(C) He lost a train ticket.
(D) He is on the wrong train.

66. Look at the graphic. At which station should the man change trains?

(A) Glendale
(B) Englewood
(C) Westchester
(D) St. Louis

67. What is the man concerned about?

(A) He will be late for lunch.
(B) He has to catch a flight.
(C) He needs to get to work earlier than usual.
(D) He has to give a talk at a seminar.

Terms of Warranty
-Limitations-

The following cases won't be covered :
1. Items purchased over two years ago
2. Non-Adams components
3. Missing items
4. Damaged items by accident

68. What kind of product are the speakers discussing?

(A) A mobile device
(B) A copy machine
(C) A projector
(D) A television set

69. Look at the graphic. Which case does the man refer to?

(A) Case 1
(B) Case 2
(C) Case 3
(D) Case 4

70. What will the man most likely do next?

(A) Show a cost estimate
(B) Order some new products
(C) Fill out a request form
(D) Provide a brochure

PART 4

Directions: You will hear some talks given by a single speaker. You will be asked to answer three questions about what the speaker says in each talk. Select the best response to each question and mark the letter (A), (B), (C), or (D) on your answer sheet. The talks will not be printed in your test book and will be spoken only one time.

71. Why does the speaker say, "Four months can be too long for our customers to wait for an order"?
(A) To cancel an order
(B) To compensate customers for inconvenience
(C) To acknowledge some complaints
(D) To blame current workers

72. According to the speaker, what will happen later this week?
(A) An employee will be transferred to another branch.
(B) New work crews will join the company.
(C) Some products are going to be discontinued.
(D) A store will hold a promotional event.

73. Why does the speaker ask for some help?
(A) To prepare a presentation
(B) To pick up a new machine
(C) To fix some broken equipment
(D) To reorganize some products

74. What type of business does the speaker work for?
(A) A food manufacturer
(B) A tour agency
(C) A restaurant
(D) A hotel chain

75. What project is the speaker discussing?
(A) Merging companies
(B) Updating technology
(C) Expanding a market
(D) Purchasing a building

76. What does the business decide to do?
(A) Research other hotels
(B) Carry out a survey
(C) Change a plan
(D) Design a program

77. Where most likely are the listeners?
(A) In a theater
(B) In an art museum
(C) In a clothing store
(D) In a company headquarters

78. What is mentioned about the paintings?
(A) Their sizes are so small.
(B) One of them won an award.
(C) Their materials are very unique.
(D) One of them is for sale.

79. What are the listeners advised to do before they start?
(A) Obtain an information packet
(B) Register for a seminar
(C) Store their personal items
(D) Apply for membership

80. Who most likely are the listeners?
(A) New staff members
(B) Some tourists
(C) Company executives
(D) Volunteer workers

81. Why does the speaker say, "All the areas in the building are equipped with a security system"?
(A) A facility has recently been renovated.
(B) Employees need to carry their badges.
(C) Employees should come to work on time.
(D) A building requires regular maintenance.

82. According to the speaker, what information is incorrect?
(A) Some items in a menu
(B) A list of clients
(C) A floor plan
(D) Working hours

GO ON TO THE NEXT PAGE ➡

83. Where do the listeners most likely work?

(A) At an international travel agency
(B) At a shoe manufacturing company
(C) At a marketing firm
(D) At a sports center

84. What is the speaker mainly talking about?

(A) A revised dress code
(B) A new product line
(C) An upcoming seminar
(D) A new hire

85. What will most likely happen next?

(A) A presenter will talk about a marketing plan.
(B) Some directions to an office will be described.
(C) New product designs will be introduced.
(D) An advertisement will be filmed.

86. What is the main purpose of the man's call?

(A) To apply for an open position
(B) To inquire about his paycheck
(C) To ask for a loan
(D) To submit an order

87. What information does the speaker mention has been changed?

(A) A meeting schedule
(B) A current mailing address
(C) An office location
(D) A phone number

88. What does the speaker imply when he says, "but I need to pay some bills"?

(A) He is still looking for a job.
(B) He is reluctant to make a change.
(C) He wants to correct wrong information.
(D) He expects a quick response.

89. What is the talk mainly about?

(A) A movie release
(B) A book publishing firm
(C) A project for new writers
(D) A new educational course

90. What are the participants in the project asked to do?

(A) Write regular columns
(B) Go on a book tour
(C) Make a donation to charity
(D) Arrange educational programs

91. What will most likely happen next?

(A) Some writers will give a speech.
(B) An award will be given to a winner.
(C) Several films will be screened.
(D) An annual banquet will start.

92. Where most likely are the listeners?

(A) At a conference
(B) At an electronics store
(C) At a manufacturing facility
(D) At an office supply shop

93. What does the speaker ask the listeners to do at the beginning of every shift?

(A) Keep track of inventory
(B) Wear protective gear
(C) Report their work hours
(D) Clean some machines

94. According to the speaker, what will be done next?

(A) A lunch break will start.
(B) Some samples will be distributed.
(C) Questionnaires will be filled out.
(D) A demonstration will be given.

Friday schedule	
10:00 A.M.	Staff Meeting
Noon	Lunch with Clients
13:00 P.M.	Interview
14:00 P.M.	Meeting with RF Recreation
15:30 P.M.	Seminar at Headquarters

Shop Information
Fourth floor: Furniture, Household Appliances, Restaurant & Café
Third Floor: Women's Clothing
Second Floor: Men's Clothing & Sportswear
First Floor: Cosmetics & Accessories

95. What does the speaker want to discuss?

(A) A sales policy
(B) An annual sports event
(C) A messenger service
(D) A trade show

96. Look at the graphic. Which of the speaker's appointments was canceled?

(A) Staff meeting
(B) Interview
(C) Meeting with RF Recreation
(D) Seminar at Headquarters

97. What is the listener asked to do?

(A) Bring some samples
(B) Calculate an estimate
(C) Set up an interview time
(D) Send an updated résumé

98. What is the main reason for holding a sales event?

(A) To make room for new products
(B) To celebrate an anniversary
(C) To promote a new store
(D) To express appreciation to customers

99. Look at the graphic. On which floor will the prices be lowered next week?

(A) The fourth floor
(B) The third floor
(C) The second floor
(D) The first floor

100. What does the speaker say the customers can obtain at the entrance?

(A) A list of local businesses
(B) Some free samples
(C) A brochure
(D) Transportation information

This is the end of the Listening test.

정답 p. 157 / 점수 환산표 p. 159 / 스크립트 p. 173

TEST

04

PART 1
PART 2
PART 3
PART 4

토익 Listening Comprehension은 약 45분 동안 진행됩니다.
반드시 녹음 파일의 재생 시간 내에
모든 문제 풀이를 완료하세요.

LISTENING TEST

In the Listening test, you will be asked to demonstrate how well you understand spoken English. The entire Listening test will last approximately 45 minutes. There are four parts, and directions are given for each part. You must mark your answers on the separate answer sheet. Do not write your answers in your test book.

PART 1

Directions: For each question in this part, you will hear four statements about a picture in your test book. When you hear the statements, you must select the one statement that best describes what you see in the picture. Then find the number of the question on your answer sheet and mark your answer. The statements will not be printed in your test book and will be spoken only one time.

Statement (C), "They are sitting at a table," is the best description of the picture, so you should select answer (C) and mark it on your answer sheet.

1.

2.

GO ON TO THE NEXT PAGE

3.

4.

5.

6.

GO ON TO THE NEXT PAGE

PART 2

Directions: You will hear a question or statement and three responses spoken in English. They will not be printed in your test book and will be spoken only one time. Select the best response to the question or statement and mark the letter (A), (B), or (C) on your answer sheet.

7. Mark your answer on your answer sheet.

8. Mark your answer on your answer sheet.

9. Mark your answer on your answer sheet.

10. Mark your answer on your answer sheet.

11. Mark your answer on your answer sheet.

12. Mark your answer on your answer sheet.

13. Mark your answer on your answer sheet.

14. Mark your answer on your answer sheet.

15. Mark your answer on your answer sheet.

16. Mark your answer on your answer sheet.

17. Mark your answer on your answer sheet.

18. Mark your answer on your answer sheet.

19. Mark your answer on your answer sheet.

20. Mark your answer on your answer sheet.

21. Mark your answer on your answer sheet.

22. Mark your answer on your answer sheet.

23. Mark your answer on your answer sheet.

24. Mark your answer on your answer sheet.

25. Mark your answer on your answer sheet.

26. Mark your answer on your answer sheet.

27. Mark your answer on your answer sheet.

28. Mark your answer on your answer sheet.

29. Mark your answer on your answer sheet.

30. Mark your answer on your answer sheet.

31. Mark your answer on your answer sheet.

PART 3

Directions: You will hear some conversations between two or more people. You will be asked to answer three questions about what the speakers say in each conversation. Select the best response to each question and mark the letter (A), (B), (C), or (D) on your answer sheet. The conversations will not be printed in your test book and will be spoken only one time.

32. Where is the conversation taking place?
(A) At a bank
(B) At a supermarket
(C) At a clinic
(D) In a restaurant

33. What did the woman tell the man to do on the phone?
(A) Send an invoice
(B) Bring a form
(C) Visit a warehouse
(D) Complete a proposal

34. What does the woman ask for?
(A) A ticket
(B) A coupon
(C) Contact information
(D) Identification

35. What does the man ask the woman to do?
(A) Review presentation materials
(B) Order new computers
(C) Fix some light fixtures
(D) Reschedule a meeting

36. Why is the woman not able to go to the meeting room right now?
(A) She has to do other work.
(B) She is having a break.
(C) She is not feeling well.
(D) She cannot find some data.

37. What will the man most likely do today?
(A) Go on a business trip
(B) Revise some information
(C) Complete a request form
(D) Make a presentation

38. What is the purpose of the man's call?
(A) To make comments
(B) To resubscribe to a publication
(C) To update personal information
(D) To request a repair service

39. What does the woman apologize for?
(A) A discount is not applicable.
(B) Operating hours have changed.
(C) A magazine will be discontinued.
(D) No employee is available.

40. What will the woman most likely do next?
(A) Change a venue
(B) Meet with a client
(C) Have a break
(D) Forward a booklet

41. What problem are the speakers talking about?
(A) An outdated facility
(B) A shortage of skilled staff
(C) Decreasing ticket sales
(D) Customer complaints

42. According to the woman, what should be considered?
(A) Organizing various shows
(B) Expanding a facility
(C) Hiring new performers
(D) Putting in more advertising effort

43. What will be held this week?
(A) An interview
(B) A new product release
(C) A budget meeting
(D) An anniversary party

GO ON TO THE NEXT PAGE

44. Where do the speakers work?

    (A) At a utility company
    (B) At a food service business
    (C) At an educational institution
    (D) At a health care center

45. What does the man mean when he says, "She'll be there early in the afternoon"?

    (A) He may encounter a scheduling conflict.
    (B) He needs to leave in the middle of the day.
    (C) He has already met a repair person before.
    (D) He can change his schedule.

46. What does the man mention about Janet?

    (A) She has recently participated in a training course.
    (B) She is more skilled than any other employees.
    (C) She just came back from her holiday.
    (D) She is willing to work additional hours.

47. Who is Rubin Williams?

    (A) A hotel manager
    (B) A product designer
    (C) A Web design specialist
    (D) A magazine editor

48. What will take place tomorrow?

    (A) An orientation session
    (B) A site inspection
    (C) A company banquet
    (D) A staff seminar

49. What will the woman and Rubin Williams do next?

    (A) Conduct an interview
    (B) Welcome some guests
    (C) Go to the reception area
    (D) Attend a meeting

50. What are the speakers mainly talking about?

    (A) Whom to invite to a seminar
    (B) Where to hold an annual event
    (C) How to draw more applicants
    (D) When to leave for an interview

51. What suggestion does the man make?

    (A) Hiring an advertising company
    (B) Shortening the interview process
    (C) Contacting a local college
    (D) Lowering an enrollment fee

52. What does the woman suggest doing?

    (A) Arranging a conference room
    (B) Delaying a deadline
    (C) Consulting with a coworker
    (D) Searching for other information sources

53. What is the woman asked to do?

    (A) Solve a problem
    (B) Go over some slides
    (C) Send out invitations
    (D) Postpone an event

54. What is the man going to do this afternoon?

    (A) Request some help
    (B) Arrange important materials
    (C) Reserve a flight ticket
    (D) Book a hotel room

55. What does the man imply when he says, "I've only recently started my new job"?

    (A) He is unwilling to transfer to another department.
    (B) He wants to express his appreciation for a promotion.
    (C) He is trying to make an excuse for some mistakes.
    (D) He is worried about doing an important task by himself.

56. Where do the speakers most likely work?

(A) At a hospital
(B) At a pharmaceutical company
(C) At an advertising agency
(D) At a department store

57. What problem does the man report?

(A) A product is not attractive to some people.
(B) A company's sales are declining.
(C) A work team needs more members.
(D) A product has a problem.

58. What will the speakers most likely do next?

(A) Develop a new medicine
(B) Launch another product
(C) Change a project timeline
(D) Take some work home

---

59. What division does the woman want to reach?

(A) Archives
(B) Accounting
(C) Customer service
(D) Personnel

60. What is the main reason of the woman's call?

(A) To arrange a meeting
(B) To request technical support
(C) To ask about a vacation policy
(D) To order office supplies

61. What does the man offer to do for the woman?

(A) Sign up for an event
(B) Give contact information
(C) Hand in a receipt
(D) Book a meeting room

Monthly Report	
Equipment Maintenance	£9,500
Shipping Service	£11,000
Facility Rental	£10,000
Supplies	£20,000

62. What type of merchandise does the company produce?

(A) Shoes
(B) Shipping trucks
(C) Appliances
(D) Office equipment

63. What does the woman mention about the report?

(A) The company did not meet their goal.
(B) Some figures are wrong.
(C) The company's expenses have gone up.
(D) A report is not prepared.

64. Look at the graphic. Which amount does the woman say needs to be changed?

(A) £9,500
(B) £11,000
(C) £10,000
(D) £20,000

GO ON TO THE NEXT PAGE

④	Fitness Center	
③	Food Court	
②	Law Offices	
①	Lobby	

65. What problem does the woman mention?

(A) The elevator is out of order.
(B) She cannot find an office.
(C) Some documents have been misplaced.
(D) Some equipment is malfunctioning.

66. Look at the graphic. On which floor does the conversation take place?

(A) Floor 4
(B) Floor 3
(C) Floor 2
(D) Floor 1

67. What does the man say he will do for the woman?

(A) Deliver a memo
(B) Notify a lawyer of a delay
(C) Help the woman fill out some paperwork
(D) Take the woman to a location

Beijing to Vancouver		
Flight No.	**Departure**	**Arrival**
203	8:25 AM	2:00 PM
205	9:25 AM	1:10 PM
312	3:05 PM	7:25 PM
405	4:35 PM	8:35 PM

68. What does the woman apologize for?

(A) A reservation cannot be made online.
(B) A service is temporarily not available.
(C) A ticket is no longer valid.
(D) A flight has been fully booked.

69. Look at the graphic. Which flight ticket will the man most likely book?

(A) Flight No. 203
(B) Flight No. 205
(C) Flight No. 312
(D) Flight No. 405

70. What does the man say he is planning to do in Vancouver?

(A) Meet his relatives
(B) Demonstrate some products
(C) Attend an important meeting
(D) Start his new job

PART 4

Directions: You will hear some talks given by a single speaker. You will be asked to answer three questions about what the speaker says in each talk. Select the best response to each question and mark the letter (A), (B), (C), or (D) on your answer sheet. The talks will not be printed in your test book and will be spoken only one time.

71. Where does the speaker most likely work?

(A) At a delivery company
(B) At a hospital
(C) At a restaurant
(D) At a food mart

72. Why is the listener asked to get to work early today?

(A) To remove some equipment
(B) To receive a phone call
(C) To arrange for an event
(D) To take care of a shipment

73. What most likely will the listener be allowed to do?

(A) Take some time off
(B) Get a bonus
(C) Transfer to another branch
(D) Attend a training session

74. What is the instruction mainly about?

(A) Applying for an ID badge
(B) Completing paperwork
(C) Registering for a training session
(D) Updating a computer system

75. What does the speaker say would happen if the listeners miss a deadline?

(A) Some shipments will be delayed.
(B) A project will not be approved.
(C) Some employees will work overtime.
(D) A payment will not be provided on time.

76. What will the speaker most likely do next?

(A) Receive questions
(B) Print out some documents
(C) Go to another office
(D) Conduct an interview

77. What department do the listeners most likely work in?

(A) Accounting and auditing
(B) Recruiting and training
(C) Warehousing and shipping
(D) Sales and marketing

78. What does the speaker mean when he says, "a box will be placed in the staff lounge"?

(A) A solution will apply to a problem.
(B) An additional supply is arriving soon.
(C) A project needs to be delayed.
(D) Some space is going to be expanded.

79. What will happen every Monday morning?

(A) A meeting will take place.
(B) Feedback will be summarized.
(C) Facilities will be inspected.
(D) A shipment will be sent.

80. What is the speaker mainly talking about?

(A) An annual town festival
(B) A road construction plan
(C) A town's seasonal programs
(D) An educational course

81. What will most likely be changed soon?

(A) The transportation fee
(B) The location of a town center
(C) The tax rates for local businesses
(D) The director of a local authority

82. What will the listeners probably do next?

(A) Organize a training event
(B) Share the latest news
(C) Order office supplies
(D) Meet with a new colleague

GO ON TO THE NEXT PAGE

83. Why does the speaker say, "Traffic is really backed up now"?

(A) To advise the listener to take a detour
(B) To give an excuse
(C) To ask the listener to leave early
(D) To postpone a schedule

84. What will the speaker e-mail to the listener?

(A) Promotional materials
(B) An agenda
(C) Some guest files
(D) Some driving directions

85. What will the speaker ask Timmy to do?

(A) Set up a conference call
(B) Text a message
(C) Circulate some materials
(D) Conduct some research

86. What type of business does Mr. Stone work for?

(A) A computer manufacturing firm
(B) A broadcasting station
(C) A construction company
(D) A software developer

87. What is the purpose of the software system Mr. Stone developed?

(A) To handle accounting work quickly
(B) To help schedule a meeting
(C) To take care of client information
(D) To keep track of inventory

88. What does the speaker ask the listeners to do?

(A) Provide new topic ideas
(B) Make a phone call to ask questions
(C) Try the latest product
(D) Sign up for an event

89. What does the speaker thank the listener for?

(A) Providing training
(B) Reserving a flight
(C) Contacting a business
(D) Placing an order

90. What does the speaker imply when he says, "I'm just about to board a flight"?

(A) He will not arrive on time.
(B) He cannot respond immediately.
(C) He does not need a ride.
(D) He forgot to bring an itinerary.

91. According to the speaker, what will take place tomorrow?

(A) Some clients will visit.
(B) A new shipment will arrive.
(C) A dinner reception will be held.
(D) New employees will start the job.

92. What is mainly discussed in the news report?

(A) A company acquisition
(B) A new transportation system
(C) A new recycling policy
(D) A town election

93. According to the news report, why is the new system not implemented immediately?

(A) To take a public-opinion poll
(B) To renovate an old facility
(C) To create a news release
(D) To conduct an investigation

94. What does the speaker encourage listeners to do?

(A) Submit an entry
(B) Register for a contest
(C) Express their opinions
(D) Attend a council meeting

TRAIN (Blue Line) SCHEDULE	
Beckton Ave.	6:45
Bermondsey Rd.	7:05
Devons St.	7:35
Putney Bridge	7:55

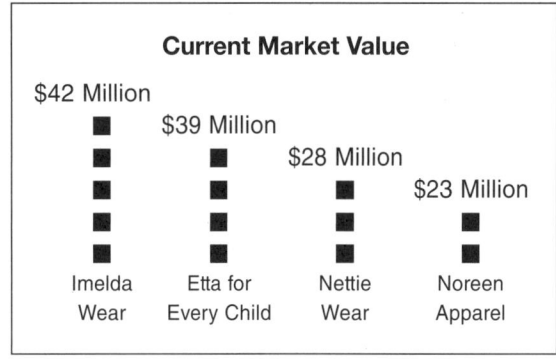

Current Market Value

$42 Million

$39 Million

$28 Million

$23 Million

| Imelda Wear | Etta for Every Child | Nettie Wear | Noreen Apparel |

95. What type of business does the speaker most likely work for?

(A) A local hotel
(B) An employment agency
(C) A real estate office
(D) A moving company

96. According to the speaker, what does the listener need to do before moving in?

(A) Obtain some keys
(B) Sign a contract
(C) Make payments
(D) Pick up a vehicle

97. Look at the graphic. Which train should the listener take?

(A) Train 6:45
(B) Train 7:05
(C) Train 7:35
(D) Train 7:55

98. Who is the talk most likely intended for?

(A) New employees
(B) Sales representatives
(C) Business owners
(D) Members of the board

99. Look at the graphic. Which company will most likely be acquired?

(A) Imelda Wear
(B) Etta for Every Child
(C) Nettie Wear
(D) Noreen Apparel

100. What will Wendy West talk about next?

(A) A project deadline
(B) Changes to some leadership
(C) A promotion budget
(D) Career development opportunities

This is the end of the Listening test.

정답 p. 157 / 점수 환산표 p. 159 / 스크립트 p. 179

TEST

PART 1
PART 2
PART 3
PART 4

토익 Listening Comprehension은 약 45분 동안 진행됩니다.
반드시 녹음 파일의 재생 시간 내에
모든 문제 풀이를 완료하세요.

LISTENING TEST

In the Listening test, you will be asked to demonstrate how well you understand spoken English. The entire Listening test will last approximately 45 minutes. There are four parts, and directions are given for each part. You must mark your answers on the separate answer sheet. Do not write your answers in your test book.

PART 1

Directions: For each question in this part, you will hear four statements about a picture in your test book. When you hear the statements, you must select the one statement that best describes what you see in the picture. Then find the number of the question on your answer sheet and mark your answer. The statements will not be printed in your test book and will be spoken only one time.

Statement (C), "They are sitting at a table," is the best description of the picture, so you should select answer (C) and mark it on your answer sheet.

1.

2.

GO ON TO THE NEXT PAGE

3.

4.

5.

6.

GO ON TO THE NEXT PAGE

PART 2

Directions: You will hear a question or statement and three responses spoken in English. They will not be printed in your test book and will be spoken only one time. Select the best response to the question or statement and mark the letter (A), (B), or (C) on your answer sheet.

7. Mark your answer on your answer sheet.

8. Mark your answer on your answer sheet.

9. Mark your answer on your answer sheet.

10. Mark your answer on your answer sheet.

11. Mark your answer on your answer sheet.

12. Mark your answer on your answer sheet.

13. Mark your answer on your answer sheet.

14. Mark your answer on your answer sheet.

15. Mark your answer on your answer sheet.

16. Mark your answer on your answer sheet.

17. Mark your answer on your answer sheet.

18. Mark your answer on your answer sheet.

19. Mark your answer on your answer sheet.

20. Mark your answer on your answer sheet.

21. Mark your answer on your answer sheet.

22. Mark your answer on your answer sheet.

23. Mark your answer on your answer sheet.

24. Mark your answer on your answer sheet.

25. Mark your answer on your answer sheet.

26. Mark your answer on your answer sheet.

27. Mark your answer on your answer sheet.

28. Mark your answer on your answer sheet.

29. Mark your answer on your answer sheet.

30. Mark your answer on your answer sheet.

31. Mark your answer on your answer sheet.

PART 3

Directions: You will hear some conversations between two or more people. You will be asked to answer three questions about what the speakers say in each conversation. Select the best response to each question and mark the letter (A), (B), (C), or (D) on your answer sheet. The conversations will not be printed in your test book and will be spoken only one time.

32. What does the woman comment on about the company cafeteria?

(A) Its low number of diners
(B) Its skilled servers
(C) Its opening hours
(D) Its limited menu items

33. What does the man suggest the woman do?

(A) Leave work early
(B) Skip a meal
(C) Order some food
(D) Hand in a request

34. Why does the woman not want to accept the man's recommendation?

(A) She is reluctant to spend extra money.
(B) She does not know how to drive.
(C) She does not have any free time.
(D) She has no contact information.

35. What is the purpose of the man's call?

(A) To sign up for an event
(B) To ask about accommodation
(C) To confirm a hotel reservation
(D) To check the location

36. What does the woman say will be offered?

(A) Complimentary meals during an event
(B) A discount on some hotels
(C) A free shuttle bus service
(D) Maps for an area

37. Why does the woman apologize?

(A) Tickets are sold out.
(B) She has incorrect information.
(C) Some benefits are limited.
(D) Accommodation is unavailable.

38. What do the women intend to do?

(A) Arrange for a video conference
(B) Request some extra equipment
(C) Prepare a business trip
(D) Apply for financial support

39. According to the women, who is the man?

(A) An event organizer
(B) A maintenance worker
(C) An office manager
(D) A security guard

40. What does the man suggest the women do?

(A) Consult a note
(B) Use another room
(C) Leave some comments
(D) Purchase new equipment

41. Why does the woman like the complex's location?

(A) The rental fee is not so high.
(B) Travel costs can be reduced.
(C) It has a great view of the area.
(D) It is close to public transportation.

42. What is mentioned about the woman's company?

(A) It was recently established.
(B) It is growing rapidly.
(C) It doesn't have many staff members.
(D) It will merge with another company.

43. What does the man indicate about the lease contract?

(A) A deposit must be paid in advance.
(B) Tenants can access some shared spaces.
(C) The contract needs to be renewed every year.
(D) A space will be renovated soon.

GO ON TO THE NEXT PAGE

44. Where most likely are the speakers?

    (A) At a job interview
    (B) At an annual conference
    (C) At a business luncheon
    (D) At an award banquet

45. What does the man's organization carry?

    (A) Office equipment
    (B) Home appliances
    (C) Potted plants
    (D) Delivery vehicles

46. What will the woman most likely do this week?

    (A) Visit a client's office
    (B) Attend another event
    (C) Go on a business trip abroad
    (D) Contact the man for more information

47. What has the man done recently?

    (A) He has opened his own store.
    (B) He has come back from his business trip.
    (C) He has designed some new furniture.
    (D) He has transferred to a new branch.

48. Why does the woman mention a particular store?

    (A) It offers a free guide.
    (B) Its prices are inexpensive.
    (C) It is near her office.
    (D) Its workers are well trained.

49. What does the woman offer to do?

    (A) E-mail a client
    (B) Share her vehicle
    (C) Talk with a colleague
    (D) Search for other stores

50. What are the speakers talking about?

    (A) Arranging a party
    (B) Refurbishing a lounge
    (C) Developing new products
    (D) Buying office equipment

51. What will most likely happen in the first week of March?

    (A) A company will be closed.
    (B) Some employees will be retiring.
    (C) Several workshops for staff will take place.
    (D) An event for new employees will be held.

52. What does the woman say she will send today?

    (A) A blueprint
    (B) A copy of a brochure
    (C) An estimate
    (D) A list of local vendors

53. What type of business does the woman work for?

    (A) A toy store
    (B) A flower store
    (C) A bakery
    (D) A restaurant

54. Why does the woman say, "Did you see the pictures of our cakes"?

    (A) She wanted the man to see their product decorations.
    (B) She would like to change a birthday cake.
    (C) She is offering a special price.
    (D) She forgot to tell the man the delivery time.

55. What does the woman say she will do on Monday?

    (A) Deliver an order in the morning
    (B) Bring an item back to her home
    (C) Attend an event
    (D) Purchase some toys

56. What kind of event are the speakers talking about?

(A) A training seminar
(B) A job interview
(C) A retirement party
(D) A business trip

57. What problem does the woman mention occurred last quarter?

(A) A travel document was misplaced.
(B) Some flights were canceled.
(C) No room was available.
(D) Travel costs were too high.

58. What will Lewis most likely do next?

(A) Book flight tickets
(B) Complete an itinerary
(C) Call a company
(D) Request full payment

59. What are the speakers mainly talking about?

(A) A regular meeting
(B) A tour to a research lab
(C) A construction project
(D) A job interview

60. Why does the woman say, "Do we still have to complete the drawings by the beginning of next week"?

(A) She does not want to work overtime.
(B) She is not happy with a situation.
(C) She did not know an exact schedule.
(D) She was planning to go on a holiday.

61. What does the man say he will do next?

(A) Inspect a research facility
(B) Change his schedule
(C) Meet with a client
(D) Arrange a meeting

We invite you to a Special Banquet!
Friday, June 19, 6:30 P.M.
Please Reply to Paul Taylor 332-3429

Meal Choices:
A. Beef Steak
B. Chicken Pasta
C. Mushroom Soup Noodle
D. Tofu Steak with Honey Sauce

---

62. What type of event will the woman be attending?

(A) An awards banquet
(B) A farewell party
(C) A charity gala
(D) An opening ceremony

63. Look at the graphic. Which meal choice will the woman have?

(A) Option A
(B) Option B
(C) Option C
(D) Option D

64. What does the man suggest the woman do?

(A) Arrive in advance
(B) Bring a present
(C) Take a free parking ticket
(D) Dress formally

GO ON TO THE NEXT PAGE

Shelf 4	Accessories		T-shirts
Shelf 3	Jackets	Jackets	Jackets
Shelf 2	Coats	Coats	Coats
Shelf 1	Trousers		Shirts

65. According to the man, what needs to be done?

(A) Delivering some items
(B) Making room for new products
(C) Decorating a store
(D) Designing a new sign

66. Look at the graphic. Which shelf will be rearranged by the woman today?

(A) Shelf 4
(B) Shelf 3
(C) Shelf 2
(D) Shelf 1

67. What does the man ask the woman to do?

(A) Put up some signs
(B) Clean the staff lounge
(C) Bring a display shelf
(D) Contact an employee

**Town Concert Hall Introduces
A Summer Performance**

Ticket Office Hours	2:00 P.M.-7:00 P.M.
Open Doors	6:00 P.M.
Concert Starts	7:00 P.M.
Limit Entrance	After 7:15 P.M.

68. Look at the graphic. What time will the speakers most likely get to the concert hall?

(A) At 2:00 P.M.
(B) At 6:00 P.M.
(C) At 7:00 P.M.
(D) At 7:15 P.M.

69. Why does the woman mention people like the concert?

(A) It has been praised by critics.
(B) It is held in a historic venue.
(C) It is very popular around the world.
(D) It is played by a local band.

70. What does the woman suggest they do before the concert?

(A) Obtain a pamphlet
(B) Meet with friends
(C) Eat a meal
(D) Finish a report

Directions: You will hear some talks given by a single speaker. You will be asked to answer three questions about what the speaker says in each talk. Select the best response to each question and mark the letter (A), (B), (C), or (D) on your answer sheet. The talks will not be printed in your test book and will be spoken only one time.

71. What is the announcement mainly about?

(A) Safety regulations
(B) A health exam
(C) Factory equipment
(D) A training session

72. According to the speaker, who will visit the factory?

(A) Inspectors
(B) Health professionals
(C) Mechanics
(D) Overseas clients

73. What will listeners do at the end of the meeting?

(A) Provide feedback
(B) Speak to a manager
(C) Complete a form
(D) Check their e-mails

74. What is the broadcast mainly about?

(A) A museum's opening celebration
(B) A town's election result
(C) A change in the ownership of a building
(D) A new hotel construction project

75. According to the speaker, why was Megan Construction chosen?

(A) Because of its experience
(B) Because of its location
(C) Because of its estimate
(D) Because of its licence

76. What is the town expecting once the renovation is complete?

(A) A new transportation system
(B) More employment opportunities
(C) Modernization of the town
(D) An increase in tourism

77. What event is being organized?

(A) An opening ceremony
(B) A trade fair
(C) A farewell party
(D) A training session

78. What does the speaker mean when she says, "you know about fifty people will be attending"?

(A) More people than expected will come to an event.
(B) A suggested place is not large enough.
(C) The budget for an event is limited.
(D) A venue is too far away.

79. What will the speaker most likely do on Thursday?

(A) Have a meeting
(B) Book a restaurant
(C) Tour a city
(D) Complete a form

80. Why is the talk being given?

(A) To announce a change to a policy
(B) To celebrate an anniversary
(C) To introduce a new staff member
(D) To inform employees of an award winner

81. According to the speaker, what has gone up significantly?

(A) The number of employees
(B) Yearly production rate
(C) The volume of traffic on a Web site
(D) Annual total expenditures

82. What will Phyllis Russell be doing next month?

(A) Leading a course
(B) Interviewing job applicants
(C) Introducing a new software program
(D) Arranging an award banquet

GO ON TO THE NEXT PAGE

83. What field do the listeners most likely work in?

(A) Online marketing
(B) Real estate
(C) Lodging industry
(D) Food and beverage

84. What does the speaker imply when she says, "I hope everyone is wearing comfortable shoes"?

(A) Participants need to move quickly.
(B) Some tasks will be harder than expected.
(C) An event tends to involve a lot of walking.
(D) Some items are already sold out.

85. According to the speaker, what is difficult for her?

(A) Obtaining good products
(B) Stepping down from a position
(C) Reserving a venue
(D) Inviting some presenters

86. Where most likely are the listeners?

(A) On a train
(B) At a local bookstore
(C) On an aircraft
(D) At a cinema

87. What kind of service is mainly explained by the speaker?

(A) Meal options
(B) Entertainment
(C) Membership
(D) Rental cars

88. According to the speaker, what needs to be done to use a new service?

(A) Filling out a request form
(B) Registering in advance
(C) Calling an attendant
(D) Using a credit card

89. What is the main issue the company has been encountering over the last few months?

(A) They have been facing intensive competition.
(B) They have been understaffed.
(C) They have not been able to meet their manufacturing goals.
(D) They have failed to launch a new product.

90. What does the speaker imply when he says, "this is very important to our firm's success"?

(A) He is trying to recognize the listeners' hard work.
(B) He is looking for an alternative method.
(C) He wants employees to attend an event.
(D) He is willing to fill a client's order.

91. What will the listeners receive after the workshop?

(A) A list of local businesses
(B) A survey sheet
(C) A revised schedule
(D) An order form

92. What type of business does the listener most likely work for?

(A) A hotel
(B) A plant
(C) A grocery store
(D) A restaurant

93. What is the problem the speaker mentions?

(A) A decrease in sales
(B) A staff shortage
(C) A defective product
(D) A road closure

94. What will the speaker make sure the listener does?

(A) Take additional days off
(B) Leave work earlier than other staff
(C) Receive compensation for extra work
(D) Participate in an event

Wearable Device Components	
Covers : 2 Options	**Sizes : 3 Options**
Classic Modern	43 mm (for men) 39 mm (for women) 33 mm (for kids)
Bands : 4 Options	**Colors : 5 Options**
Leather Cloth Metal Rubber	Blue Red Yellow Green Striped Navy Striped

95. What is the talk mainly about?

(A) A database for target customers
(B) A marketing campaign
(C) A launching event
(D) Progress on a product development

96. Look at the graphic. Which option quantity will increase next month?

(A) 2
(B) 3
(C) 4
(D) 5

97. What is the speaker excited about?

(A) Contracts from other countries
(B) An opportunity to attend an event
(C) Newly opened branches
(D) An increased market share

Membership Application Form	
£20 Basic _____	£80 Standard _____
£40 Premier _____	£160 Platinum _____
Full Name: _____	
Mailing address: _____	
Credit Card Detail [Number and Expiration Date]	
_____ (__ / __)	

98. Where do the listeners work?

(A) At a theater
(B) At a sports center
(C) At a gallery
(D) At a city park

99. Why does the speaker thank some employees?

(A) For registering for a training session
(B) For giving assistance with a project
(C) For creating a new application form
(D) For purchasing a membership

100. Look at the graphic. Which amount has been changed this season?

(A) £20
(B) £40
(C) £80
(D) £160

This is the end of the Listening test.

정답 p. 157 / 점수 환산표 p. 159 / 스크립트 p. 185

TEST

06

PART 1
PART 2
PART 3
PART 4

토익 Listening Comprehension은 약 45분 동안 진행됩니다.
반드시 녹음 파일의 재생 시간 내에
모든 문제 풀이를 완료하세요.

LISTENING TEST

In the Listening test, you will be asked to demonstrate how well you understand spoken English. The entire Listening test will last approximately 45 minutes. There are four parts, and directions are given for each part. You must mark your answers on the separate answer sheet. Do not write your answers in your test book.

PART 1

Directions: For each question in this part, you will hear four statements about a picture in your test book. When you hear the statements, you must select the one statement that best describes what you see in the picture. Then find the number of the question on your answer sheet and mark your answer. The statements will not be printed in your test book and will be spoken only one time.

Statement (C), "They are sitting at a table," is the best description of the picture, so you should select answer (C) and mark it on your answer sheet.

1.

2.

GO ON TO THE NEXT PAGE

3.

4.

5.

6.

GO ON TO THE NEXT PAGE

PART 2

Directions: You will hear a question or statement and three responses spoken in English. They will not be printed in your test book and will be spoken only one time. Select the best response to the question or statement and mark the letter (A), (B), or (C) on your answer sheet.

7. Mark your answer on your answer sheet.

8. Mark your answer on your answer sheet.

9. Mark your answer on your answer sheet.

10. Mark your answer on your answer sheet.

11. Mark your answer on your answer sheet.

12. Mark your answer on your answer sheet.

13. Mark your answer on your answer sheet.

14. Mark your answer on your answer sheet.

15. Mark your answer on your answer sheet.

16. Mark your answer on your answer sheet.

17. Mark your answer on your answer sheet.

18. Mark your answer on your answer sheet.

19. Mark your answer on your answer sheet.

20. Mark your answer on your answer sheet.

21. Mark your answer on your answer sheet.

22. Mark your answer on your answer sheet.

23. Mark your answer on your answer sheet.

24. Mark your answer on your answer sheet.

25. Mark your answer on your answer sheet.

26. Mark your answer on your answer sheet.

27. Mark your answer on your answer sheet.

28. Mark your answer on your answer sheet.

29. Mark your answer on your answer sheet.

30. Mark your answer on your answer sheet.

31. Mark your answer on your answer sheet.

PART 3

Directions: You will hear some conversations between two or more people. You will be asked to answer three questions about what the speakers say in each conversation. Select the best response to each question and mark the letter (A), (B), (C), or (D) on your answer sheet. The conversations will not be printed in your test book and will be spoken only one time.

32. What does the man give to the woman?

(A) The location of a facility
(B) A clear deadline
(C) An invitation to an event
(D) A subway map

33. What type of event is the woman going to attend?

(A) A trade fair
(B) A performance
(C) An opening ceremony
(D) A meeting with a client

34. What does the man suggest the woman do?

(A) Postpone her appointment
(B) Purchase a map
(C) Use a different type of transportation
(D) Book a ticket

35. What is mainly being discussed by the speakers?

(A) Taking a winter break
(B) Upgrading some equipment
(C) Establishing a new branch
(D) Holding a farewell party for a coworker

36. What does the woman say about the Wembley area?

(A) Its public transportation is very convenient.
(B) The number of its residents is increasing.
(C) A new shopping center has been built.
(D) Its residents have relatively strong spending power.

37. What will the woman most likely do tomorrow?

(A) Create a new sign
(B) Arrange another meeting
(C) Purchase extra office supplies
(D) Look around a property

38. What kind of business do the women work for?

(A) A movie theater
(B) A travel agency
(C) A hotel
(D) An airline

39. What does the man say is strange?

(A) A flight ticket has been misplaced.
(B) An employee does not know about a new policy.
(C) An additional fee is required for a certain service.
(D) A hotel reservation has not been confirmed yet.

40. What type of information will the man need to provide?

(A) The confirmation code
(B) The number of group members
(C) The current address
(D) The reservation dates

41. Where does the man most likely work?

(A) At a hotel
(B) At a gym center
(C) At a school
(D) At a travel agency

42. What is the purpose of the woman's call?

(A) To look for a specific program
(B) To update an itinerary
(C) To make a reservation
(D) To confirm a payment

43. What will the man most likely do next?

(A) Speak to an instructor
(B) Transfer a call
(C) Change the time
(D) Check a schedule

GO ON TO THE NEXT PAGE

44. What type of business is the man calling?

(A) A food supplier
(B) A delivery service
(C) A restaurant
(D) A travel agency

45. According to the man, what is the problem?

(A) An order is filled incompletely.
(B) Some items went to a wrong place.
(C) No delivery truck is available.
(D) Some products are sold out.

46. What does the woman say she will offer for free?

(A) A delivery service
(B) A recipe book
(C) Advice on diet and nutrition
(D) Food samples

47. What type of product is being discussed?

(A) Household appliances
(B) Office supplies
(C) Soft drinks
(D) Sports wear

48. According to the man, what information probably makes the woman disappointed?

(A) A sports celebrity will retire.
(B) An event was canceled.
(C) Some figures are lower than expected.
(D) Advertising costs went up significantly.

49. What does the man suggest the company do?

(A) Use social media for advertising
(B) Increase the marketing budget
(C) Search for a new contractor
(D) Conduct a customer survey

50. What are the speakers mainly talking about?

(A) A presentation to make
(B) New phone service plans
(C) Findings from a survey
(D) Some recent customer complaints

51. What department do the speakers most likely work in?

(A) Maintenance
(B) Personnel
(C) Customer service
(D) Product development

52. What does the woman suggest?

(A) Extending work hours
(B) Using an automated system
(C) Rewarding some employees
(D) Purchasing more telephones

53. Where most likely are the speakers?

(A) In an art supply store
(B) In a museum
(C) In a hotel
(D) In a cinema

54. Why does the woman say, "It's my first time visiting this city"?

(A) To excuse a mistake
(B) To ask for a recommendation
(C) To express her excitement
(D) To delay an appointment

55. Why does the man suggest purchasing a ticket online?

(A) It is much quicker.
(B) It is cheaper.
(C) It is accessible 24 hours.
(D) It is easy to use.

56. Where most likely are the speakers?

(A) At a company-wide conference
(B) At a management seminar
(C) At an art exposition
(D) At a new employee orientation

57. What project are the speakers discussing?

(A) A Web site improvement
(B) A work hour reporting system
(C) A new marketing campaign
(D) An office expansion

58. What does the man say he was responsible for?

(A) Arranging quarterly seminars
(B) Analyzing user comments
(C) Redesigning a customer survey
(D) Holding job interviews

59. What was a client unhappy with about the exterior wall?

(A) Its size
(B) Its material
(C) Its color
(D) Its cost

60. What does the woman imply when she says, "the project has to be completed no later than this week"?

(A) She will need additional construction materials.
(B) She has to ask workers to put in overtime.
(C) She is concerned about meeting a deadline.
(D) She believes some information is wrong.

61. What does the man say he is going to do?

(A) Close a deal
(B) Revise a contract
(C) Place an order
(D) Get in touch with a client

Seating Chart

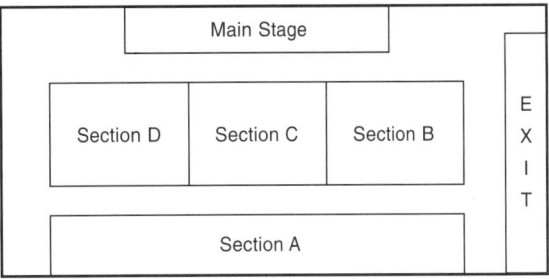

62. What is the woman trying to do?

(A) Register for a trade fair
(B) Book a flight for a business trip
(C) Purchase tickets for a concert
(D) Make a room reservation

63. Look at the graphic. Which seat will the speakers reserve?

(A) Section A
(B) Section B
(C) Section C
(D) Section D

64. What suggestion does the woman make?

(A) Use public transportation
(B) Arrive early at a venue
(C) Share a car from the office
(D) Check a location in advance

GO ON TO THE NEXT PAGE

Service Bill	
Size of Frame	**Charge**
22 X 19 inch	$63
13 X 35 inch	$45
9 X 9 inch	$37
5 X 8 inch	$25
Total	**$170**

To	Sutton, Kristi
From	Torres, Roger

Office location	**Opening schedule**
Kenton City	March 9
Devon	April 14
Wanstead	June 21
South Park	July 10

65. What does the man say he will do with the framed pictures?

(A) Decorate his house
(B) Donate them to an event
(C) Give them to a friend as a gift
(D) Display them in a store

66. Look at the graphic. Which amount will be taken out from the bill?

(A) $63
(B) $45
(C) $37
(D) $25

67. What does the woman say her coworker will do?

(A) Print out some information
(B) Move some items to a car
(C) Give the man a survey sheet
(D) Put the man's name on a list

68. What are the speakers discussing?

(A) A renovation plan
(B) An equipment inspection
(C) A business meeting
(D) An expansion plan

69. Look at the graphic. Which schedule must be revised?

(A) March 9
(B) April 14
(C) June 21
(D) July 10

70. Why has the construction work been delayed?

(A) Because of defective equipment
(B) Because of heavy weather conditions
(C) Because of a limited budget
(D) Because of a shortage of labor

Directions: You will hear some talks given by a single speaker. You will be asked to answer three questions about what the speaker says in each talk. Select the best response to each question and mark the letter (A), (B), (C), or (D) on your answer sheet. The talks will not be printed in your test book and will be spoken only one time.

71. What is the speaker discussing?

(A) Outdoor advertising
(B) Consumer spending
(C) Radio advertising
(D) Online promotion

72. According to the speaker, what might the listeners be concerned about?

(A) Location
(B) Compatibility
(C) Cost
(D) Time

73. What does the speaker say she will do during the program?

(A) Listen to commercials
(B) Interview experts
(C) Receive calls from listeners
(D) Evaluate a report

74. What type of business is the speaker working for?

(A) A local restaurant
(B) A car dealership
(C) A furniture shop
(D) A service center

75. What does the speaker mean when he says, "it seems like none of our trucks will be available for a week"?

(A) A company is growing rapidly.
(B) Some cars are being repaired.
(C) A vehicle is unavailable for rental service.
(D) Some products can not be delivered.

76. What is offered to the listener by the speaker?

(A) A free delivery
(B) A replacement item
(C) A price reduction
(D) A product sample

77. What type of business does the speaker work for?

(A) A real estate agency
(B) A legal service provider
(C) A printing shop
(D) A shipping firm

78. What is the speaker mainly talking about?

(A) Writing up a contract
(B) Scheduling a meeting
(C) Placing an order
(D) Developing a new product line

79. What will the listener most likely provide to the speaker?

(A) A service request form
(B) A copy of an agreement
(C) Some information on a budget
(D) Directions to a construction site

80. What kind of product is the speaker talking about?

(A) Delivery vans
(B) An accounting program
(C) Furnishing materials
(D) Packaging machinery

81. According to the speaker, what will the product help avoid?

(A) Increasing the number of defective products
(B) Ordering from an outside supplier
(C) Growing customer complaints
(D) Damaging some items

82. What will the listeners most likely do next?

(A) Watch a demonstration
(B) Read a brochure
(C) Sign a contract
(D) Create their own design

GO ON TO THE NEXT PAGE

83. What is the museum exhibit about?

(A) Cities
(B) Celebrities
(C) Tourism
(D) Museum history

84. Why does the speaker say, "That's why I'm here"?

(A) To hand out a museum map
(B) To provide assistance for a tour
(C) To apply for a position
(D) To collect mobile phones

85. What does the speaker ask the listeners to do?

(A) Ask questions after a tour ends
(B) Turn off an electronic device
(C) Touch some artifacts
(D) Take a picture

86. According to the speaker, what did the city council approve?

(A) The expansion of a subway station
(B) The construction of some houses
(C) The relocation of a city hall
(D) The renovation of some office buildings

87. What is mentioned about the location of the complex?

(A) Street parking is accessible.
(B) There are many cafés and restaurants.
(C) Public transportation is located nearby.
(D) It is the busiest area in the city.

88. What is available on a Web site for the listeners?

(A) Some floor plans
(B) A discount coupon
(C) Some comments
(D) A list of council members

89. What is being advertised?

(A) An electric cleaner
(B) A mobile phone
(C) A battery
(D) Portable furniture

90. What feature does the speaker say is good about the product?

(A) Its durability
(B) Its color
(C) Its price
(D) Its size

91. What does the speaker say is available on a Web site?

(A) A list of stores
(B) A discount coupon
(C) Payment information
(D) Customer comments

92. What is the talk intended for?

(A) Product developers
(B) Personnel managers
(C) Salespeople
(D) Bank tellers

93. What does the speaker mean when he says, "many people have a limited understanding of the subject"?

(A) Some equipment has to be updated.
(B) A project is more difficult than expected.
(C) Something should be described in detail.
(D) An employee is available for customer inquiries.

94. What does the speaker say is the listeners' goal?

(A) To get along with coworkers
(B) To have more meetings with clients
(C) To communicate efficiently
(D) To fulfill a sales quota

Possibility of Rain				
Wednesday 20%	Thursday 50%	Friday 90%	Saturday 0%	Sunday 100%

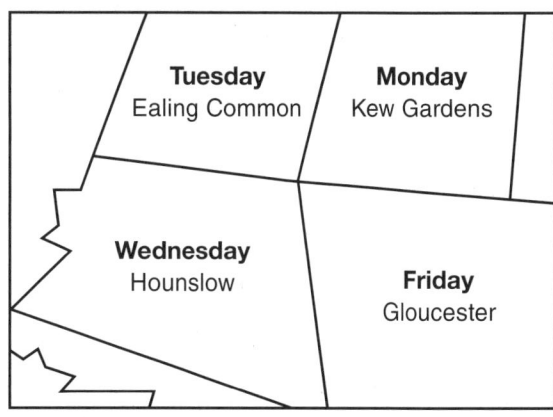

95. For whom most likely is the announcement intended?

(A) Hotel employees
(B) Coach drivers
(C) Tourists
(D) Shop assistants

96. Look at the graphic. On which day did the listeners visit the Ruislip Hotel?

(A) Thursday
(B) Friday
(C) Saturday
(D) Sunday

97. What does the speaker encourage the listeners to do?

(A) Explore a museum
(B) Stop by a shop
(C) Reserve a ticket
(D) Purchase a gift

98. What is the speaker mainly talking about?

(A) A construction project
(B) A new work schedule
(C) An office expansion plan
(D) A brand new vehicle

99. Look at the graphic. In which area will the service be provided more frequently?

(A) Ealing Common
(B) Kew Gardens
(C) Hounslow
(D) Gloucester

100. According to the speaker, what will be purchased for business?

(A) Some office supplies
(B) More service vehicles
(C) A construction site
(D) Additional recycling bins

This is the end of the Listening test.

정답 p. 157 / 점수 환산표 p. 159 / 스크립트 p. 191

TEST 07

PART 1
PART 2
PART 3
PART 4

토익 Listening Comprehension은 약 45분 동안 진행됩니다.
반드시 녹음 파일의 재생 시간 내에
모든 문제 풀이를 완료하세요.

LISTENING TEST

In the Listening test, you will be asked to demonstrate how well you understand spoken English. The entire Listening test will last approximately 45 minutes. There are four parts, and directions are given for each part. You must mark your answers on the separate answer sheet. Do not write your answers in your test book.

PART 1

Directions: For each question in this part, you will hear four statements about a picture in your test book. When you hear the statements, you must select the one statement that best describes what you see in the picture. Then find the number of the question on your answer sheet and mark your answer. The statements will not be printed in your test book and will be spoken only one time.

Statement (C), "They are sitting at a table," is the best description of the picture, so you should select answer (C) and mark it on your answer sheet.

1.

2.

GO ON TO THE NEXT PAGE

3.

4.

5.

6.

GO ON TO THE NEXT PAGE

PART 2

Directions: You will hear a question or statement and three responses spoken in English. They will not be printed in your test book and will be spoken only one time. Select the best response to the question or statement and mark the letter (A), (B), or (C) on your answer sheet.

7. Mark your answer on your answer sheet.

8. Mark your answer on your answer sheet.

9. Mark your answer on your answer sheet.

10. Mark your answer on your answer sheet.

11. Mark your answer on your answer sheet.

12. Mark your answer on your answer sheet.

13. Mark your answer on your answer sheet.

14. Mark your answer on your answer sheet.

15. Mark your answer on your answer sheet.

16. Mark your answer on your answer sheet.

17. Mark your answer on your answer sheet.

18. Mark your answer on your answer sheet.

19. Mark your answer on your answer sheet.

20. Mark your answer on your answer sheet.

21. Mark your answer on your answer sheet.

22. Mark your answer on your answer sheet.

23. Mark your answer on your answer sheet.

24. Mark your answer on your answer sheet.

25. Mark your answer on your answer sheet.

26. Mark your answer on your answer sheet.

27. Mark your answer on your answer sheet.

28. Mark your answer on your answer sheet.

29. Mark your answer on your answer sheet.

30. Mark your answer on your answer sheet.

31. Mark your answer on your answer sheet.

Directions: You will hear some conversations between two or more people. You will be asked to answer three questions about what the speakers say in each conversation. Select the best response to each question and mark the letter (A), (B), (C), or (D) on your answer sheet. The conversations will not be printed in your test book and will be spoken only one time.

32. Where in Cleveland is the woman planning to go?
(A) To a city hall
(B) To a theater
(C) To an art museum
(D) To a city park

33. What does the man suggest?
(A) Reserving a hotel in advance
(B) Reading online reviews
(C) Getting a city map
(D) Taking the bus

34. What will the man probably do next?
(A) Give a phone number
(B) Provide a site address
(C) Download an expense form
(D) Get an access code

35. Where does the man most likely work?
(A) At a home improvement firm
(B) At a furniture store
(C) At a real estate agency
(D) At a housekeeping firm

36. Why does the man say, "Our crew is going to be here all day"?
(A) To ask for some help
(B) To offer assistance
(C) To decline a request
(D) To confirm his location

37. What does the woman say she will do?
(A) Call a customer
(B) Check a schedule
(C) Place an order
(D) Visit a house

38. Where does the man most likely work?
(A) At a television studio
(B) At an apartment complex
(C) At an advertising company
(D) At a fitness center

39. What is the woman concerned about?
(A) She a difficulties with stairs.
(B) She wants a short term lease.
(C) An elevator is too small.
(D) A work site is too far away.

40. What will the woman most likely do next?
(A) Sign a contract
(B) Decorate a living space
(C) Discuss a rent fee
(D) Set up an appointment

41. What department does the man work in?
(A) Engineering
(B) Marketing
(C) Accounting
(D) Personnel

42. What does the man say will be discussed on Tuesday?
(A) A recruiting policy
(B) A company event
(C) An investment plan
(D) A newly installed program

43. What does the woman offer to do?
(A) Send an e-mail
(B) Prepare for a meeting
(C) Update a change
(D) Reserve a flight

GO ON TO THE NEXT PAGE

44. What is the conversation mainly about?

(A) A company acquisition
(B) New employees
(C) Results of a survey
(D) Price estimates

45. What does the man mention about the main problem?

(A) There seems to be a budget cut.
(B) A project is being delayed.
(C) More parking spaces are required.
(D) Noise distracts employees from their work.

46. What does the man suggest doing?

(A) Asking for a deadline extension
(B) Conducting a regular inspection
(C) Transferring to another branch
(D) Letting staff know about a policy

47. What does the woman imply when she says, "I've never expected to live abroad"?

(A) She won't accept a job offer.
(B) She will be retiring soon.
(C) She is concerned about a change.
(D) She wants to advise a colleague.

48. According to the man, what can a mobile app be used for?

(A) For securing personal information
(B) For obtaining appropriate accommodation
(C) For finding social networks
(D) For searching for legal assistance

49. What does the man offer to do?

(A) Update a staff directory
(B) Pick up a business card
(C) Bring a book
(D) Print out a form

50. Who most likely is the man?

(A) A reporter
(B) A photographer
(C) A publisher
(D) A technician

51. Why does the woman want to reschedule an appointment?

(A) A meeting is running behind schedule.
(B) Some equipment is being upgraded.
(C) Some facilities will be closed for repairs.
(D) Some employees will be unavailable.

52. What does the man say he needs?

(A) A conference hall
(B) An official place
(C) A copy of an invoice
(D) Some contact information

53. What event are the speakers discussing?

(A) An investment presentation
(B) A press conference
(C) A yearly dinner
(D) A grand opening

54. How do the speakers know Jarvis Taylor?

(A) He recently made an investment contract.
(B) He is one of the executives.
(C) He is one of the loyal customers.
(D) He organized last year's event.

55. What does the woman say she will do?

(A) Send a speaker list
(B) Delay some speeches
(C) Review a food order
(D) Update a list

56. What type of event did the man recently attend?

(A) A product launch
(B) A sports match
(C) A business fair
(D) An anniversary party

57. According to the woman, what have customers been suggesting?

(A) Extending business hours
(B) Operating an online store
(C) Using different local suppliers
(D) Creating additional menu options

58. What does the man say he will do next?

(A) Meet with a manager
(B) Cook some food
(C) Set up tables
(D) Put up a new sign

59. What type of business do the speakers most likely work for?

(A) A graphic design agency
(B) A printing company
(C) An educational institution
(D) A magazine company

60. What problem do the speakers discuss?

(A) Images need to be replaced.
(B) A deadline has passed.
(C) Writing is not clearly legible.
(D) An article is too short.

61. What does the woman promise to do in an hour?

(A) Renew her subscription
(B) Have a new sample ready
(C) Speak to a technician
(D) Correct an estimate

Classic Jacket Brand : Ann Myer	**Leather Jacket** Brand : Stella Tillerson
Casual Jacket Brand : Timothy Denim	**Sports Jacket** Brand : Ellen Sports

62. Who most likely is the woman?

(A) A tailor
(B) A marketing specialist
(C) A sales associate
(D) A fashion designer

63. Look at the graphic. Which brand does the man say he likes?

(A) Ann Myer
(B) Stella Tillerson
(C) Timothy Denim
(D) Ellen Sports

64. What does the woman offer to do?

(A) Give a brochure
(B) Stock some goods
(C) Check an inventory
(D) Read a contract

GO ON TO THE NEXT PAGE →

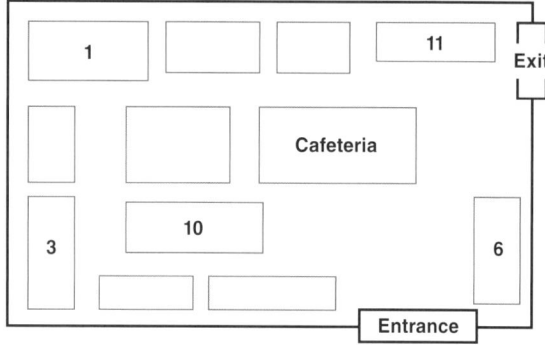

65. According to the woman, what is the news about?

(A) A budget will be cut.
(B) A colleague got a promotion.
(C) An office will be relocated.
(D) A contract has been renewed.

66. Look at the graphic. Which discount will be applied to the speakers' bill?

(A) 20%
(B) 25%
(C) 30%
(D) 35%

67. What does the man suggest the woman do?

(A) Share a car
(B) Meet other employees
(C) Try a new dish
(D) Arrive in advance

68. What do the speakers plan to give away at the trade show?

(A) Free refreshments
(B) Discount coupons
(C) Promotional items
(D) Meal vouchers

69. Look at the graphic. Which booth do the speakers want to reserve?

(A) Booth 1
(B) Booth 3
(C) Booth 6
(D) Booth 11

70. What does the man offer to do?

(A) Call his manager
(B) Submit the planned budget
(C) Contact an event organizer
(D) Arrange a client meeting

Directions: You will hear some talks given by a single speaker. You will be asked to answer three questions about what the speaker says in each talk. Select the best response to each question and mark the letter (A), (B), (C), or (D) on your answer sheet. The talks will not be printed in your test book and will be spoken only one time.

71. According to Ms. Silva, what will not be done as scheduled?
    (A) Signing a contract
    (B) Finishing roadwork
    (C) Installing doors
    (D) Paying a rental fee

72. Why does the speaker apologize?
    (A) She did not contact a client.
    (B) She ordered some wrong products.
    (C) She was late for a meeting.
    (D) She needs to leave work early.

73. What will the listener most likely do next?
    (A) Deliver some supplies
    (B) Set up some equipment
    (C) Prepare for replacement work
    (D) Confirm the dimensions of a room

74. What is the main purpose of today's meeting?
    (A) To present an award
    (B) To arrange a conference
    (C) To welcome new employees
    (D) To invite employees to a banquet

75. According to the speaker, what will be done later today?
    (A) Preparing a presentation
    (B) Printing out some documents
    (C) Submitting a request
    (D) Booking a meeting room

76. What are the listeners asked to do?
    (A) Be present at the next meeting
    (B) Contact a travel agency
    (C) Attend a training session
    (D) Revise a contract

77. What is the workshop mainly about?
    (A) Creating effective proposals
    (B) Improving presentation skills
    (C) Learning company policies
    (D) Getting a job

78. What will the listeners be doing at the end of today?
    (A) Introducing themselves
    (B) Presenting a current project
    (C) Assessing their works
    (D) Receiving a certificate

79. What will the listeners do next?
    (A) Complete a form
    (B) Adjust tables
    (C) Read some manuals
    (D) Work with a partner

80. Where does the talk most likely take place?
    (A) At a garden
    (B) At an old apartment
    (C) At a construction site
    (D) At a city park

81. What is the purpose of the talk?
    (A) To give some advice about gardening
    (B) To promote a new exhibit
    (C) To discuss a policy
    (D) To explain a tour

82. According to the speaker, what can the listeners do at Cream House?
    (A) Purchase some gifts
    (B) Eat lunch
    (C) Look at some photographs
    (D) Take a group picture

TEST 07

GO ON TO THE NEXT PAGE

83. What are the listeners encouraged to do?

(A) Confirm a list of available items
(B) Provide customers with free samples
(C) Notify customers of a special menu
(D) Address complaints immediately

84. What does the speaker mean when he says, "it's not your first day working here"?

(A) New employees need to attend a training session.
(B) Further information is unnecessary for the listeners.
(C) The listeners will get a promotion soon.
(D) The quality of service should be improved.

85. What is mentioned about the time sheets?

(A) They can be completed online.
(B) They require a manager's signature.
(C) They will be sent to a different place.
(D) They need to be submitted earlier.

86. According to the speaker, what equipment has been set up?

(A) Fax machines
(B) Coffee makers
(C) Copiers
(D) Monitors

87. What feature of the equipment does the speaker mention?

(A) Its speed
(B) Its price
(C) Its durability
(D) Its security

88. Why does the speaker say, "they're usually tied up with other work"?

(A) To suggest recruiting additional workers
(B) To inform the listeners of a possible delay
(C) To complain about a tight schedule
(D) To ask the listeners to work overtime

89. What field do the listeners work in?

(A) Medical service
(B) Car manufacturing
(C) Public transportation
(D) Book publishing

90. What will most likely happen on Thursday?

(A) A construction project will begin.
(B) An important announcement will be made.
(C) A journalist will visit a company.
(D) A company will move to a different location.

91. What does the speaker ask the listeners to do?

(A) Submit their progress reports
(B) Review a survey result
(C) Come to work early
(D) Talk with a visitor about their jobs

92. What does the speaker mention about himself?

(A) He has worked as a broadcaster for a long time.
(B) He will publish a book soon.
(C) He has his own business.
(D) He is resigning from his current position.

93. Why does the speaker say, "I know it sounds very costly"?

(A) To turn down a request
(B) To acknowledge a common thought
(C) To negotiate a price
(D) To disagree with some opinions

94. What will most likely happen next?

(A) Some suggestions will be given.
(B) A guest will be introduced.
(C) A list of events will be provided.
(D) Some questions will be received.

Product names	Discounted prices
Folding chair	£30
Armchair	£35
Stacking chair	£37
Side chair	£40

City Hall	Post Office	Joe's Café
Lincoln Street		
Grocery Store	HSB Bank	Auto Repair Shop

95. Look at the graphic. Which price of the chair is being advertised?

(A) £30
(B) £35
(C) £37
(D) £40

96. What is the main reason many customers like the chair?

(A) It is very durable.
(B) It comes with a lifetime warranty.
(C) It is much cheaper than other chairs.
(D) It does not take a long time to assemble.

97. According to the advertisement, what is available on a Web site?

(A) A discount coupon
(B) Technical assistance
(C) The exact size of a product
(D) Simple instructions

98. Who most likely is the speaker?

(A) An apartment manager
(B) A real estate agent
(C) A café owner
(D) A sales manager

99. Look at the graphic. Which location is the speaker talking about?

(A) City Hall
(B) Grocery Store
(C) HSB Bank
(D) Auto Repair Shop

100. What plan does the speaker suggest changing?

(A) A store renovation
(B) A blueprint
(C) A work schedule
(D) A budget

This is the end of the Listening test.

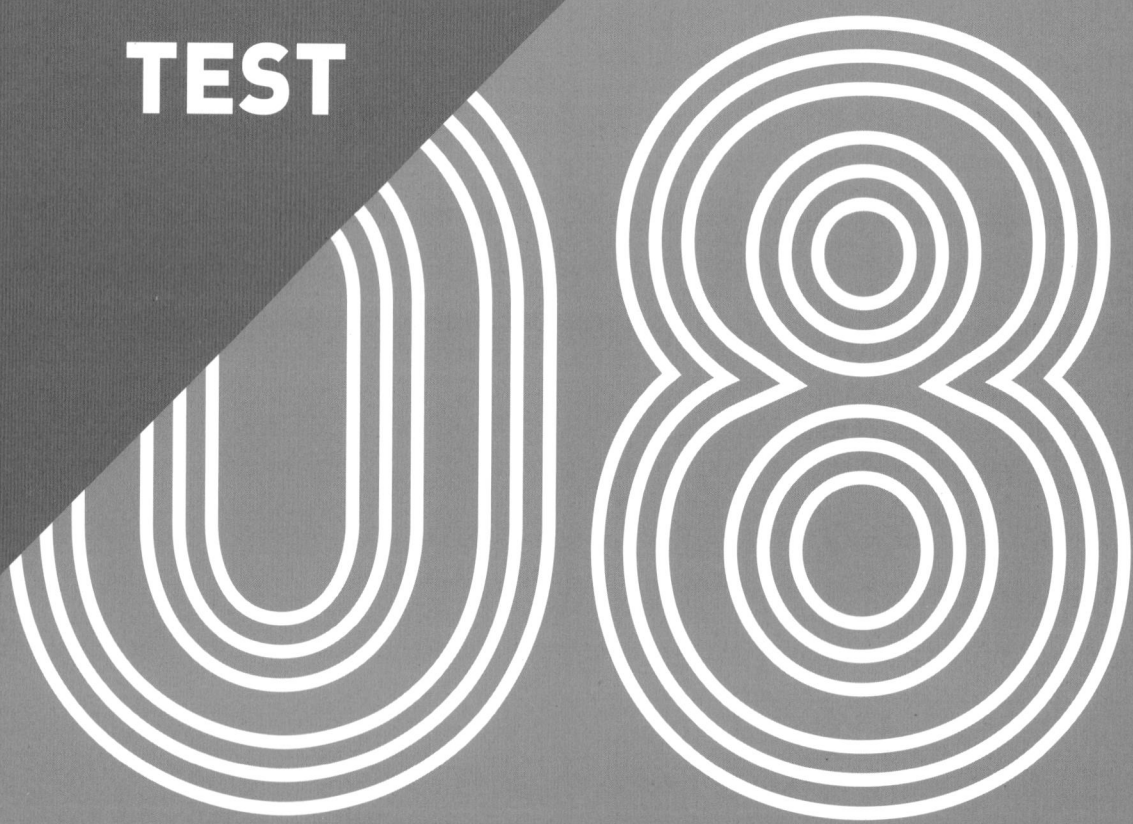

TEST 08

PART 1
PART 2
PART 3
PART 4

토익 Listening Comprehension은 약 45분 동안 진행됩니다.
반드시 녹음 파일의 재생 시간 내에
모든 문제 풀이를 완료하세요.

LISTENING TEST

In the Listening test, you will be asked to demonstrate how well you understand spoken English. The entire Listening test will last approximately 45 minutes. There are four parts, and directions are given for each part. You must mark your answers on the separate answer sheet. Do not write your answers in your test book.

PART 1

Directions: For each question in this part, you will hear four statements about a picture in your test book. When you hear the statements, you must select the one statement that best describes what you see in the picture. Then find the number of the question on your answer sheet and mark your answer. The statements will not be printed in your test book and will be spoken only one time.

Statement (C), "They are sitting at a table," is the best description of the picture, so you should select answer (C) and mark it on your answer sheet.

1.

2.

GO ON TO THE NEXT PAGE

3.

4.

5.

6.

GO ON TO THE NEXT PAGE

PART 2

Directions: You will hear a question or statement and three responses spoken in English. They will not be printed in your test book and will be spoken only one time. Select the best response to the question or statement and mark the letter (A), (B), or (C) on your answer sheet.

7. Mark your answer on your answer sheet.

8. Mark your answer on your answer sheet.

9. Mark your answer on your answer sheet.

10. Mark your answer on your answer sheet.

11. Mark your answer on your answer sheet.

12. Mark your answer on your answer sheet.

13. Mark your answer on your answer sheet.

14. Mark your answer on your answer sheet.

15. Mark your answer on your answer sheet.

16. Mark your answer on your answer sheet.

17. Mark your answer on your answer sheet.

18. Mark your answer on your answer sheet.

19. Mark your answer on your answer sheet.

20. Mark your answer on your answer sheet.

21. Mark your answer on your answer sheet.

22. Mark your answer on your answer sheet.

23. Mark your answer on your answer sheet.

24. Mark your answer on your answer sheet.

25. Mark your answer on your answer sheet.

26. Mark your answer on your answer sheet.

27. Mark your answer on your answer sheet.

28. Mark your answer on your answer sheet.

29. Mark your answer on your answer sheet.

30. Mark your answer on your answer sheet.

31. Mark your answer on your answer sheet.

Directions: You will hear some conversations between two or more people. You will be asked to answer three questions about what the speakers say in each conversation. Select the best response to each question and mark the letter (A), (B), (C), or (D) on your answer sheet. The conversations will not be printed in your test book and will be spoken only one time.

32. What does the man want to do?

(A) Repair a vehicle
(B) Pick up a car
(C) Draft an agreement
(D) Reserve a room

33. What is the man concerned about?

(A) His credit card details
(B) His driver licence
(C) His confirmation number
(D) His home address

34. What will the woman most likely do next?

(A) Sign an agreement
(B) Look up some information
(C) Refer to an e-mail
(D) Contact another department

35. What most likely is the woman's job?

(A) Carpenter
(B) Bus driver
(C) Realtor
(D) Plumber

36. According to the woman, what is the problem?

(A) One of the workers called in sick.
(B) More materials are needed.
(C) A tool is not working.
(D) There is a scheduling conflict.

37. What does the man suggest that the woman do?

(A) Complete a job as soon as possible
(B) Bring a receipt
(C) Use a different route
(D) Correct some information

38. What kind of product are the speakers talking about?

(A) Household appliances
(B) Office supplies
(C) Formal clothes
(D) Commercial properties

39. What does the woman mean when she says, "Only a few boxes are left in the storage room"?

(A) She needs to order more containers.
(B) Some products are almost sold out.
(C) A shop requires proper inventory management.
(D) Some records indicate wrong figures.

40. What does the woman say she will do?

(A) Contact a sales person
(B) Invest more in advertisement
(C) Print out more brochures
(D) Open more branches

41. What is the man's job?

(A) Journalist
(B) Professor
(C) Librarian
(D) Publisher

42. What does the woman say about some books?

(A) They are available as e-books.
(B) They are available in France only.
(C) They cannot be open to the public.
(D) They cannot be taken from the building.

43. What will the woman do next?

(A) Make an appointment
(B) Send an application form
(C) Transfer a phone call
(D) Check the schedule

GO ON TO THE NEXT PAGE

44. What type of industry do the speakers work in?

(A) Tourism
(B) Financial service
(C) Car manufacturing
(D) Software development

45. What did Anthony Lee encourage the man to do?

(A) Talk with individual workers
(B) Attend some online courses
(C) Participate in various social gatherings
(D) Issue a company newsletter

46. What does the man indicate he will do?

(A) Submit some application forms
(B) Post a notice on the bulletin board
(C) Find out some cost information
(D) Schedule a meeting

47. What is the purpose of the man's call?

(A) To put in an order
(B) To reserve a room
(C) To inquire about a problem
(D) To arrange an event

48. Who most likely is the woman?

(A) An Internet engineer
(B) A software designer
(C) A hotel employee
(D) A security officer

49. According to the woman, what can be found when the man checks out?

(A) A list of local attractions
(B) Transportation information
(C) An adjusted detail of a bill
(D) Directions to a bank

50. What does the woman thank the man for?

(A) Giving a presentation
(B) Arranging a meeting
(C) Meeting a project deadline
(D) Organizing a company event

51. What does the man say about the sales department?

(A) It faces a staff shortage.
(B) It was relocated to another place.
(C) It had a poor performance last month.
(D) It will receive an award.

52. What does the man ask about?

(A) The evaluation of his work
(B) The availability of office space
(C) The possibility of a transfer
(D) The qualifications for a promotion

53. What type of business do the speakers most likely work for?

(A) A hotel
(B) A real estate office
(C) A travel agency
(D) An advertising company

54. What does the man mean when he says, "the holiday season is nearly over"?

(A) He wanted to go on a vacation earlier.
(B) An advertising campaign may not be very effective.
(C) He has a deadline to meet.
(D) A new product design should be released soon.

55. What will the woman most likely do next?

(A) Print out some flyers
(B) Review customer comments
(C) Call some business partners
(D) Submit a report

56. What is the main topic of the conversation?

(A) A hotel grand opening
(B) A company reorganization
(C) A renovation project
(D) A product launch

57. According to Peter, what problem will be corrected on Friday?

(A) An inaccurate work schedule
(B) A delivery issue
(C) A supply order mistake
(D) A lack of light fixtures

58. What will the woman most likely do next?

(A) Reserve an event space
(B) Make a phone call
(C) Revise an oder
(D) Stick to the original plan

59. What kind of business do the speakers work for?

(A) A culinary school
(B) A supermarket
(C) A local restaurant
(D) A real estate agency

60. What does the man want to ask the management to consider?

(A) Allowing staff to change shifts
(B) Upgrading old appliances
(C) Changing hours of operation
(D) Giving a discount to frequent customers

61. What will the woman most likely do next?

(A) Call a manager
(B) Post the daily special
(C) Place an order
(D) Change a work shift

Town Public Park Picnic Facilities	
Available Capacity	List of Shelters
70 people	Finchley Hill
60 people	Hendon Green
45 people	Tufnell Lake
30 people	Archway

62. According to the man, what was approved this morning?

(A) The date of a picnic
(B) The budget for an event
(C) The menu options
(D) The place to go

63. Look at the graphic. Which shelter was chosen by the speakers?

(A) Finchley Hill
(B) Hendon Green
(C) Tufnell Lake
(D) Archway

64. What does the woman say she will do?

(A) Search for a map
(B) Arrange transportation
(C) Print out some documents
(D) Rent some tables and chairs

GO ON TO THE NEXT PAGE

Vehicle Rentals

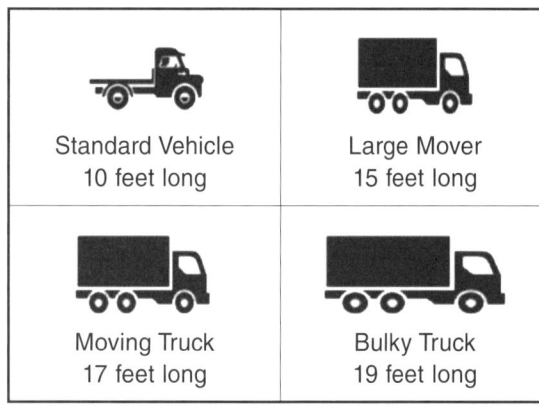

Standard Vehicle 10 feet long	Large Mover 15 feet long
Moving Truck 17 feet long	Bulky Truck 19 feet long

65. Why is the man trying to rent a vehicle?

(A) He wants to move some building supplies.

(B) He is relocating to a new office.

(C) His truck is in a service center.

(D) His client needs an express shipping service.

66. Look at the graphic. Which vehicle will the man rent?

(A) Standard Vehicle

(B) Large Mover

(C) Moving Truck

(D) Bulky Truck

67. What information does the woman ask about?

(A) Where the new office is located

(B) When a car will be rented

(C) How to make a payment

(D) Whether she needs a driving licence

---

the Process for Financial Planning

Stage A ➜	Stage B ➜	Stage C ➜	Stage D
Accessing current financial status	Creating a list of future aims	Designing an action plan	Overseeing outcomes

68. What type of business is the woman running?

(A) A second-hand bookshop

(B) A car service center

(C) A Web site design company

(D) A household appliance store

69. What does the woman say she intends to do in the near future?

(A) Resign from her current position

(B) Enlarge her business

(C) Finish her study at university

(D) Publish her own novel

70. Look at the graphic. Which stage does the woman want to talk about?

(A) Stage A

(B) Stage B

(C) Stage C

(D) Stage D

Directions: You will hear some talks given by a single speaker. You will be asked to answer three questions about what the speaker says in each talk. Select the best response to each question and mark the letter (A), (B), (C), or (D) on your answer sheet. The talks will not be printed in your test book and will be spoken only one time.

71. What type of business does the speaker work for?

(A) An advertising agency
(B) A mobile phone manufacturer
(C) An appliance store
(D) A shipping company

72. What problem does the speaker mention?

(A) Low sales
(B) A budget cut
(C) Poor quality
(D) A project delay

73. What does the speaker ask the listeners to do?

(A) Volunteer to stay late
(B) Submit some documents
(C) Look through a schedule
(D) Speak to their supervisor

74. Who is the speaker most likely talking to?

(A) Tourists
(B) Safety inspectors
(C) New employees
(D) Overseas investors

75. What about the company is the speaker most proud of?

(A) Its long history
(B) Its market share
(C) The quality of its products
(D) Its up-to-date equipment

76. What will the listeners do next?

(A) Receive some materials
(B) Visit the assembly area
(C) Wear safety equipment
(D) Return some samples

77. Where most likely are the listeners?

(A) At a trade show
(B) At a tourist attraction
(C) At a local restaurant
(D) At a shopping center

78. Why does the speaker say, "think about enjoying artworks in the gallery"?

(A) To change a schedule
(B) To remind the listeners of a plan
(C) To suggest a tourist spot
(D) To talk about an experience

79. According to the speaker, what are the listeners scheduled to do at six o'clock?

(A) Attend a lecture
(B) Go to a bus stop
(C) See a performance
(D) Have a dinner

80. Where does the speaker most likely work?

(A) At a law office
(B) At a construction firm
(C) At an office supply store
(D) At a news agency

81. What is mentioned about the office?

(A) Its location will be changed.
(B) It will have a new director.
(C) It is under renovation.
(D) Its opening hours will be shortened.

82. What does the speaker instruct the listeners to do?

(A) Access a Web site regularly
(B) Send a message by e-mail
(C) Complete a request form
(D) Make a phone call

GO ON TO THE NEXT PAGE

83. According to the broadcast, what has been announced?

(A) Some road maintenance work
(B) A store's relocation
(C) An international trade fair
(D) Unemployment rates

84. Who most likely is Brett Armstrong?

(A) A technician
(B) A business executive
(C) A news reporter
(D) A city official

85. What is Casey Appliances going to do next winter?

(A) Open an online store
(B) Extend its business hours
(C) Recruit more employees
(D) Unveil a new product line

86. What event is the speaker discussing?

(A) A staff orientation
(B) An industrial design contest
(C) A musical festival for tourists
(D) A conference

87. What does the speaker imply when she says, "we have another week until the deadline"?

(A) There is inaccurate information on the brochure.
(B) The listeners have time to submit proposals.
(C) Some more time is needed.
(D) She wants to hire more workers.

88. Why should the listeners visit the speaker after the meeting?

(A) To request some time off
(B) To contact every participant
(C) To become a member of a team
(D) To interview some candidates

89. Who is the talk most likely intended for?

(A) Technical experts
(B) Small-business owners
(C) Sales representatives
(D) University professors

90. What does the speaker want to help the listeners do?

(A) Set up a business network
(B) Lead a successful online business
(C) Operate a Web site better
(D) Improve presentation skills

91. What are the listeners asked to do?

(A) Ask a question at any time
(B) Keep quiet during the talk
(C) Hold a question until the end of the talk
(D) Buy tickets for the event

92. Where do the listeners most likely work?

(A) At a manufacturing facility
(B) At a construction site
(C) At a newspaper company
(D) At a conference center

93. Why does the speaker say, "Many clients have recently talked about this issue"?

(A) To recognize an employee for hard work
(B) To emphasize the importance of a procedure
(C) To assign new work to each worker
(D) To announce business growth

94. According to the speaker, what will be done by a new team?

(A) Special machines will be designed.
(B) Work areas will be expanded.
(C) Items will be checked.
(D) Temporary workers will be hired.

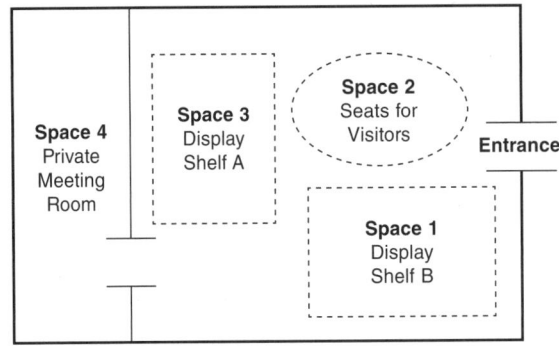

Weather Report				
Monday	Tuesday	Wednesday	Thursday	Friday
Light Rain	Humid [partly cloudy]	Heavy Rain	Sunny [moderate wind]	Sunny [extreme heat]

95. Who is leaving the message?

(A) A building constructor
(B) An event organizer
(C) A delivery person
(D) A technician

96. What is mentioned about the digital cameras?

(A) They are currently on sale.
(B) They can not be used during the event.
(C) They come with a limited warranty.
(D) They will be located in the center.

97. Look at the graphic. Which space has been added?

(A) Space 1
(B) Space 2
(C) Space 3
(D) Space 4

98. What event is the speaker talking about?

(A) A tour to the museum
(B) An outdoor concert
(C) A charity race
(D) An annual celebration

99. Look at the graphic. Which day was originally planned for the event?

(A) Monday
(B) Tuesday
(C) Wednesday
(D) Friday

100. What does the speaker suggest doing tomorrow?

(A) Having a meeting
(B) Mailing some flyers
(C) Purchasing additional raincoats
(D) Designing a new sign

This is the end of the Listening test.

TEST

09

PART 1
PART 2
PART 3
PART 4

토익 Listening Comprehension은 약 45분 동안 진행됩니다.
반드시 녹음 파일의 재생 시간 내에
모든 문제 풀이를 완료하세요.

LISTENING TEST

In the Listening test, you will be asked to demonstrate how well you understand spoken English. The entire Listening test will last approximately 45 minutes. There are four parts, and directions are given for each part. You must mark your answers on the separate answer sheet. Do not write your answers in your test book.

PART 1

Directions: For each question in this part, you will hear four statements about a picture in your test book. When you hear the statements, you must select the one statement that best describes what you see in the picture. Then find the number of the question on your answer sheet and mark your answer. The statements will not be printed in your test book and will be spoken only one time.

Statement (C), "They are sitting at a table," is the best description of the picture, so you should select answer (C) and mark it on your answer sheet.

1.

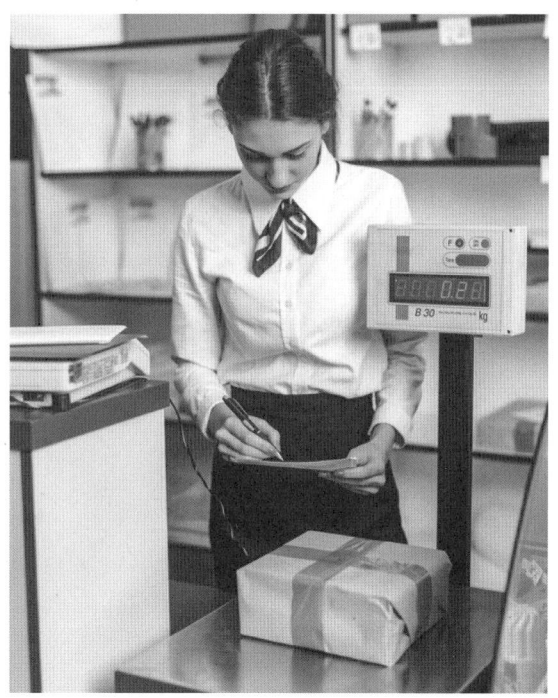

2.

GO ON TO THE NEXT PAGE

3.

4.

5.

6.

GO ON TO THE NEXT PAGE

PART 2

Directions: You will hear a question or statement and three responses spoken in English. They will not be printed in your test book and will be spoken only one time. Select the best response to the question or statement and mark the letter (A), (B), or (C) on your answer sheet.

7. Mark your answer on your answer sheet.

8. Mark your answer on your answer sheet.

9. Mark your answer on your answer sheet.

10. Mark your answer on your answer sheet.

11. Mark your answer on your answer sheet.

12. Mark your answer on your answer sheet.

13. Mark your answer on your answer sheet.

14. Mark your answer on your answer sheet.

15. Mark your answer on your answer sheet.

16. Mark your answer on your answer sheet.

17. Mark your answer on your answer sheet.

18. Mark your answer on your answer sheet.

19. Mark your answer on your answer sheet.

20. Mark your answer on your answer sheet.

21. Mark your answer on your answer sheet.

22. Mark your answer on your answer sheet.

23. Mark your answer on your answer sheet.

24. Mark your answer on your answer sheet.

25. Mark your answer on your answer sheet.

26. Mark your answer on your answer sheet.

27. Mark your answer on your answer sheet.

28. Mark your answer on your answer sheet.

29. Mark your answer on your answer sheet.

30. Mark your answer on your answer sheet.

31. Mark your answer on your answer sheet.

PART 3

Directions: You will hear some conversations between two or more people. You will be asked to answer three questions about what the speakers say in each conversation. Select the best response to each question and mark the letter (A), (B), (C), or (D) on your answer sheet. The conversations will not be printed in your test book and will be spoken only one time.

32. Who most likely is the man?

(A) A restaurant supervisor
(B) A café owner
(C) A receptionist
(D) A factory manager

33. Why does Lola say she feels sorry?

(A) An item is currently out of stock.
(B) A bill is incorrect.
(C) A worker is not friendly.
(D) An order has not been brought out yet.

34. What does the man say he will do?

(A) Change a request
(B) Talk with a coworker
(C) Cancel an order
(D) Discount an item

35. Where does the man most likely work?

(A) At a hotel
(B) At a restaurant
(C) At an event-planning company
(D) At a party-supply store

36. Why does the woman say, "The Queen's Café charges 120 dollars"?

(A) To negotiate a price
(B) To notify the man of her decision
(C) To express her satisfaction
(D) To prevent a wrong charge

37. What will the man do next?

(A) Call the woman back
(B) Speak with a manager
(C) Provide some samples
(D) Cancel an order

38. What type of business do the speakers most likely work for?

(A) A local museum
(B) A shoe manufacturing firm
(C) A fitness center
(D) An employment agency

39. What is the woman concerned about?

(A) Revising a policy
(B) Finding a way to increase sales
(C) Solving recent customer complaints
(D) Finishing a task by a deadline

40. What does the man ask the woman to do?

(A) Revise a report
(B) E-mail the status of a job
(C) Prepare a presentation
(D) Repair some equipment

41. What dream is the woman trying to achieve?

(A) To become an author
(B) To open a book store
(C) To visit other countries
(D) To join a publishing company

42. What does the man offer to do for the woman?

(A) Design a survey
(B) Review some paperwork
(C) Revise a proposal
(D) Get in touch with his friend

43. What information is given to the woman?

(A) Some directions to a building
(B) A list of local businesses
(C) Some contact information
(D) A home address

GO ON TO THE NEXT PAGE

44. What did the man not expect to see?

(A) Some documents containing wrong information
(B) A coworker staying late at work
(C) An office space under renovation
(D) Some vehicles parked on the street

45. What was the problem Lucy encountered in the morning?

(A) Her car had an unexpected glitch.
(B) Her purse was missing.
(C) She got off at the incorrect location.
(D) She lost her smart phone.

46. What does Lucy offer to do for Hilda?

(A) Search for some information
(B) Share a cost
(C) Hand in a document
(D) Make a phone call

47. What type of business do the speakers most likely work for?

(A) A construction company
(B) A shipping firm
(C) A retail store
(D) A cleaning company

48. According to the man, why will customers like new goods?

(A) Because of its user-friendly design
(B) Because of its price that is much cheaper than other products
(C) Because of its ingredients that do not harm the environment
(D) Because of its online ordering system

49. What does the woman suggest the man do?

(A) Design a new model
(B) Revise a report
(C) Contact a supplier
(D) Put up a new sign

50. What type of business do the speakers most likely work for?

(A) A marketing agency
(B) A medical institution
(C) A conference center
(D) A flooring company

51. What does the man mean when he says, "Vicky is tied up with some other reports"?

(A) A deadline is expected to be extended.
(B) A colleague cannot participate in a meeting.
(C) He thinks they are understaffed.
(D) He has to work overtime for several months.

52. What will take place next year?

(A) A renovation project
(B) New training sessions
(C) An internship program
(D) Organizational reform

53. What does the woman indicate about the refrigerator?

(A) It is inexpensive.
(B) It will receive an award.
(C) It is in great demand.
(D) It consumes less energy.

54. What is the man concerned about?

(A) Insufficient work hours
(B) A limited budget
(C) Old equipment
(D) A shortage of labour

55. What does the woman suggest the man do on Thursday?

(A) Come to a meeting
(B) Hand in a report
(C) Review some data
(D) Lead a training session

56. What does the woman ask the man to do?

(A) Lead music classes
(B) Promote new recordings
(C) Fix some equipment
(D) Arrange transportation

57. Why is the woman not able to visit the store on Friday?

(A) She needs to meet a client.
(B) Her studio will be renovated.
(C) She will be on a business trip.
(D) Her family will be staying in town.

58. What does the man advise the woman to do?

(A) Print out some instructions
(B) Park her car in an area
(C) Bring enough cash
(D) Fill out a request form

---

59. Who is the woman?

(A) A business owner
(B) A construction worker
(C) A property developer
(D) A real estate agent

60. What does the man say about the TM 400 Watcher?

(A) It can be used to anticipate weather.
(B) It records cash transactions.
(C) It keeps track of the levels of moisture.
(D) It monitors system failures.

61. Why does the woman say she will call back?

(A) She wants to talk with her manager.
(B) She has a meeting to attend.
(C) She has to review her finances.
(D) She needs more information about the equipment.

Request Form	
Supplies & Equipment	**Number**
☐ Tables	13
☐ Chairs	60
☐ Podium	0
☐ Projectors	1
☐ Microphones	4

62. Look at the graphic. Which number on the request form needs to be updated?

(A) 13
(B) 60
(C) 0
(D) 4

63. According to the man, who is Mr. Collins?

(A) A conference speaker
(B) An event organizer
(C) A building inspector
(D) A news reporter

64. What does the woman say she will do next?

(A) Make a phone call
(B) Purchase some office supplies
(C) Go out for lunch
(D) Print out some documents

GO ON TO THE NEXT PAGE

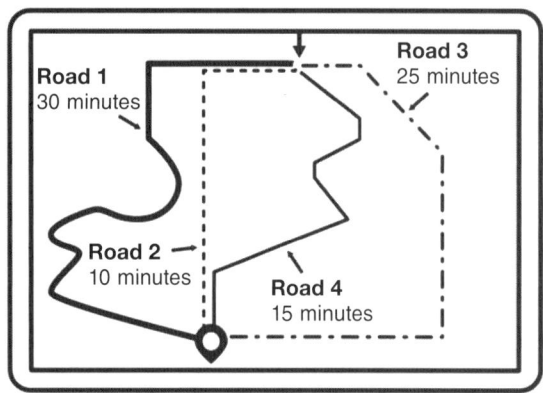

Fee list for Social Marketing		
	Students	**Professional**
Advance Registration (before Jun 10)	$50	$150
Standard Registration (After June 10)	$100	$250

65. Why is the man offering the woman a ride?

(A) Her train has been delayed.

(B) She has just moved to the area.

(C) Her car is being repaired.

(D) She left her car at home.

66. According to the man, what event is being held this evening?

(A) A marathon

(B) A musical event

(C) A sports game

(D) A parade

67. Look at the graphic. Which road will the speakers use?

(A) Road 1

(B) Road 2

(C) Road 3

(D) Road 4

68. What field does the man most likely work in?

(A) Financial management

(B) Research and development

(C) Sales and marketing

(D) Social studies

69. Look at the graphic. How much will the firm most likely pay for the event?

(A) $50

(B) $100

(C) $150

(D) $250

70. What will the man forward the woman by e-mail?

(A) An application form

(B) A registration number

(C) An event schedule

(D) A signed contract

Directions: You will hear some talks given by a single speaker. You will be asked to answer three questions about what the speaker says in each talk. Select the best response to each question and mark the letter (A), (B), (C), or (D) on your answer sheet. The talks will not be printed in your test book and will be spoken only one time.

71. What type of event was canceled this Friday?

(A) A sports match
(B) An outdoor exhibition
(C) A music concert
(D) A new product release

72. What is the reason for the cancellation of an event?

(A) Because of a technical problem
(B) Because of a construction project
(C) Because of severe weather conditions
(D) Because of a delay in government approval

73. What will most likely be aired next?

(A) Some local news
(B) Some advertisements
(C) Business reports
(D) Weather forecasts

74. Why is the speaker leaving the message?

(A) To give a notice to move out
(B) To complain about a fitness center
(C) To talk about a parking problem
(D) To request a repair service

75. According to the speaker, what happened a few days ago?

(A) She contacted a real estate agency.
(B) She lost her car key.
(C) She came home earlier than usual.
(D) She spoke to her neighbors.

76. What does the speaker say she wants to do on Monday afternoon?

(A) Rent a car
(B) Visit an office
(C) Meet her friends
(D) Go on a vacation

77. What does the speaker imply when he says, "it will only take a couple of minutes"?

(A) An inspection will not last long.
(B) Employees will get back to work soon.
(C) His office is close to the headquarters.
(D) A meeting will start in a minute.

78. What does the speaker say happened last Friday?

(A) A factory was renovated.
(B) A business was inspected.
(C) New equipment arrived.
(D) A power failure occurred.

79. What is Jeff Clark supposed to do this afternoon?

(A) Give some tips for working efficiently
(B) Provide a guide for safety management
(C) Replace some equipment
(D) Promote a new product

80. Where is the speaker reporting from?

(A) A radio station
(B) An art museum
(C) A community center
(D) A public library

81. What does the speaker say about paintings?

(A) They are leased from an art center.
(B) They can be purchased.
(C) They will be given as a gift.
(D) They are originally from other countries.

82. According to the speaker, what can the listeners do online?

(A) Join a membership program
(B) Get some information about paintings
(C) Register for an event
(D) Check a tour schedule

GO ON TO THE NEXT PAGE

83. What kind of business does the speaker work for?

(A) An electronics company
(B) A car dealership
(C) A home appliance store
(D) A marketing company

84. Why does the speaker say, "only the appearance of the phone will be examined by the reviewers at this time"?

(A) To make a change to a product
(B) To make the listener less worried
(C) To remind the listener of a deadline
(D) To express dissatisfaction with an arrangement

85. What is the listener asked to do?

(A) Start a new project
(B) Prepare a meeting
(C) Clarify a date
(D) Change a design

86. According to the speaker, what does the company do?

(A) Organize personal classes
(B) Provide online learning opportunities
(C) Provide driving instructions
(D) Help finding a job

87. What does the speaker say is surprising about the program?

(A) Its price
(B) Its instructors
(C) Its period
(D) Its flexibility

88. What does the speaker invite the listeners to do?

(A) Take an online test
(B) Download a discount coupon
(C) Watch an instructional video
(D) Quit a current job

89. Where do the listeners work?

(A) At a car wash
(B) At a post office
(C) At a car dealership
(D) At an advertising agency

90. According to the speaker, what is the purpose of the survey?

(A) To invite customers to an event
(B) To find out the level of customer satisfaction
(C) To decide the location of a new store
(D) To create a new vehicle

91. What incentive was offered to the customers who returned the survey?

(A) A car wash
(B) A car maintenance service
(C) A set of car tires
(D) A parking pass

92. Where most likely are the listeners?

(A) At an anniversary banquet
(B) At an award ceremony
(C) At an investor meeting
(D) At a retirement party

93. Why does the speaker say, "I always stopped by her office and asked questions"?

(A) To suggest an idea
(B) To remind a schedule
(C) To give a compliment
(D) To get some feedback

94. What does the speaker say she and her coworkers did?

(A) They purchased a present.
(B) They conducted a survey.
(C) They prepared their own meals.
(D) They made a contract.

Full Name : Barry Garza
ID Code : 00234-B

Department : Accounting
Extension Number : 3456
Telephone No. : 322-4431

Result of the Survey

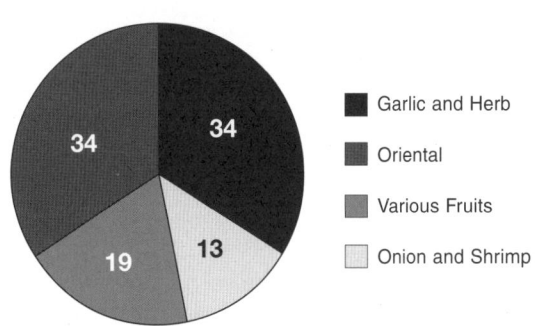

- ■ Garlic and Herb
- ■ Oriental
- ■ Various Fruits
- □ Onion and Shrimp

95. Which department does the listener work for?

(A) Accounting
(B) Personnel
(C) Security
(D) Sales

96. Look at the graphic. What information does the speaker mention is wrong?

(A) Barry Garza
(B) 00234-B
(C) 3456
(D) 322-4431

97. What is the listener asked to do?

(A) Forward some information
(B) Make a phone call
(C) Compile some documents
(D) Arrange a meeting

98. Which team does the speaker mostly likely work in?

(A) Sales and marketing
(B) Product development
(C) Accounting
(D) Purchasing

99. According to the speaker, what factor influenced a decision?

(A) Recent trends
(B) Budget limits
(C) Preference in other countries
(D) Similar products in a market

100. Look at the graphic. Which salad dressing will be produced?

(A) Garlic and herb
(B) Oriental
(C) Various fruits
(D) Onion and shrimp

This is the end of the Listening test.

정답 p. 158 / 점수 환산표 p. 159 / 스크립트 p. 211

TEST 10

⬇ Test10.mp3

MP3 다운로드
eng.conects.com

QR 코드로 바로가기

PART 1
PART 2
PART 3
PART 4

토익 Listening Comprehension은 약 45분 동안 진행됩니다.
반드시 녹음 파일의 재생 시간 내에
모든 문제 풀이를 완료하세요.

LISTENING TEST

In the Listening test, you will be asked to demonstrate how well you understand spoken English. The entire Listening test will last approximately 45 minutes. There are four parts, and directions are given for each part. You must mark your answers on the separate answer sheet. Do not write your answers in your test book.

PART 1

Directions: For each question in this part, you will hear four statements about a picture in your test book. When you hear the statements, you must select the one statement that best describes what you see in the picture. Then find the number of the question on your answer sheet and mark your answer. The statements will not be printed in your test book and will be spoken only one time.

Statement (C), "They are sitting at a table," is the best description of the picture, so you should select answer (C) and mark it on your answer sheet.

1.

2.

3.

4.

5.

6.

GO ON TO THE NEXT PAGE →

PART 2

Directions: You will hear a question or statement and three responses spoken in English. They will not be printed in your test book and will be spoken only one time. Select the best response to the question or statement and mark the letter (A), (B), or (C) on your answer sheet.

7. Mark your answer on your answer sheet.

8. Mark your answer on your answer sheet.

9. Mark your answer on your answer sheet.

10. Mark your answer on your answer sheet.

11. Mark your answer on your answer sheet.

12. Mark your answer on your answer sheet.

13. Mark your answer on your answer sheet.

14. Mark your answer on your answer sheet.

15. Mark your answer on your answer sheet.

16. Mark your answer on your answer sheet.

17. Mark your answer on your answer sheet.

18. Mark your answer on your answer sheet.

19. Mark your answer on your answer sheet.

20. Mark your answer on your answer sheet.

21. Mark your answer on your answer sheet.

22. Mark your answer on your answer sheet.

23. Mark your answer on your answer sheet.

24. Mark your answer on your answer sheet.

25. Mark your answer on your answer sheet.

26. Mark your answer on your answer sheet.

27. Mark your answer on your answer sheet.

28. Mark your answer on your answer sheet.

29. Mark your answer on your answer sheet.

30. Mark your answer on your answer sheet.

31. Mark your answer on your answer sheet.

PART 3

Directions: You will hear some conversations between two or more people. You will be asked to answer three questions about what the speakers say in each conversation. Select the best response to each question and mark the letter (A), (B), (C), or (D) on your answer sheet. The conversations will not be printed in your test book and will be spoken only one time.

32. Which department do the speakers work in?
(A) Sales
(B) Human Resources
(C) Information Technology
(D) Finance

33. What does the man want employees to know?
(A) The company will not dismiss anyone.
(B) The company will hire some new employees.
(C) A confidential survey will be conducted.
(D) Some employees are not satisfied.

34. What does the man say he will do next?
(A) Distribute an employee handbook
(B) Lead a seminar
(C) Arrange an information session
(D) Request some research data

35. How did the woman learn about Stanmore Gym?
(A) From an acquaintance
(B) From a TV advertisement
(C) From a poster
(D) From a magazine article

36. Why are Stanmore Gym's facilities more convenient than some of its competitors?
(A) Because of its multiple locations
(B) Because of its new equipment
(C) Because of its affordable prices
(D) Because of its longer operating hours

37. What is the woman going to do in October?
(A) Take part in a sports event
(B) Become a professional trainer
(C) Join a new company
(D) Publish a book

38. What are the speakers discussing?
(A) A musical performance
(B) A dance festival
(C) A photography exhibit
(D) A sales presentation

39. Why does the woman apologize to the man?
(A) A ticket is no longer valid.
(B) A parking area is full.
(C) A poster has changed.
(D) All seats have been sold out.

40. What will the man probably do on Saturday?
(A) Call back later
(B) Visit the gift shop
(C) Arrive early
(D) Buy a poster

41. What event is the man most likely attending?
(A) A sports game
(B) A convention
(C) A movie preview
(D) A book fair

42. What does the woman offer to do for the man?
(A) Provide some local information
(B) Issue a new pass
(C) Find a lost item
(D) Give a refund

43. What will the man most likely do next?
(A) Present some identification
(B) Proceed to the security office
(C) Make a reservation
(D) Contact his manager

44. What are the speakers discussing?

(A) Purchasing computer software
(B) Meeting a budget
(C) Hiring a service company
(D) Promoting store managers

45. According to the man, what should be considered?

(A) The times of cleaning service
(B) Budgetary restrictions
(C) Safety concerns
(D) Optional features

46. What does the man suggest doing?

(A) Checking online reviews
(B) Reviewing a proposal
(C) Contacting a service provider
(D) Working on a document

47. Who most likely is the man talking with?

(A) Legal assistants
(B) Researchers
(C) New hires
(D) Technicians

48. What does the man say about the fitness facility?

(A) It requires a nominal fee.
(B) It has been under renovation.
(C) It is not accessible early in the morning.
(D) It can be accessed by using an employee ID.

49. What will the women most likely do next?

(A) Go to the personnel office
(B) Arrange a regular meeting
(C) Meet with other workers
(D) Talk with a manager

50. According to the woman, why were some orders shipped later than scheduled?

(A) Some products were sold out.
(B) An employee called in sick.
(C) The order system had a problem.
(D) None of the delivery vehicles were available.

51. What does the woman suggest to make the process better?

(A) Outsourcing some work
(B) Texting customers when their order will arrive
(C) Taking inventory more often
(D) Hiring additional workers for the shipping department

52. What will the man most likely do today?

(A) Interview applicants
(B) Visit another branch
(C) Meet with some clients
(D) Announce a change

53. What kind of information does the woman ask about?

(A) An office address
(B) The status of an application
(C) A company's new Web site
(D) A university curriculum

54. What does the man imply when he says, "the position requires some previous work experience"?

(A) Many candidates have failed to get a job.
(B) The woman's qualifications may not be enough for a position.
(C) Some work can be more difficult than expected.
(D) The man will give up applying for a job.

55. What will the woman most likely do next?

(A) Set up a software program
(B) Visit the man's office
(C) Forward a link to the man
(D) Search for other open positions

56. What is the reason for the man's visit?

    (A) To tour a facility
    (B) To introduce a new product
    (C) To have an interview with a person
    (D) To register for an event

57. What is the man asked to do?

    (A) Read some documents
    (B) Present his identification
    (C) Come back later
    (D) Leave some information

58. What is the reason for Ms. Griffin's apology?

    (A) Some documents are missing.
    (B) Mr. Gregory needs to wait.
    (C) An appointment has been canceled.
    (D) An employee made a mistake.

59. Where most likely are the speakers?

    (A) At a real estate office
    (B) At a convention center
    (C) At a furniture store
    (D) At a restaurant

60. Why does the man say, "we do have a balcony table upstairs"?

    (A) To suggest an alternative
    (B) To verify that the payment and bill amount match
    (C) To change a seat
    (D) To show more items

61. What does the woman decide to do?

    (A) Place an order
    (B) Sit in the shade
    (C) Reserve a table
    (D) Visit another business

Final Destination	Departure time	Current Status
Vancouver	9:30	On time
Toronto	10:00	Delayed [one hour]
Calgary	10:30	Delayed [30 minutes]
Ottawa	12:15	On time

62. According to the man, what is the problem?

    (A) One of the speakers is late for an event.
    (B) A train is out of service for a few days.
    (C) He is not able to get somewhere in time.
    (D) A colleague of his called in sick.

63. Look at the graphic. Which destination do the speakers need to go?

    (A) To Vancouver
    (B) To Toronto
    (C) To Calgary
    (D) To Ottawa

64. What is the woman asked to do?

    (A) Make a call to someone
    (B) Call off a meeting
    (C) Ask for a deadline extension
    (D) Purchase tickets

Apricot Tree Measurement Chart

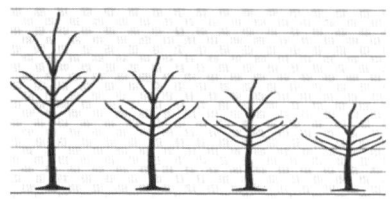

Size	1	2	3	4
Height	4.5 meters	3.5 meters	2.5 meters	1.5 meters

Harman International building
Directory
second floor

201	Cleary Recording Studio
202	Bryant Employment Services
203	Sally Beauty Holdings
204	World Languages Translations

65. Why does the man want to purchase some trees?

(A) To grow organic fruits
(B) To use for a memorial event
(C) To give them to his coworkers
(D) To enhance the appearance of a building

66. Look at the graphic. Which height of trees does the man intend to buy?

(A) 4.5 meters
(B) 3.5 meters
(C) 2.5 meters
(D) 1.5 meters

67. What extra service does the woman mention to the man?

(A) Lawn mowing
(B) Free tree planting
(C) Regular cleaning
(D) Express shipping

68. Look at the graphic. Which office will the man visit?

(A) Office 201
(B) Office 202
(C) Office 203
(D) Office 204

69. What does the woman offer the man?

(A) Some food
(B) Some information
(C) A beverage
(D) A message

70. Why was the man late?

(A) He was stuck in traffic.
(B) His phone was misplaced.
(C) He was not informed.
(D) He has a busy schedule.

Directions: You will hear some talks given by a single speaker. You will be asked to answer three questions about what the speaker says in each talk. Select the best response to each question and mark the letter (A), (B), (C), or (D) on your answer sheet. The talks will not be printed in your test book and will be spoken only one time.

71. Where most likely are the listeners?

(A) At a pharmacy
(B) In a food mart
(C) In a local café
(D) At a department store

72. What are the listeners encouraged to do?

(A) Buy new cooking equipment
(B) Obtain a discount coupon
(C) Eat some sample food
(D) Proceed to the checkout counter

73. What is mentioned about the bakery goods?

(A) They can be delivered.
(B) The prices are much cheaper.
(C) The ingredients are organic.
(D) They are cooked by a famous chef.

74. Which department in Newark City most likely created the message?

(A) Transportation
(B) Sanitation
(C) Construction
(D) Education

75. According to the message, what has caused a problem?

(A) The license fee was increased.
(B) An application process was shortened.
(C) More people want to travel overseas.
(D) A new policy will go into effect next year.

76. What does the message remind the listeners to do?

(A) Visit a Web site
(B) Return an old license
(C) Sign up for a membership
(D) Provide a registration number

77. What event is the speaker discussing?

(A) A staff orientation
(B) A corporate luncheon
(C) A product development
(D) A customer survey

78. What does the speaker ask the listeners to do?

(A) Fill out the survey
(B) Check an attendance list
(C) Devise some questions
(D) Invite a guest speaker

79. What does the speaker imply when he says, "I don't have much experience with this"?

(A) He does not want to take on a new task.
(B) He wants someone to teach him.
(C) He wants to learn more about this job.
(D) He cannot answer listeners' questions.

80. Where do the listeners work?

(A) At a community center
(B) At a clinic
(C) At a store
(D) At a factory

81. What does the speaker say will be changed?

(A) A chip-based ID card will be used.
(B) Some members will move to another office.
(C) A hiring policy will be revised.
(D) Security officers will be replaced.

82. What are the listeners asked to do by the end of the month?

(A) Visit the security office
(B) Submit opinions
(C) Download coupons
(D) Sign up for membership

83. What type of business does the speaker work for?

(A) A travel firm
(B) An advertising agency
(C) A hotel
(D) A recreation company

84. What are the listeners encouraged to do at today's meeting?

(A) Conduct a market survey
(B) Test a sample product
(C) Find some agencies
(D) Make a suggestion

85. What will the speaker do next?

(A) Distribute a document
(B) Accept volunteers
(C) Collect donations
(D) Answer some questions

86. What does the speaker apologize for?

(A) Being difficult to register online
(B) Informing an incorrect place
(C) Cancelling an appointment
(D) Arriving late to an event

87. Who is William Wiseman?

(A) A financial expert
(B) An architect
(C) A business owner
(D) A communication consultant

88. What will William Wiseman talk about?

(A) Securing data
(B) Developing collaboration skills
(C) Creating a proposal
(D) Evaluating a report

89. What is the speaker mainly talking about?

(A) Reviewing some information
(B) Making a plan for a party
(C) Attending a promotional event
(D) Arranging a business conference

90. What does the speaker imply when she says, "I think you remember how the last party was"?

(A) She is requiring more specific information.
(B) She did not need more help from her colleagues.
(C) She is not completely happy with the preceding event.
(D) She will arrange a meeting regularly.

91. What does the speaker say she is going to do tomorrow night?

(A) Order some food supplies
(B) Visit a restaurant
(C) Request some catering services
(D) Sign up for an event

92. What is the main topic of the broadcast?

(A) Overseas investment
(B) Finding a right location
(C) Hiring good workers
(D) Cost-effective advertising

93. What does the speaker imply when she says, "it seems very successful"?

(A) A marketing method may be effective.
(B) A training event should take place regularly.
(C) A store has been in business for a long time.
(D) A new business needs to focus on a product line.

94. What does the speaker say will happen next?

(A) A traffic update will be given.
(B) A commercial break will start.
(C) A guest will share some details.
(D) A list of sponsors will be announced.

Title	Time
How to be a farmer	09:00 A.M.
How to export agricultural and marine products	10:00 A.M.
The plan for construction of an Agricultural and Marine Products Distribution Center	03:00 P.M.
Marketing economics of agricultural products	05:00 P.M.

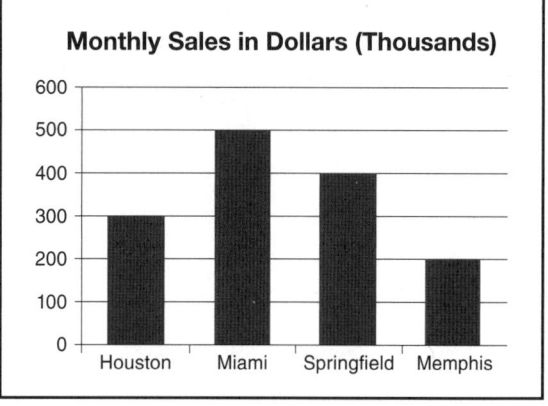

Monthly Sales in Dollars (Thousands)

95. Where is the announcement most likely being made?

(A) At a conference center
(B) At a community park
(C) At a market
(D) At a school

96. Look at the graphic. What time will the speaker be leading a talk?

(A) At 09:00 A.M.
(B) At 10:00 A.M.
(C) At 03:00 P.M.
(D) At 05:00 P.M.

97. What can the listeners find near the entrance?

(A) Brochures
(B) Light food and drinks
(C) Promotional gifts
(D) Area maps

98. What kind of business does the speaker work for?

(A) A consumer-research agency
(B) An office supplies store chain
(C) A real estate company
(D) A supermarket chain

99. Look at the graphic. According to the speaker, which location will have more space?

(A) Houston
(B) Miami
(C) Springfield
(D) Memphis

100. What does the speaker say she will do?

(A) Recruit more employees
(B) Praise a team's performance
(C) Order additional supplies
(D) Contact a local manager

This is the end of the Listening test.

정답&
스크립트

정답

점수 환산표

스크립트

ANSWER SHEETS

ANSWER KEYS 정답

TEST 01

PART 1	1 (D)	2 (B)	3 (C)	4 (C)	5 (D)
	6 (A)				

PART 2	7 (C)	8 (C)	9 (C)	10 (A)	11 (C)
	12 (A)	13 (B)	14 (A)	15 (B)	16 (B)
	17 (C)	18 (A)	19 (A)	20 (A)	21 (A)
	22 (A)	23 (C)	24 (B)	25 (B)	26 (A)
	27 (C)	28 (C)	29 (B)	30 (B)	31 (B)

PART 3	32 (B)	33 (C)	34 (D)	35 (A)	36 (C)
	37 (D)	38 (C)	39 (B)	40 (A)	41 (C)
	42 (B)	43 (A)	44 (B)	45 (D)	46 (C)
	47 (B)	48 (D)	49 (B)	50 (C)	51 (B)
	52 (B)	53 (B)	54 (C)	55 (D)	56 (C)
	57 (B)	58 (C)	59 (A)	60 (A)	61 (C)
	62 (A)	63 (C)	64 (C)	65 (C)	66 (D)
	67 (B)	68 (C)	69 (C)	70 (D)	

PART 4	71 (A)	72 (D)	73 (C)	74 (C)	75 (B)
	76 (A)	77 (C)	78 (D)	79 (C)	80 (B)
	81 (B)	82 (A)	83 (C)	84 (B)	85 (A)
	86 (D)	87 (B)	88 (B)	89 (D)	90 (C)
	91 (D)	92 (B)	93 (D)	94 (A)	95 (C)
	96 (C)	97 (D)	98 (B)	99 (D)	100 (C)

TEST 02

PART 1	1 (C)	2 (C)	3 (B)	4 (B)	5 (D)
	6 (C)				

PART 2	7 (C)	8 (C)	9 (B)	10 (B)	11 (A)
	12 (C)	13 (B)	14 (C)	15 (C)	16 (C)
	17 (A)	18 (C)	19 (A)	20 (A)	21 (C)
	22 (A)	23 (C)	24 (A)	25 (C)	26 (A)
	27 (C)	28 (A)	29 (B)	30 (C)	31 (C)

PART 3	32 (B)	33 (A)	34 (B)	35 (C)	36 (B)
	37 (B)	38 (D)	39 (C)	40 (A)	41 (B)
	42 (B)	43 (A)	44 (C)	45 (D)	46 (C)
	47 (C)	48 (C)	49 (A)	50 (D)	51 (A)
	52 (A)	53 (A)	54 (C)	55 (C)	56 (B)
	57 (A)	58 (B)	59 (A)	60 (C)	61 (C)
	62 (D)	63 (A)	64 (C)	65 (A)	66 (C)
	67 (D)	68 (D)	69 (C)	70 (B)	

PART 4	71 (C)	72 (C)	73 (A)	74 (D)	75 (C)
	76 (B)	77 (C)	78 (C)	79 (D)	80 (C)
	81 (C)	82 (D)	83 (C)	84 (B)	85 (D)
	86 (C)	87 (A)	88 (D)	89 (D)	90 (B)
	91 (A)	92 (C)	93 (B)	94 (D)	95 (B)
	96 (C)	97 (C)	98 (B)	99 (C)	100 (C)

TEST 03

PART 1 1 (C) 2 (B) 3 (A) 4 (C) 5 (D)
6 (D)

PART 2 7 (A) 8 (B) 9 (B) 10 (B) 11 (C)
12 (C) 13 (A) 14 (C) 15 (C) 16 (A)
17 (A) 18 (A) 19 (C) 20 (B) 21 (B)
22 (B) 23 (C) 24 (A) 25 (B) 26 (C)
27 (B) 28 (C) 29 (A) 30 (A) 31 (A)

PART 3 32 (B) 33 (C) 34 (D) 35 (C) 36 (B)
37 (C) 38 (B) 39 (D) 40 (C) 41 (B)
42 (D) 43 (A) 44 (C) 45 (C) 46 (B)
47 (D) 48 (C) 49 (A) 50 (C) 51 (D)
52 (C) 53 (B) 54 (A) 55 (D) 56 (D)
57 (C) 58 (B) 59 (A) 60 (B) 61 (C)
62 (B) 63 (C) 64 (B) 65 (D) 66 (B)
67 (D) 68 (A) 69 (D) 70 (A)

PART 4 71 (C) 72 (B) 73 (B) 74 (B) 75 (C)
76 (B) 77 (B) 78 (A) 79 (C) 80 (A)
81 (B) 82 (C) 83 (B) 84 (B) 85 (A)
86 (B) 87 (B) 88 (D) 89 (C) 90 (D)
91 (A) 92 (C) 93 (D) 94 (D) 95 (D)
96 (C) 97 (A) 98 (B) 99 (C) 100 (C)

TEST 04

PART 1 1 (B) 2 (D) 3 (B) 4 (B) 5 (D)
6 (A)

PART 2 7 (C) 8 (A) 9 (A) 10 (B) 11 (B)
12 (C) 13 (C) 14 (B) 15 (B) 16 (B)
17 (A) 18 (B) 19 (B) 20 (B) 21 (C)
22 (B) 23 (A) 24 (B) 25 (B) 26 (A)
27 (C) 28 (C) 29 (C) 30 (A) 31 (B)

PART 3 32 (C) 33 (B) 34 (D) 35 (C) 36 (A)
37 (D) 38 (B) 39 (A) 40 (D) 41 (C)
42 (D) 43 (C) 44 (B) 45 (A) 46 (D)
47 (C) 48 (D) 49 (C) 50 (C) 51 (C)
52 (C) 53 (B) 54 (C) 55 (D) 56 (B)
57 (C) 58 (C) 59 (D) 60 (C) 61 (A)
62 (A) 63 (C) 64 (B) 65 (B) 66 (B)
67 (D) 68 (A) 69 (B) 70 (C)

PART 4 71 (C) 72 (D) 73 (A) 74 (B) 75 (D)
76 (A) 77 (C) 78 (A) 79 (B) 80 (C)
81 (A) 82 (B) 83 (B) 84 (B) 85 (C)
86 (D) 87 (B) 88 (A) 89 (A) 90 (B)
91 (A) 92 (C) 93 (D) 94 (C) 95 (C)
96 (A) 97 (B) 98 (D) 99 (C) 100 (B)

TEST 05

PART 1 1 (B) 2 (A) 3 (D) 4 (B) 5 (B)
6 (C)

PART 2 7 (C) 8 (B) 9 (C) 10 (B) 11 (A)
12 (A) 13 (A) 14 (C) 15 (B) 16 (C)
17 (C) 18 (C) 19 (A) 20 (C) 21 (C)
22 (C) 23 (B) 24 (C) 25 (B) 26 (B)
27 (C) 28 (C) 29 (A) 30 (B) 31 (A)

PART 3 32 (D) 33 (C) 34 (A) 35 (B) 36 (B)
37 (C) 38 (A) 39 (C) 40 (B) 41 (B)
42 (C) 43 (B) 44 (B) 45 (A) 46 (D)
47 (D) 48 (B) 49 (C) 50 (B) 51 (D)
52 (C) 53 (C) 54 (A) 55 (A) 56 (D)
57 (D) 58 (C) 59 (C) 60 (B) 61 (B)
62 (C) 63 (C) 64 (A) 65 (B) 66 (B)
67 (C) 68 (B) 69 (D) 70 (C)

PART 4 71 (B) 72 (B) 73 (C) 74 (C) 75 (A)
76 (D) 77 (C) 78 (B) 79 (A) 80 (D)
81 (C) 82 (A) 83 (B) 84 (C) 85 (B)
86 (C) 87 (B) 88 (D) 89 (A) 90 (C)
91 (B) 92 (D) 93 (B) 94 (B) 95 (D)
96 (D) 97 (A) 98 (C) 99 (B) 100 (D)

TEST 06

PART 1 1 (D) 2 (C) 3 (B) 4 (B) 5 (D)
6 (C)

PART 2 7 (C) 8 (A) 9 (C) 10 (C) 11 (A)
12 (B) 13 (C) 14 (C) 15 (B) 16 (B)
17 (B) 18 (C) 19 (C) 20 (C) 21 (A)
22 (C) 23 (C) 24 (C) 25 (B) 26 (B)
27 (A) 28 (C) 29 (B) 30 (A) 31 (A)

PART 3 32 (A) 33 (B) 34 (C) 35 (C) 36 (B)
37 (D) 38 (B) 39 (C) 40 (D) 41 (B)
42 (A) 43 (D) 44 (A) 45 (A) 46 (D)
47 (C) 48 (C) 49 (A) 50 (D) 51 (C)
52 (B) 53 (C) 54 (B) 55 (B) 56 (B)
57 (A) 58 (B) 59 (C) 60 (C) 61 (D)
62 (C) 63 (D) 64 (A) 65 (B) 66 (C)
67 (B) 68 (D) 69 (D) 70 (B)

PART 4 71 (A) 72 (C) 73 (B) 74 (C) 75 (D)
76 (C) 77 (B) 78 (A) 79 (C) 80 (D)
81 (B) 82 (A) 83 (A) 84 (B) 85 (B)
86 (D) 87 (C) 88 (A) 89 (C) 90 (D)
91 (D) 92 (C) 93 (C) 94 (D) 95 (C)
96 (B) 97 (B) 98 (B) 99 (C) 100 (B)

TEST 07

PART 1
1 (C) 2 (B) 3 (C) 4 (A) 5 (A)
6 (B)

PART 2
7 (A) 8 (A) 9 (B) 10 (C) 11 (A)
12 (B) 13 (B) 14 (C) 15 (C) 16 (C)
17 (A) 18 (C) 19 (B) 20 (B) 21 (C)
22 (C) 23 (B) 24 (B) 25 (C) 26 (C)
27 (B) 28 (A) 29 (A) 30 (C) 31 (B)

PART 3
32 (D) 33 (D) 34 (B) 35 (A) 36 (C)
37 (B) 38 (B) 39 (A) 40 (D) 41 (C)
42 (D) 43 (C) 44 (C) 45 (D) 46 (D)
47 (C) 48 (C) 49 (C) 50 (A) 51 (A)
52 (B) 53 (C) 54 (B) 55 (D) 56 (C)
57 (D) 58 (B) 59 (D) 60 (C) 61 (B)
62 (C) 63 (A) 64 (C) 65 (B) 66 (C)
67 (A) 68 (C) 69 (D) 70 (C)

PART 4
71 (C) 72 (B) 73 (C) 74 (B) 75 (C)
76 (A) 77 (B) 78 (A) 79 (A) 80 (A)
81 (D) 82 (B) 83 (C) 84 (B) 85 (D)
86 (C) 87 (D) 88 (B) 89 (B) 90 (C)
91 (D) 92 (C) 93 (B) 94 (A) 95 (B)
96 (D) 97 (D) 98 (B) 99 (D) 100 (D)

TEST 08

PART 1
1 (C) 2 (D) 3 (D) 4 (C) 5 (B)
6 (C)

PART 2
7 (B) 8 (A) 9 (B) 10 (B) 11 (C)
12 (B) 13 (C) 14 (C) 15 (A) 16 (C)
17 (C) 18 (C) 19 (C) 20 (C) 21 (B)
22 (B) 23 (C) 24 (C) 25 (C) 26 (A)
27 (A) 28 (A) 29 (B) 30 (A) 31 (B)

PART 3
32 (B) 33 (C) 34 (A) 35 (A) 36 (B)
37 (C) 38 (C) 39 (B) 40 (A) 41 (A)
42 (D) 43 (C) 44 (B) 45 (B) 46 (C)
47 (C) 48 (C) 49 (C) 50 (C) 51 (A)
52 (C) 53 (C) 54 (C) 55 (C) 56 (C)
57 (C) 58 (B) 59 (C) 60 (C) 61 (B)
62 (A) 63 (A) 64 (C) 65 (B) 66 (B)
67 (B) 68 (A) 69 (C) 70 (C)

PART 4
71 (A) 72 (D) 73 (C) 74 (C) 75 (A)
76 (A) 77 (B) 78 (C) 79 (D) 80 (A)
81 (C) 82 (B) 83 (C) 84 (B) 85 (D)
86 (D) 87 (B) 88 (C) 89 (B) 90 (A)
91 (A) 92 (A) 93 (B) 94 (C) 95 (B)
96 (D) 97 (D) 98 (C) 99 (C) 100 (A)

TEST 09

PART 1
1 (C) 2 (D) 3 (A) 4 (A) 5 (C)
6 (D)

PART 2
7 (B) 8 (B) 9 (B) 10 (C) 11 (A)
12 (B) 13 (C) 14 (C) 15 (C) 16 (B)
17 (B) 18 (A) 19 (B) 20 (C) 21 (B)
22 (B) 23 (A) 24 (B) 25 (A) 26 (A)
27 (C) 28 (B) 29 (B) 30 (C) 31 (B)

PART 3
32 (A) 33 (D) 34 (B) 35 (B) 36 (A)
37 (B) 38 (B) 39 (D) 40 (B) 41 (A)
42 (D) 43 (C) 44 (B) 45 (A) 46 (B)
47 (C) 48 (C) 49 (C) 50 (B) 51 (B)
52 (A) 53 (C) 54 (D) 55 (A) 56 (C)
57 (C) 58 (B) 59 (A) 60 (C) 61 (C)
62 (B) 63 (A) 64 (D) 65 (C) 66 (B)
67 (D) 68 (C) 69 (D) 70 (C)

PART 4
71 (C) 72 (C) 73 (B) 74 (C) 75 (D)
76 (B) 77 (B) 78 (B) 79 (A) 80 (C)
81 (B) 82 (B) 83 (A) 84 (B) 85 (C)
86 (B) 87 (D) 88 (A) 89 (C) 90 (B)
91 (A) 92 (D) 93 (C) 94 (A) 95 (C)
96 (C) 97 (B) 98 (B) 99 (C) 100 (B)

TEST 10

PART 1
1 (B) 2 (D) 3 (A) 4 (B) 5 (A)
6 (D)

PART 2
7 (B) 8 (B) 9 (B) 10 (A) 11 (B)
12 (B) 13 (C) 14 (A) 15 (B) 16 (B)
17 (B) 18 (B) 19 (B) 20 (C) 21 (B)
22 (A) 23 (C) 24 (B) 25 (A) 26 (A)
27 (B) 28 (B) 29 (A) 30 (C) 31 (B)

PART 3
32 (B) 33 (A) 34 (C) 35 (B) 36 (D)
37 (A) 38 (A) 39 (D) 40 (C) 41 (B)
42 (B) 43 (A) 44 (C) 45 (B) 46 (D)
47 (C) 48 (D) 49 (C) 50 (C) 51 (B)
52 (D) 53 (B) 54 (C) 55 (C) 56 (C)
57 (D) 58 (B) 59 (D) 60 (A) 61 (D)
62 (C) 63 (C) 64 (A) 65 (D) 66 (C)
67 (B) 68 (C) 69 (B) 70 (D)

PART 4
71 (B) 72 (C) 73 (C) 74 (A) 75 (D)
76 (D) 77 (D) 78 (C) 79 (D) 80 (D)
81 (A) 82 (A) 83 (C) 84 (D) 85 (A)
86 (B) 87 (A) 88 (C) 89 (B) 90 (C)
91 (B) 92 (D) 93 (A) 94 (C) 95 (C)
96 (C) 97 (B) 98 (B) 99 (B) 100 (D)

점수 환산표

맞은 개수	환산 점수	맞은 개수	환산 점수
96–100	485–495	41–45	140–180
91–95	440–490	36–40	115–150
86–90	400–445	31–35	95–130
81–85	360–410	26–30	80–115
76–80	330–375	21–25	60–95
71–75	300–345	16–20	40–65
66–70	270–315	11–15	25–45
61–65	245–285	6–10	15–30
56–60	220–260	1–5	5–15
51–55	195–235	0	5
46–50	165–205		

나의 점수 향상표

TEST	맞은 개수	환산 점수
TEST 01		
TEST 02		
TEST 03		
TEST 04		
TEST 05		
TEST 06		
TEST 07		
TEST 08		
TEST 09		
TEST 10		

▶각 TEST 채점 후 향상표를 작성하여 나의 실력 향상을 확인하세요.

PART 1

1
US
(A) One of the men is typing on a keyboard.
(B) One of the men is putting on his watch.
(C) The men are leaning over the railing.
(D) The men are looking at a computer.

2
US
(A) Some people are working on the sign.
(B) Some people are crossing a street.
(C) Some people are waiting for a bus.
(D) Some people are entering an outdoor café.

3
AU
(A) Some people are getting on a boat.
(B) Some people are resting on the deck.
(C) Some people are strolling along a pier.
(D) Some people are walking on a bridge.

4
BR
(A) A man is operating a truck.
(B) Some workers are taking a break at the corner.
(C) Some construction materials have been stacked.
(D) Some bricks have fallen out of a cart.

5
US
(A) They're looking in the same direction.
(B) They're assembling some shelving units.
(C) They're having a discussion.
(D) They're seated across from each other.

6
BR
(A) Trees have been planted near some buildings.
(B) A concrete path goes down to a forest.
(C) Lampposts are being fixed.
(D) Some stairs lead to a garden.

PART 2

7
US
US
Does this train go to the Huston National Park?
(A) It has a limited parking space.
(B) I left it on the bus.
(C) Yes, it does.

8
AU
US
Where is the nearest hospital located?
(A) Not so good.
(B) Ten floors.
(C) On Queen's Avenue.

9
BR
US
How was the trade convention last week?
(A) It was on June 12.
(B) I do have a seminar.
(C) It was extremely well attended.

10
US
US
Who's going to pick up the clients from the hotel?
(A) I will pick them up at eleven.
(B) It's my favorite hotel.
(C) At the lobby.

11
US
BR
When is the marketing budget due?
(A) Yes, the monthly payment is due today.
(B) In the accounting department.
(C) In a month.

12
AU
BR
Which restaurant do you want me to make the reservation at?
(A) The Chinese restaurant next to Sky Tower.
(B) Through the Web site.
(C) At least ten.

13
US
AU
Would you like some help in packaging trial products?
(A) Sure, I'd love to help you.
(B) Sandra has already sent them out yesterday.
(C) No, I didn't.

14
BR
AU
How many more are we interviewing this afternoon?
(A) That was the last applicant.
(B) He will interview the rest.
(C) No, we don't need it any more.

15
US
US
Why is the pharmacy at the corner of Michigan Avenue closed today?
(A) The corner of Santa Monica and Winter streets.
(B) For some renovations.
(C) In the next building.

16
US
BR
Do you have a customer account with our store?
(A) No, he is not our customer.
(B) Yes, you should have my address.
(C) A month ago.

17
AU
US
Where can I find the list of guests for the banquet?
(A) Outside of London.
(B) That's a nice party.
(C) On the Web site.

18 AU BR Why don't we get rid of the old stocks and boxes in storage?
(A) Sure, but let me finish this first.
(B) To make more space.
(C) Oh, did she?

19 US US Didn't you come here for lunch yesterday?
(A) Yes, around noon.
(B) At the restaurant.
(C) A reservation for 6.

20 US AU I heard that Kathy moved to the human resources department in January.
(A) Oh, I didn't know that.
(B) Yes, they moved in.
(C) The winter sales event.

21 BR US Do you need to review the monthly bank statement or the yearly one?
(A) The one for this fiscal year.
(B) I will get a new one.
(C) Every two months.

22 BR AU Could I use your computer for a while?
(A) My graphic card is not working currently.
(B) Yes, you did.
(C) I couldn't buy it.

23 US US When are you available to talk about the product designs with me?
(A) In my office.
(B) No, they didn't.
(C) I'm free all this afternoon.

24 US BR These blue pants look good on you.
(A) No, I am not able to go with you.
(B) I think I should try this pair instead.
(C) Yes, it was good to see her.

25 AU US The elevator in the main building was fixed yesterday, right?
(A) Five is enough.
(B) None of our technicians were available.
(C) Yes, the right building.

26 AU BR Who will be invited as a keynote speaker for the workshop?
(A) Adrian has made the list.
(B) They will close soon.
(C) I ordered Asian food as well.

27 US US Do you want me to select the candidates?
(A) Yes, he did a good job.
(B) They warned me about the trails.
(C) We're still accepting applications.

28 US AU How long will it take to become a professional carpenter?
(A) For a price estimate.
(B) Since the last year.
(C) Are you interested in training for that job?

29 BR US The photo shooting for the magazine is finished, right?
(A) A yearly subscription.
(B) The studio had to start over.
(C) No, I didn't mean that.

30 BR AU Would you like to address the board of directors first or shall I?
(A) Quality issues.
(B) Why don't you start?
(C) About ten board members.

31 AU BR We are struggling to attract new customers in the Asian market.
(A) Only for a couple of months.
(B) You should offer the cash incentive to first time buyers.
(C) Yes, they performed very well.

PART 3

Questions 32-34 refer to the following conversation.
| US - AU |

W   I'd like to rent kayaks for two days. They will be for myself and my husband.

M   Right, the total fee will be £70. The kayaks can be picked up from the deck right over there. And, please bring them back to the same place by 11 o'clock on the day you return them. There will be a small additional charge if you're late.

W   Well, I don't think we'll be late. By the way, would you recommend any good rivers or lakes for kayaking around the area?

M   Yeah, there is a scenic river nearby. We have some maps showing directions to some good places for kayaking including that one. Please take a copy. It's free.

Questions 35-37 refer to the following conversation.

| US - US |

W   Good afternoon, Mr. Allen. Baker is not in his office and I was asked to hand in a request for some new office chairs to him no later than today. I brought the form with me. Could you give it to him?

M   Sure, no problem. He's attending a meeting with one of his clients, and he'll be back soon.

W   Thank you. I have to leave for an interview with a job candidate this afternoon.

Questions 38-40 refer to the following conversation.

| US - BR |

M   Hilda. I just spoke with our TV program's producer, and he informed me that Erica Riley, the famous chef, agreed to appear on one of our afternoon programs next week. She would like to promote her new cookbook.

W   That's great. That would be very interesting. I'm sure she'll demonstrate one of her special recipes.

M   Right! That's why we need to have our kitchen set arranged for her. Tomorrow, Chef Riley will be e-mailing us a list of all of the ingredients and equipment required for her show.

W   Alright, I'll be expecting her e-mail and we can talk about it then.

Questions 41-43 refer to the following conversation with three speakers.

| AU - BR - US |

M   Hello, Terri and Debra. I was just informed by the e-mail you sent me that the machines on the assembly line have some problems. What seems to be wrong?

W1   Well, the packing unit is not as fast as it should be. Debra already contacted a technician to get help.

W2   Yes. The technician came and found that some of the conveyer belts are not working properly. So the overall process is taking far longer than it used to.

M   That sounds serious. We should set up a time when the line can be shut down for the repair work.

Questions 44-46 refer to the following conversation.

| US - US |

W   Hi, Robin. We're scheduled to launch a new line of leather shoes next month. So, my biggest issue is how we market the shoes better. And I'm trying to find some low-cost ways to promote them. Do you have any suggestions?

M   You know that it is important to target the right customers and that makes the advertisement more cost-efficient. Also you will need to focus on the fact that they are made with collaboration of a famous jewelry brand.

W   Definitively. Why don't we offer a discount to all return customers who have purchased our shoes for the last two years? And if they bring their friends we also offer the same discount to them.

Questions 47-49 refer to the following conversation.

| US - US |

M   Technical Support, how can I help you?

W   Hi, I'm having difficulty using the time reporting software. Since last week, it hasn't allowed me to log in to my account, and I'm very concerned my paycheck won't be issued on time.

M   We're sorry to hear that. The software was recently updated. Would you describe what information your login screen shows?

W   Actually, I'm out of the office at the moment. I'm on my way to meet one of my clients and won't be back to my office.

M   OK. Then, why don't I e-mail you some instructions? So you can consult them to solve the problem.

W   Oh, that sounds great. Thank you.

Questions 50-52 refer to the following conversation.

| BR - AU |

W   Hello, Jack. How did last week's employee award banquet go?

M   It was pretty good. Actually, I received a prize for accomplishing the highest sales numbers.

W   Oh, congratulations. But that does not really surprise me. Your sales number always impresses me. By the way, what's the prize?

M   Well, it was a couple of tickets to a baseball game on Saturday.

W That's great.

M Yeah, but you know, I'm planning to go on holiday this weekend. So I don't think I'll be able to go.

W That's too bad. Then, are you going to give the tickets away to someone?

M Yes, would you like to go to the game?

Questions 53-55 refer to the following conversation.

| BR - US |

W Bennie, you've been working on the new personal directory application for mobile device, haven't you? How is it coming along?

M The tech development division has been helping us make the app ready to run. But it seems there are still several problems in the final stage when it displays specific information related to home addresses.

W Okay. Then, how long do you believe it will take to make the app ready?

M Well, someone from the software team might be able to tell you that. I hope it won't take long, but it seems...

W Hmm... I should talk with them about it. I'm concerned about the launch we have scheduled for the beginning of the next month. Before the event, consumer testing should be done.

Questions 56-58 refer to the following conversation.

| AU - US |

M Good morning. I'm Noel Torres. I phoned you yesterday about visiting your office complex to check if I can rent an office for my dental clinic.

W Alright, Dr. Torres. I've been waiting for you. My name is Alicia and I'm property manager for the complex.

M Pleased to meet you. I would like to rent space on the first floor, which makes my clinic more easily accessible for my patients.

W Sure, let me show you around some offices on the first floor. By the way, do you know we have a parking lot beside the building? It's only for this office complex, so your patients and employees can readily use it.

Questions 59-61 refer to the following conversation with three speakers.

| BR - US - AU |

W1 Hello, Steven. I'm Edith Henry, human resources manager at Horton Marketing, and this is my coworker, Sadie Jackson.

W2 Glad to meet you, Steven.

W1 Could you tell us about your previous work experience?

M Well, I have extensive experience in Web design. I believe you can see it in my portfolio.

W2 Oh, it's quite fascinating. Would you tell us any specialties you have?

M I have participated in creating many Web pages for large international organizations.

W2 It seems you have been doing great at your previous job. What made you decide to leave?

M I liked my work, but it was only a temporary position. I was told that Horton offers permanent positions. I think Horton considers its employees important assets. I'm quite impressed.

Questions 62-64 refer to the following conversation and schedule.

| AU - BR |

M Hi, Jessy. You're on the team that will be giving a presentation of our new packaging design at the international design conference, right?

W That's right, James. We introduced a more sophisticated packaging design. According to our recent market research, most consumers greatly preferred the new design to traditional ones.

M You know, I have some new clients in Paris and they said that they would also like to see it if possible. Do you think you can add one more stop to your next month's trip?

W Well, we could go to Paris the day after we're in Amsterdam and move Firenze's design exhibition to Thursday.

Questions 65-67 refer to the following conversation and window.

| US - AU |

W Hello, Misty. We need to leave for the annual conference soon, right? Actually, I need some help before we go. I wanted to open some files on my computer, but this window popped up.

M Hmm... Let me see. Well, it's asking you to choose an option among four to install the software which is needed to open the files.

W Do you know which option would be better than the others?

M Well, I used the third one, but it had me spend too much time to install the software. I asked some of my friends and they said the last one is the best.

W Oh, thank you. I should finish installing it right now before joining you to the conference.

Questions 68-70 refer to the following conversation and table of contents.
I US - US I

M Ms. Hicks. I've just reviewed the business plan you created, and it seems you made a great one. You've got an intriguing idea for your new hotel. I think you've taken much account of your main customer base.

W That's right. From my previous business, I learned that attracting everyone is impossible and inefficient. So, to avoid making the same mistake, I tried to focus more on the concept for certain customers.

M Excellent. OK, now you're going to use this plan to get a loan, right? So, I think you need to revise the budget you estimated. Especially, since staffing tends to cost much higher than this, more of the expense should be allocated to it.

PART 4

Questions 71-73 refer to the following introduction.
I US I

M Welcome to the Annual Businessman of the Year Banquet and thank you for being with us tonight. Now, it's time to present the award to this year's winner. Each year we honor a local entrepreneur who has succeeded in business and ultimately benefited the community. This year's award will go to Suzanne Horton, founder of the Brandy Restaurant, which is well known as one of the most popular spots in the area. Ms. Horton has been supporting young people willing to begin their own

business and recently set up the Suzanne scholarship program to assist students with their educational expenses. Let's give her a round of applause.

Questions 74-76 refer to the following talk.
I US I

W Good afternoon, welcome to Maxine Research Firm's staff training course for new employees. I believe you'll love market research work with us very much. I'm Thelma and I will lead today's training. This afternoon, we'll go over the employee handbook. But before we start, you've received an application form, so please fill it out for the employee ID badge. You will need the badge when you access any of our facilities. During the training, please help yourself to snacks and beverages on the table by the window. Thank you.

Questions 77-79 refer to the following tour information.
I BR I

W Well, this is the end of our tour of Euston History Museum. I hope all of you have found today's tour both exciting and informative. Well, before leaving today, I'd like you all to visit our souvenir shop on the first floor. There are a wide selection of items that would make today's tour more memorable. In addition, you can learn more about our art restoration processes. If you come to the reception desk now, you can meet some of our restoration specialists.

Questions 80-82 refer to the following telephone message.
I US I

M Hi, Ms. Herrera. This is Kurt Howell living in Apartment 201 and I'm returning your call regarding the annual building inspection. Thank you for reminding me about this. But I didn't realize it's scheduled to be inspected this Wednesday. Is it possible to do it this Friday instead? Some of my family members are coming to see me on Wednesday. So, it would be great if you reschedule the inspection for Friday. I'll be expecting your call soon. Thank you.

Questions 83-85 refer to the following excerpt from a meeting.

| AU |

M Thank you for attending today's staff meeting. Before we talk about our agenda, let me remind you that the time sheet needs to be completed and handed in by Thursday. Now, first I'd like to tell you about some great news. We've experienced dramatic increases in sales for the last three months. I really appreciate your hard work and dedication. I'm well aware that our quarterly report about our top-selling goods should have been prepared for this staff meeting, but you know, some important clients from Washington are visiting us for a week. So, it won't be ready until tomorrow afternoon. You all will receive it by e-mail.

Questions 86-88 refer to the following broadcast.

| BR |

W And now for our local news. The town's public transit authority will introduce a new payment system for public transportation. As of next week, commuters will have the option of paying their fares with an electronic card when they use public transportation. The cards can be considered as debit cards. Commuters can use the card multiple times as long as they put enough money into it. The cash-only system often caused people to waste time, trying to find change for their fare. Some commuters we interviewed are pleased with the new system because it allows them to travel a lot more conveniently. However, at the moment this system is only limited to some parts of the town. In July, the authority is planning to expand this service into the other areas in the town.

Questions 89-91 refer to the following talk.

| US |

M Welcome to this month's career development seminar. We'll be focusing on the problem that our staff members frequently experience cultural misunderstandings in their foreign assignments. Many business relationship related issues can be caused by unfamiliarity with what is usual for the host culture. We are currently working very much with international clients. Thus, it is important for us to improve relationships across other cultures. You can check other things in the packet you have received – such as how to make a good impression, exchange greetings or make an appointment. Let's go through it together.

Question 92-94 refer to the following talk.

| BR |

W Well, I'm pleased to meet you all here at JR Constructions. And thank you for inviting me to introduce the Reymo Online Meeting System. Since your company has many international projects as well as local ones, in order to meet your clients and on-site staff you need to visit them. However, with this system, you can reduce the need for on-site meetings, which means you will improve efficiency in time and money. Just say there are some concerns about your project in New York. You don't need to travel immediately. First you can figure out what the concerns are through the online meeting with your on-site managers. Okay, now I'd like to show you how to use this system. Please check your computer is turned on.

Questions 95-97 refer to the following announcement and train ticket.

| US |

W Attention, please! We are sorry to inform all the passengers on board train 34 to Grand Canyon of a delay. Due to the heavy snow, our train needs to stop at the next station while our work crew clears the train tracks. Passengers are allowed to get off the train, but please stay within the train station. An announcement will be made when our train is ready to depart. We apologize for this delay once again. We expect that we will arrive at Grand Canyon station at around 7 P.M., which is an hour later than originally scheduled. A voucher for a complimentary meal will be passed out to each passenger to compensate for the unexpected delay. The voucher can be used at any café or restaurant in the station.

Questions 98-100 refer to the following talk and chart.

| AU |

M   Yesterday, we talked about how to handle the most frequent customer inquiries. At today's workshop, we'll focus on upgrading satellite TV service when a subscriber makes a request. Take a look at the chart on page 43 in your handbook, which shows the package options. Among the four options, most subscribers are currently using the one which includes only national channels. However, we can suggest them to use the best deal with national channels plus movies and dramas. When you sell this option to more than fifteen customers by next month, a bonus will be added to your paycheck as an incentive.

PART 1

1
AU
(A) He's holding onto a door handle.
(B) He's entering a restaurant.
(C) He's walking through a revolving door.
(D) He's carrying some plants.

2
US
(A) The woman is inspecting some toys.
(B) The woman is holding a box.
(C) The man is handing over an item to a customer.
(D) The man is wiping a countertop with a cloth.

3
US
(A) One of the men is taking a shovel out of a box.
(B) They're wearing safety helmets.
(C) They're putting on safety vests.
(D) They're washing their hands.

4
BR
(A) People are getting out of the train.
(B) Some people are standing on a platform.
(C) Some train tracks are being fixed.
(D) A train has stopped at a platform.

5
AU
(A) Some racks are arranged in front of the house.
(B) Some people are fixing the door.
(C) Potted plants are growing on balconies.
(D) A staircase leads to the entrance of the house.

6
US
(A) A sofa is located between round tables.
(B) A light fixture is being removed from the ceiling.
(C) Some artwork has been mounted on the wall.
(D) Some furniture is being carried inside.

PART 2

7
US
US
When are you placing an order for the parts?
(A) From the purchasing department.
(B) In order to get more replacements.
(C) Next week, actually.

8
US
BR
Have you decided which restaurant to go?
(A) It's already closed.
(B) I'll give you a ride.
(C) Not yet, do you have any recommendations?

9
AU
US
How long will it take to drive to the grocery store?
(A) You don't need to bring anything.
(B) Just 5 minutes.
(C) Sure, when would you like to go?

10
AU
BR
Where should I put these boxes?
(A) They are from the supplier.
(B) In the cabinet is fine.
(C) At three o'clock.

11
US
US
Wasn't that a great film premiere?
(A) Yes, the movie was quite impressive.
(B) The show was filmed in China.
(C) Exhibitors should arrive early.

12
US
AU
Why is it taking so long to get to the airport?
(A) A flight for Hong Kong.
(B) Well, it's no longer available.
(C) Because of the parade on Jason Avenue.

13
BR
US
Where is the box office?
(A) An informative guidebook.
(B) Right in front of the theater.
(C) I always go to the office supply store.

14
BR
AU
This building is very well maintained.
(A) The maintenance department.
(B) No, Kevin is in charge of that.
(C) We inspect it regularly.

15
US
US
What is on the agenda for today's meeting?
(A) Yes, it will be handled today.
(B) At the convention center.
(C) Recent updates on the merger.

16
US
BR
Do you want me to book a hotel for you?
(A) Sorry, I can't stay longer.
(B) A higher ticket price.
(C) Yes, I'd appreciate that.

17
AU
US
What are people saying about our new customer service center?
(A) Let's look at the online reviews.
(B) 24 hours a day.
(C) It's nearly done.

18
AU
BR
Aren't we supposed to send our design samples to Mr. Gordon?
(A) No. I didn't.
(B) Yes, he is my assistant.
(C) I was told to send them by overnight express mail.

19
US
US
Did you purchase the tickets for the concert?
(A) Not yet, I'll get them this afternoon.
(B) 30 dollars per month.
(C) A local charity event.

20
US
AU
Is there any computer I could use?
(A) This is my only one.
(B) That doesn't work properly.
(C) A used one is fine with me.

21
BR
US
The store has a delivery service, right?
(A) It's out of order.
(B) That's my favorite food.
(C) Here's their phone number.

22
BR
AU
Are we planning to conduct a videoconference or hold a meeting here at our company?
(A) Actually, we'll have to postpone the meeting.
(B) How about a seminar on business communication skills?
(C) In about two months.

23
US
US
Can I speak to the editor about today's article?
(A) Here's your copy.
(B) Your article will be on page 7.
(C) Her next meeting is about to start.

24
US
BR
Am I supposed to give a presentation on behalf of our department?
(A) Your supervisor will help you with that.
(B) Let's get started.
(C) All of us should be there.

25
AU
US
How many employee handbooks do we need for the orientation?
(A) The company rules.
(B) No, we do not need anymore.
(C) You should check the attendee list.

26
AU
BR
You've been to Australia before, haven't you?
(A) It was held in Sydney.
(B) I've never tried that brand.
(C) I was there ten years ago.

27
US
US
How come our sales were so high during the last summer?
(A) By airplane.
(B) Mostly summer items.
(C) Probably because of the sales promotions.

28 Who's leading the training workshop next Monday?
US AU
(A) Let me check the schedule.
(B) It's on the ground floor.
(C) I was told so.

29 Would you like your coffee with milk or just black?
BR US
(A) She prefers black.
(B) Isn't there any tea?
(C) Sure, we are so thirsty.

30 Have you decided to hire the law firm that I
BR AU
recommended?
(A) The first row in the aisle.
(B) We needed rental accommodation.
(C) Don't they specialize in our case?

31 It's probably too late to grab some groceries and
AU BR
medicine.
(A) I have been there before.
(B) Just a small amount for me, please.
(C) The lights are still on in the store.

PART 3

Questions 32-34 refer to the following conversation.
| US - US |

M Thank you for visiting Jack's Camera Store.
W Good afternoon. I purchased this video camera from this store just a week ago, and it seems to have some kind of problem.
M That's too bad. So, could you tell me what the problem is?
W It suddenly stopped working only four days after I bought it. Although I turned it on, nothing seems to function.
M That's very weird. Maybe, that's because of the battery. Have you replaced the battery?
W Yes, I have. But, it didn't work. Could you repair the camera for me?
M I'm afraid we don't do any repair service in the shop. You should contact the manufacturer. They will be able to fix the camera for you.

Questions 35-37 refer to the following conversation with three speakers.
| BR - AU - US |

W Hi, gentlemen. I'm the chef. Did you enjoy your meal?

M1 Yes, it was so delicious, and absolutely well worth driving a long distance.
W Oh, that sounds like you live quite far from here.
M2 Yeah, we both live in Hanger Lane – about 3 hours away.
W Wow, you came quite a long way. How did you learn about us?
M1 Well, we happened to read a review in a local newspaper last week and the food today was much better than we had expected from the review. You should consider opening a branch near Hanger Lane.
W Actually, we're going to open a new one in the area next month. Then, you'll be able to try our dishes more often.

Questions 38-40 refer to the following conversation.
| US - AU |

W Hi, I'm calling to learn more about your display shelves. I'm starting my own clothing shop next month, and I'm looking for some shelves for my business.
M Sure. We carry a large selection of racks for commercial use. Do you have anything in mind?
W Well, the design is the most important. It has to be modern and simple. Actually, I found some on your online store. I like the one that is currently advertised on your main page.
M I see. Well, but you should consider that the model with the design is rather smaller than expected. So I think you need to take thorough measurements to find right ones for your shop before making an order.

Questions 41-43 refer to the following conversation.
| BR - US |

W Hello. Is it possible to make a reservation for flight 32 to New York at 11 A.M. tomorrow?
M OK, let me check in the system. The rainstorm we've been experiencing since last week is causing a lot of travel disruptions. So many of our flights have been canceled and other flights are almost fully booked.
W Yeah, I'm already aware of that. But, I'm trying to book a ticket at the last minute because I have an urgent meeting with an investor there tomorrow evening.

M Well, the system indicates that there is no seat left on the 11 A.M. flight, but we have a few seats left on the 2 P.M. flight.

W OK, then I'd like to reserve a seat on that one, please. I really need to be there tomorrow.

Questions 44-46 refer to the following conversation.
| AU - BR |

M Dave, I just got off the phone with Billy Shoes Firm about their advertisement which we're currently working on.

W OK. It's for their new line of running shoes for kids, right? Do they want to add something to the ad?

M Right. They want to emphasize their various designs available. So, we need to highlight the shoes available in many patterns and colors to attract kids' attention.

W Oh, I think that'd be a great way to appeal to customers. Let's talk about that at today's meeting for the ad.

Questions 47-49 refer to the following conversation.
| US - US |

M Ms. Ellis, this is Cedric Fleming and I'm returning your call about the order you requested. I'm sorry to tell you that only 5 boxes of organic spinach can be delivered to your restaurant today.

W Oh, that's not good. They're not going to be enough. There will be a large event in our restaurant tomorrow, and I'm planning to serve spinach salads for the side dish.

M We're really sorry, but there isn't much we can do about it since those are all we have this week. Would you like to use other vegetables instead?

W Well, the client requested to use the ingredient.

M Then, here is something I can do. I'll contact other vendors in the area and ask if they can give us some.

W That'd be nice. If needed, I don't mind paying extra.

Questions 50-52 refer to the following conversation.
| BR - US |

W Sam, do you think the plan to relocate our clothing store to the new place next month is

on schedule?

M Yes, it is. But I believe we should give a notice to the landlord that we're moving out once the lease ends. Would you mind giving him a call?

W Not at all, I'll do that after lunch.

M Thank you. And the signs informing customers of our new location just arrived. I'm going to put them up in front of our shop.

W Excellent. Then, I guess everything is on track.

Questions 53-55 refer to the following conversation.
| AU - US |

M Hi, is this the information desk for the local farmers' outdoor market? I'm running a small café in the area and searching for some seasonal fruits to use for my juice beverages.

W Oh, you are in the right place. If you turn left at the corner over there, you'll find the Powell Orchard booth on your right. They should carry various seasonal fruits.

M Perfect! Thanks for your great help. This is my first time here and I just didn't know where I should go.

W No problem. And you know, actually we are celebrating our fifth anniversary of this market. A free music concert will be held in the evening. The first performance will begin at 6:30 P.M. Don't miss it.

Questions 56-58 refer to the following conversation.
| AU - BR |

M Hi, Ms. Cohen. My name is Jeffery Chavez from the Juan Gallery. I'm calling to express my gratitude for your generous donation to our gallery's educational programs. We will surely benefit from your donation.

W Oh, my pleasure. Right after I learned about the programs when I visited the gallery last time, I decided to make a contribution to your educational programs.

M Thank you so much. Now, as a token of our appreciation, we'd like to send you a set of bath towels with the gallery logo. Your current address is the same as the one you gave me last time, right?

W Yeah, that's right.

M Perfect. You should receive the towels in a week.

Questions 59-61 refer to the following conversation with three speakers.

| US - US - BR |

M   Diane and Karen, can I meet with both of you today? I would like to know how the trip to Kenton City yesterday went.

W1   Hello, Zachary. Actually, it went very well. Four appliance stores we visited have agreed to sell our new line of refrigerators.

M   Well done! And Karen, I believe it was the first business trip you went on as a sales person. Did you like it?

W2   Yeah, but I had some problems. It was so hard to answer all the questions the clients asked about some of our products that I haven't become familiar with yet. So, Diane helped me a lot.

M   I see. Actually, we're creating a new manual for our sales representatives to consult when they go on sales calls. With it, they will be able to handle most of our clients' questions about our products.

W1   That would be great, Zachary.

Questions 62-64 refer to the following conversation and form.

| US - US |

M   Hello, could I wire some money to Washington?

W   Certainly, I can help you, sir. Have you filled out the request form?

M   Yeah, here is the form. It's £1.50, right?

W   Exactly, since the total amount is less than £300.

M   Right, and I'd like the money to be there as soon as possible because it's very urgent.

W   Well, transferring money to other countries can take up to a week. But it's normally done much sooner. It can be expected to be there in about 4 days.

M   Oh, that's good. I'm glad your store provides this service. It's so convenient since my apartment is just around the corner.

W   We're happy to help you, sir.

Questions 65-67 refer to the following conversation and menu.

| US - BR |

M   Allison. Before starting your shift this evening,

would you change one of today's specials on the board? We had so many diners at lunch and we ran out of chicken already.

W   No problem. Could you tell me what we should replace it with?

M   We'll provide salmon steaks with fresh vegetables instead of roasted chicken salads.

W   So, the price will remain the same, right?

M   Exactly, it won't be different from the chicken's.

W   Sure, I'll get it done right now.

Questions 68-70 refer to the following conversation and signs.

| BR - AU |

W   Hi, my name is Tina Terry. The sign says all vehicles are required to check in here at the security office.

M   Yeah, right. What is the purpose of your visit to the research facility?

W   Well, I need to meet the research lab manager for a job interview at 3 o'clock.

M   OK. Let me check if your name is on the scheduled visitors' list. Right, I found it.

W   Thank you. Where should I park my car?

M   Just, turn right at the corner over there and leave your vehicle at parking lot D. But, take this tag and don't forget to display it on your car's windshield. You will be ticketed if you don't.

PART 4

Questions 71-73 refer to the following telephone message.

| US |

W   Hi, Trent. It's Kathy calling from sales and marketing department. We've set a meeting for tomorrow, remember? We were going to revise the technical specifications for the Web site development, but I won't be able to make it. Some major clients from Europe are visiting tomorrow, and I was asked to show them around the factory. So I will be out of the office all day. Why don't you ask Frederic to explain them to you? Actually, he knows more than I do, since he was one of the members who initiated the project.

Questions 74-76 refer to the following podcast.

| US |

M Welcome to our Business Podcast. This is produced for those running their own large and small businesses. One of the most important things most of business owners want to have is decent accounting software to handle their finance. Today's podcast will be focusing on several accounting software programs that I've used over the years. But, before we start, I'd like to remind you that the generous support from our listeners makes this podcast possible. If you think what you hear is useful, please think about giving a donation, which will be a big support for us. We'd appreciate even the smallest amount.

Questions 77-79 refer to the following advertisement.

| BR |

W Here is some fantastic news for you! Goodwin Apparel is relocating to the city center this November. To celebrate our relocation, a huge sale will be held at the current location. It begins next Monday from 10 A.M. In spite of the limited inventory, various products will still be available from trousers to T-shirts. In addition, if you simply access our online store at www.goodwinapparel.com, the coupons for much bigger discounts can be printed out! Don't miss this great opportunity. We'll expect to see you next Monday.

Questions 80-82 refer to the following excerpt from a meeting.

| AU |

M OK! The next item on the agenda is the new software program we installed on our computer system last month. Some of its new functions need to be addressed. Thus, we invited Ethel Mason from the Tech Support to lead a series of training sessions. She will ensure that every employee is familiarized with the new software. Please don't forget to register for the course no later than this week.

Questions 83-85 refer to the following excerpt from a meeting.

| US |

M Thank you all for attending this week's marketing meeting. Today, we're going to focus on our fruit juice drinks. After looking through the quarterly sales for the products, we decided to make some changes to our advertising strategy. We'll start with our TV advertisements, and of course our Internet and print ads will need to be changed, too. The packaging will be redesigned by adding photos of celebrities. A brief slide show has been prepared to give an overview of some of our future directions we will follow. OK, everyone. Let's take a look at it now.

Questions 86-88 refer to the following talk.

| US |

W Hi, my name is Colleen Gibson and I'm the one who will be leading the orientation for you here at Graham Financial Academy. I believe enrolling in our college's accounting program will help you with successful careers. During your study here, you'll be able to acquire the wide knowledge to qualify for various accounting positions. Also I suggest that you frequently check current job postings on our Web site. They can give you an idea of what courses you should take. OK, it's time to give you a tour of our computer lab and library. We might have a chance to see what the actual classes you'll take are like.

Questions 89-91 refer to the following telephone message.

| BR |

W Hi, Mr. Hector. This is Noelle Shelton returning your phone call about organizing your company's staff training program. I'm willing to meet with you in person to talk about it in more detail to help your business reach its potential. We can organize various training programs with our highly skilled and experienced coordinators to meet your needs. Jesse Computer Engineering can be a good example of how our service can help our clients. You can visit our Web site to find out more about it. I'm scheduled to be away for my vacation this week. So, if you are OK, I would like to meet you next Monday to see how we can help you.

Questions 92-94 refer to the following news report.

| AU |

M Good evening, welcome back! This is James Cohen and you're listening to Channel 9 Local News. Two years ago today, we reported that the Karlson University's library started a project to digitalize their entire collection of books, journals, and documents. It took almost two years to convert everything into electronic copies. Janet Moore, director of the library, says that she is pleased that now people can easily access them anytime anywhere. Actually, it was not an easy task. As you remember, the project was expected to be finished within a year. But there were many things happened unexpectedly.

Questions 95-97 refer to the following excerpt from a workshop and table of contents.

| US |

M Hello, everyone. Thank you for attending the last day of our training on fitted wardrobe installation. Before we start, I should say thank you for completing the questionnaire following the first day of training. I'm so grateful for giving us useful information on what other issues we should talk about. And we'll try to address all of them at today's training session. OK, now please look at your handbook, and if you turn to page 16, you'll see the section C. First, we will have a lecture here, but some hands-on practice is required for this section. So, following our lunch break, we'll move to the training area, and today's training will end there.

Questions 98-100 refer to the following excerpt from a meeting and diagram.

| BR |

W Hi, everyone. Thank you for agreeing to volunteer to arrange this year's IT conference. This conference will be led by many of the top professionals in the IT field. They will share the findings from their latest studies. So, the pre-registration has already been finished, and many more people are expected to sign up on the day of the event. Lowell Doyle, renowned researcher and IT expert will be one of our presenters. His presentation will be in room

303-A. The seating needs to be set up in a way that has all the audience members face the front, instead of making people sit across from each other. A podium for the presenter will be placed in front and several lines of chairs will be arranged. OK, let's get started.

TEST 03 스크립트

🎧 TEST03.mp3

PART 1

1
BR
(A) He's removing the label.
(B) He's carrying a shopping cart.
(C) He's holding a basket.
(D) He's moving a display rack.

2
US
(A) He's repairing a door.
(B) He's working under a sink.
(C) He's opening a toolbox.
(D) He's lying on the grass.

3
AU
(A) A woman is pointing toward a monitor.
(B) A man is taking a note.
(C) Some computers are located on a desk.
(D) Some people are sitting opposite each other.

4
US
(A) Some people are fixing a road sign.
(B) A person is hiking through a path.
(C) A person is sitting by the side of a road.
(D) Some people are resting on the grass.

5
AU
(A) People are leaving the office.
(B) A woman is reading over a man's shoulder.
(C) People are sitting around a conference table.
(D) Some people are facing away from each other.

6
BR
(A) There are lamps mounted on both sides of each window.
(B) A house is surrounded by a fence.
(C) A staircase is being swept.
(D) Some potted plants have been placed outside a building.

PART 2

7
US
US
Is your new place comfortable?
(A) Yes, fairly comfortable.
(B) It's a different place.
(C) Moving to a new apartment.

8
BR
US
How often do we have a regular meeting?
(A) 30 minutes in the afternoon.
(B) Usually once a week.
(C) How many customers?

9
AU
US
Do you work in this building?
(A) Yes, it works well.
(B) No, I'm here to meet my friend.
(C) A marketing agency.

10
AU
BR
When are we supposed to relocate our headquarters?
(A) Due to the delay.
(B) By the end of this month.
(C) A change of address.

11
US
US
How long did it take to build the Empire State Building?
(A) About 400 meters.
(B) In Midtown Manhattan.
(C) Nearly a year.

12
US
AU
What did the director say about our proposed budget?
(A) The accounting director.
(B) No, that's not what I heard.
(C) I'm meeting with him tomorrow.

13
BR
US
When do you usually receive the bank statement?
(A) At the end of the month.
(B) The local bank branch.
(C) Just this morning.

14
BR
AU
Isn't the personnel manager available this afternoon?
(A) I am not on duty today.
(B) They met at the conference.
(C) No, but he can see you early tomorrow.

15
US
US
This storage lease will be automatically renewed, right?
(A) I had them for a while.
(B) These items are for sale.
(C) Did you check the contract?

16
US
BR
Would you like to discuss the final sales report today or early tomorrow?
(A) How about tomorrow morning?
(B) We should fix this watch.
(C) This promotion plan looks good.

17
AU
US
Make sure you lock the door when you leave the warehouse.
(A) Okay, I'll remember to do that.
(B) It won't take long.
(C) Martin already checked the inventory.

18
AU BR
Is it all right if I call the manager at home this late?
(A) I think so.
(B) His desk is on your left.
(C) That's not his phone number.

19
US US
Who can help me set up the projector in the seminar room?
(A) What project are you working on?
(B) I met her earlier today.
(C) I will go with you.

20
AU US
Where is the National Museum?
(A) Five tickets, please.
(B) Turn right at the intersection.
(C) It closes at 7.

21
BR US
Why should we relocate the factory?
(A) The factory is located within ten miles.
(B) The rent has become unaffordable.
(C) Sometime next year.

22
BR AU
All the safety facilities in this factory were inspected recently, weren't they?
(A) Our customers are top priority.
(B) No, but it's scheduled for tomorrow.
(C) Only some of the potted plants.

23
US US
Why don't you join us for a coffee break downstairs?
(A) It was broken already.
(B) Thanks, I enjoyed it a lot.
(C) I have a meeting soon.

24
US BR
Isn't our company intranet supposed to be upgraded tonight?
(A) Yes, the manager said to save all important files.
(B) A local Internet provider.
(C) It's 25 dollars per computer.

25
AU US
Which company do we use to cater for the company events?
(A) It is not working now.
(B) Check the latest invoice.
(C) I have not been there.

26
AU BR
Where should I take our investors for dinner next week?
(A) Around 6 will be good for me.
(B) I can show you our investment plan.
(C) You know, most of us hardly ever eat out.

27
US US
This promotional campaign poster is attractive?
(A) He's been promoted.
(B) Yes, the design looks professional.
(C) He is not so interested.

28
US AU
Would you like to sign up for the gym only or also the pool?
(A) A gym next to the clinic.
(B) About 100 dollars a month.
(C) I don't like to swim.

29
BR US
I reserved your meeting room for 2 o'clock today.
(A) But our seminar is supposed to start at 1.
(B) A reservation is not required.
(C) Could you let me know today's meeting agenda?

30
BR AU
Were you able to change the meeting time with the director?
(A) There was no answer.
(B) At the convention hall.
(C) No, we accept only cash.

31
AU BR
Where do you recommend we should go when we visit London?
(A) To Buckingham Palace.
(B) This July.
(C) Summer is better.

PART 3

Questions 32-34 refer to the following conversation.
| US - US |

M   Hello, Annie. I've found that one of the box making machines has stopped today. Did you call a repairperson to come to examine it?

W   Yeah, I already did. She came by the plant this afternoon and mentioned that we need to replace the equipment's motor. She can fix it by tomorrow morning.

M   Excellent! By the way, we have to check if there are enough boxes to fill this week's orders. Could you check our current inventory? If there aren't, I need to get in touch with our clients.

Questions 35-37 refer to the following conversation.

| AU - BR |

M   Andrea, are you planning to come to the office on Saturday morning to participate in the accounting seminar? Could you tell me where I should go to attend it?

W   It'll be held in conference room A on the third floor. And its start time has been rescheduled. It will start at 10:30 A.M. instead of 11:00 A.M. An expert, Connie Ray, has been invited to lead the seminar.

M   Oh, that'd be great. I can't wait! Actually, Connie and I already know each other. I used to work with her at another company before.

Questions 38-40 refer to the following conversation.

| US - US |

M   Hello, my name is Dean Evans. I have a job interview with Carlton Association.

W   Good afternoon. Could you show me some form of identification? It's required to issue you a visitor's badge.

M   Of course. Here it is. And, my car is parked in the parking lot behind the building. They said it's a dollar for every 10 minutes. Is it possible to get a discount on it?

W   Well, you can get a stamp on the ticket for that. Just be sure to take it to the office where you'll have the interview. Without the stamp, you'll need to pay on your way out.

Questions 41-43 refer to the following conversation.

| BR - US |

W   Ben, why don't you come with us to the welcoming party for the new employees tomorrow night?

M   Well, I have to get ready for a presentation.

W   Alright. You will make a presentation on Wednesday, right?

M   Exactly, and I'm searching for a print shop to have several visual materials printed, which need to be ready a day before the presentation.

W   I think you should talk with the hotel reception for some recommendations.

Questions 44-46 refer to the following conversation with three speakers.

| AU - US - BR |

M   Hello, Leticia and Lucy. Before we start today's new employee training, let me give you a tour of our factory where our car parts are produced. Is there any question before we start?

W1 Yes, I have one. Do we need to put on company uniforms or is it OK with our regular clothes?

M   Well, for now you don't need to. After the tour, you can change into your uniforms. Lucy, do you have any questions?

W2 Oh, I do. I was told that many complex machines are operating here. Could you tell me how often they are inspected?

M   We conduct regular inspections on a monthly basis, and also we hired mechanics to take care of maintenance and minor repairs.

Questions 47-49 refer to the following conversation.

| US - AU |

W   Hello, Sam. It seems our business has been going quite well since we started our retail shop last February.

M   Yeah, our customers have shown a positive response as they were trying to find a furniture store which offers quality products at very reasonable prices. I think our prices are unbeatable.

W   That's right. Well, it may be a great time to consider how our business can be more profitable in the upcoming season.

M   Do you have any particular idea in mind?

W   I'm thinking about carrying brand new house-furnishing goods. I've found Eailing Furnishing is getting popular nowadays.

M   That can be a great idea. Should I go ahead and contact them to see if they can provide some more information about their products?

Questions 50-52 refer to the following conversation.

| US - US |

W   Todd, do you have a minute? I have something to talk over with you.

M   Yes, are there any problems?

W   Hmm... I have to go on a business trip, but I haven't submitted a travel expense request form yet. I should have handed in the form yesterday.

M   Oh, that's not a big issue. Just send me the
    form no later than today, and I'll have the
    approval process expedited.
W   That's great! Thank you. And I need to learn
    more about how to keep track of my expenses
    since it is my first trip.
M   We have expense-recording software for
    employees. I can give you the link to the
    program.

Questions 53-55 refer to the following conversation with
three speakers.
| AU - BR - US |

M   Julia, what are you doing here in the lobby?
W1   Hello, Ivan. I'm expecting a new staff member
     who will start working with our advertising
     firm today.
M   That's good for us. We definitely need more
     hands since we were awarded a contract with
     Fulham Appliances last week.
W1   Exactly, that will be a great chance for our
     company. Oh, here she is now. Erma Snyder,
     I would like to introduce one of our sales
     managers, Ivan Steele.
W2   Glad to meet you. It's great to work at such a
     leading advertising agency.
M   Yeah, we're pleased to work with you.
W1   And Erma, please follow me. Let me give you
     a tour of our office before starting your work
     today.

Questions 56-58 refer to the following conversation.
| BR - US |

W   Sally, I have some good news to tell you!
    Do you know the Web site we designed for
    the Plus Mate Office? They said it was so
    impressive that they have introduced some
    potential clients to us.
M   That's great! I think our business has been
    growing rapidly. We were awarded three more
    contracts last week alone.
W   Well, in order to keep up with our fast
    growing business needs, I believe an
    accountant should be hired to take care of our
    bookkeeping.
M   Well, I was told that Hicks Accounting is really
    good. Let me schedule a meeting with them.
    Are you available on Tuesday?
W   Yes, in the morning.

Questions 59-61 refer to the following conversation.
| BR - US |

W   Hello, Kevin. Could you inform all staff
    members of the maintenance work our IT team
    will conduct on the network server during the
    first weekend of June?
M   Certainly. Is the whole network system going
    to be affected?
W   Yes. So, please make sure that everyone
    knows starting Friday evening through Sunday
    afternoon on that weekend, they won't be able
    to access the system.
M   Sure, I'll highlight that in the e-mail and
    forward it to every employee right now.

Questions 62-64 refer to the following conversation and
error code list.
| US - US |

M   Valdez Tech Security. How may I help you?
W   Hello, umm... Yeah. My name is Patsy Walsh,
    one of the new laboratory employees. Well,
    you issued me the access card early today.
    But when I try to open the lab's secure door
    with the card, I can see the error code ER3 on
    the screen.
M   ER3? Give me a second and I'll check that
    code on my computer. Oh, I see what the
    problem is. I believe you need a new card.
W   Is it possible to issue the new card soon?
    I have an urgent project to complete by
    tomorrow morning.
M   It won't take long to issue one. I will take care
    of it right away. Just stop by the security desk
    now.

Questions 65-67 refer to the following conversation and
train schedule.
| AU - US |

M   Excuse me, madam. Can you help me? Here's
    my ticket. I wonder if I am on the right train. I
    have to go to Westchester.
W   Let me see, hmm... This is the 201 train. I am
    sorry but it doesn't go to the station you want.
M   Oh, no, what should I do now?
W   We just left Glendale station, but you can
    change trains at the next stop.
M   Do you happen to know how long I will need to
    wait for another train? I don't have much time
    because I have to make a presentation at a
    seminar that starts in an hour.

W No worries, your train will be less than ten minutes. You will get to your seminar on time.

Questions 68-70 refer to the following conversation and warranty information.

| AU - US |

M Adams Electronics Store. How may I help you?

W Hello, I purchased one of your tablet PCs a few weeks ago, and I accidentally broke it. I believe it comes with a two-year warranty, so is it possible to exchange it?

M Well, most of our products do, but there are some limitations of our warranty. It doesn't cover some problems, so you might not be able to exchange your device. Could you tell me what happened?

W Its screen cracked because I accidentally dropped it on the floor.

M Oh, that's too bad, but I'm sorry to tell you that it's not covered under warranty.

W Is that so? What should I do then?

M I suggest you take it to one of our service centers and get the screen replaced. It will be the cheapest option for you.

W OK. Then, is it possible to know how much I will pay for the repair service?

M No problem.

PART 4

Questions 71-73 refer to the following talk.

| US |

W Before starting today's shift, I'd like to make a brief announcement. The demand for our personalized furniture is increasing significantly, but there have been some customer complaints about our service. Four months can be too long for our customers to wait for an order. So, we've hired several additional woodworkers, skilled and experienced. They're scheduled to start later this week, which will make our work process faster for our customers. In addition, some of our equipment is too old, so the outdated machines will be replaced one by one. Actually, a new power saw will be purchased today. So, I need someone to help me load it into our vehicle at the shop.

Questions 74-76 refer to the following excerpt from a meeting.

| US |

M Now for an update on our travel agency's business plan. 'Beauty & Cuisines in China', which started out last summer, was very successful. I believe building up various local restaurants and beauty shops has been the most contributing factor for a great year. Now it's time we should enter into a bigger market. We're in talks with Moline hotel chains about combining and developing our new program with them. But their sales director wants to make sure that customers will buy this tour program exclusively on their Web site. So we're going to conduct some customer surveys about a luxury tour program combining with a five star hotel.

Questions 77-79 refer to the following talk.

| BR |

W Good morning. Thank you for visiting Harriet Gallery of Modern Art. I'll be guiding you through our special exhibit hall, showing artworks by painter Kenneth Martin. The most interesting thing about Mr. Martin's paintings is that they're very tiny. They are even as small as a grain of rice. This tour takes about one hour and a half. So, please leave your bags and jackets behind before we start. Lockers by the entrance are available to store them.

Questions 80-82 refer to the following instructions.

| AU |

M Good morning, everyone. Welcome to your first day at Gross Tech Inc. The first thing we need to do today is to walk around our premises including the employee cafeteria. It seems you are all wearing your badges. Excellent! All the areas in the building are equipped with a security system. And after the tour, I will show you your workstation and help you set up your computer. The layout has recently been rearranged, which means the floor plans you received with the employee handbook are no longer accurate, but revised ones will be distributed to each of you soon.

Questions 83-85 refer to the following excerpt from a meeting.

| US |

W Up until now, our firm has been focusing on producing footwear for sports and outdoor activities. Today's meeting has been called to announce our new plan to branch out into a new line of formal shoes for men. If the expansion is successful, we'll expand into formal footwear for women. I'm of course aware that our marketing approach will need to be changed. I brought some prototypes of the new line and let's pass it around. Ms. Hanson will share the direction which her marketing team intends to take with the new advertising campaign they'll be conducting.

Questions 86-88 refer to the following telephone message.

| US |

M Hello, Mr. Hardy. My name is Jared Harper. I hope you still remember me working as a temporary worker on your team last winter. I'm calling regarding the payment for the last month of work that I've not received yet. After I left the job, I went back to London to stay with my family. So, I believe the check you sent me probably went to the place I used to stay in Brighton. I don't work now, but I need to pay some bills. You can reach me at 4401-8832. Thanks.

Questions 89-91 refer to the following talk.

| BR |

W Thank you for joining the information course on Lyons Writers Project. I'm Harriet Lopez, the organizer. As you may already know, Lyons Writers Project offers the most promising new authors year-long financial support. In return for the support, the participants are asked to engage in our community by arranging various activities like lecture series in local schools and writing seminars. We have invited two previous recipients here with us today, who have now become well-known authors with this project. They will speak about how the project helped them. Please give them a big round of applause.

Questions 92-94 refer to the following instructions.

| US |

W Good afternoon! I'm Kristin, the head of the maintenance team. We installed a new paper cutting machine at the plant early today. The equipment is capable of cutting up to 25 layers of paper at once, and it will make our overall working process faster and even easier. At the beginning of every shift, all the gears of every machine are required to be cleaned for optimal conditions. So, please don't forget to do this. Now, I'd like to show you all how to use the equipment before you operate the machine. Please hand me a roll of paper.

Questions 95-97 refer to the following telephone message and schedule.

| AU |

M Hi, Julia. This is Paul from Dallas Sports Agency. I just received your message regarding the upcoming sporting goods trade show scheduled for this May. I was wondering if we could discuss it on Friday afternoon for about an hour. One of my afternoon meetings was just cancelled, so we could talk at two. And I'd like to see some samples you want to display at the trade show, so don't forget to bring them. Please let me know if that's convenient for you. Thanks.

Questions 98-100 refer to the following announcement and directory.

| BR |

W Thank you for shopping at Pinner Department Store. As of next month, to celebrate our 15th anniversary, there will be a lot of special deals each week for a month. Next week, all the sportswear will be on sale. So, don't miss this great opportunity to get great savings. From jogging suits to running shoes, to exercise equipment, customers will be surprised by our discounted prices. And come by our newly refurbished restaurant and café on the fourth floor for a great dining experience or even for light refreshments. For more information about the upcoming sales, take a brochure at the entrance when you leave. Enjoy your shopping. Thank you.

PART 1

1
US
(A) He's moving some wooden panels.
(B) He's standing near a wall.
(C) He's repairing some equipment.
(D) He's taking off his hat.

2
US
(A) They're assembling a box.
(B) They're arranging some furniture.
(C) They're seated at a table.
(D) They're facing each other.

3
AU
(A) A woman is hiking on a hill.
(B) A woman is resting on a bench.
(C) Some boats are lined up along the harbor.
(D) A travel bag is being unpacked.

4
BR
(A) The man is leaning against shelves.
(B) The man is talking to the woman.
(C) A rug is being unrolled on the floor.
(D) The woman is drinking from a cup.

5
US
(A) Some chairs are stacked in a corner.
(B) Menus are placed on some tables.
(C) Some pedestrians are walking beside an outdoor café.
(D) Some canopies are mounted on the wall.

6
BR
(A) Trees have been planted along the street.
(B) An outdoor market is crowded with shoppers.
(C) Leaves have covered a walkway.
(D) Some people are stopped at the side of a truck.

PART 2

7
BR
US
(A) There are more in my office.
(B) A newly launched model.
(C) I think Jeff is in charge of that.

Who conducted the survey of focus groups?

8
US
US
How can I get to the city center from here?
(A) Turn right at the next intersection.
(B) One hour.
(C) A central city.

9
US
BR
When will the seminar in the conference hall begin?
(A) In about ten minutes.
(B) They will arrive soon.
(C) We'll be there in time.

10
AU
BR
Is there a vending machine at this station?
(A) Drinks and snacks.
(B) Actually, it's out of service.
(C) We only have a few more seats available.

11
US
US
This office is a little hot, isn't it?
(A) She found that, too.
(B) I'll open the window.
(C) Yes, it was not the office.

12
AU
US
How much do you think this new jacket costs?
(A) Could you show me another?
(B) A larger size.
(C) Let's ask the clerk.

13
BR
US
Could you tell me which suitcase you want?
(A) You need it just in case.
(B) An air express service.
(C) The brown one with a yellow tag.

14
US
US
Would you like more coffee?
(A) In the menu.
(B) No, I have had enough.
(C) We liked it, too.

15
US
US
Didn't you sign up for the monthly magazine subscription?
(A) The editor's review.
(B) Actually, I decided not to.
(C) What was it about?

16
US
BR
Where did you store our printing paper?
(A) A stationery store across the street.
(B) There should be some next to the cabinet.
(C) Sure, you can use mine.

17
AU
US
Would you rather eat out or order delivery tonight?
(A) I prefer to dine out.
(B) Yes, I cook every night.
(C) It was about 9 o'clock.

18
AU
BR
Will there be heavy traffic on the highway this weekend?
(A) Okay, I'll make a detour.
(B) Yes, the snow will cause a delay.
(C) They used public transportation.

19 Can you tell me how to turn this printer on?
BR
AU
(A) The most advanced model.
(B) Just press the button on the back.
(C) No, it was on Friday.

20 The promotional campaign was canceled, wasn't
US
AU
it?
(A) It is our new logo.
(B) It was, unfortunately.
(C) No, I don't like it.

21 Shouldn't we purchase new office furniture now?
US
BR
(A) Please deliver them to our office.
(B) Some pens and note pads.
(C) There will be a clearance sale in January.

22 Thomas, why are you working so late this week?
BR
AU
(A) Sure, we'll finish the proposal tomorrow.
(B) What time is it?
(C) Thanks, but we already ate.

23 Could you fill me in on the details of what
US
US
happened at the seminar yesterday?
(A) I will have Peter tell you about that.
(B) How much time do you need?
(C) We're meeting in Seminar Room C.

24 Where should we hold the International Auto
US
AU
Show?
(A) I thought it was August.
(B) It was in Canberra last year.
(C) More than 100 vendors.

25 We need to order some letterhead stationery.
BR
US
(A) Is that the stationery store on the corner?
(B) I have a list of things we need to buy as well.
(C) For official written correspondence.

26 Won't we leave early on the day before the
AU
BR
holiday?
(A) Yes, we only work in the morning.
(B) A vacation in Hawaii.
(C) Its business hours are from 9 A.M. to 5 P.M.

27 How is it possible to prepare all the reports at
US
US
once?
(A) Sorry, I am not able to go with you.
(B) More or less.
(C) Actually, all of us are worried about that too.

28 Why haven't you sent the package by express
US
AU
mail?
(A) From Perth.
(B) Yes, it was fast enough.
(C) Didn't it arrive yet?

29 If you want to open an account, let me show you
BR
US
some options.
(A) The show was too predictable.
(B) Our new accountant will be here soon.
(C) Thanks, that would be great.

30 Why did you schedule the client meeting so early
AU
BR
in the morning?
(A) I can move it to late in the afternoon.
(B) Yes, she set up the meeting.
(C) I will get there as soon as possible.

31 Our sales team will have a meeting today to
BR
AU
discuss the customer feedback.
(A) It was going well.
(B) Rachel is still on vacation, though.
(C) Of course, but I'll need it back by today.

PART 3

Questions 32-34 refer to the following conversation.
| US - US |

M Hi, my name is Robin Myers. I'm supposed to see Dr. Munoz at 10 A.M.

W Hello, Mr. Myers. Dr. Munoz is now examining a patient, so could you wait? This is your first time to visit here, right?

M Yes, I made an appointment over the phone yesterday.

W Oh, I see. Can I have your medical history form that I requested yesterday?

M Here's the form. I've downloaded it from your Web site and completed it.

W Thank you. Also, since you're a new patient, can I see your photo identification?

Questions 35-37 refer to the following conversation.
| AU - US |

M Hi, Pauline. I would like to check if you looked at the work request I forwarded you earlier today for the meeting room downstairs. The lights have not been working properly for several days.

W Yes, I did. But, I need to set up some computers for the new employees in marketing at the moment. Right after finishing the work, I will check the meeting room.

M Alright, thank you. Could you inform me when you repair them? I have to prepare my presentation for today's meeting with my client. Without lights, we won't be able to have a meeting there.

Questions 38-40 refer to the following conversation.
| BR - US |

W Good morning, thanks for calling Austin Publishing. How can I help you today?

M Hello, my current subscription to *Financial Report Monthly* will expire soon, so is it possible to renew it now? I heard that 40% off an annual subscription is currently being offered.

W Well, we're very sorry to tell you that the discount is only for new subscribers. If you order a subscription for another magazine, you can receive the discount.

M Well... Actually, I can't afford to subscribe to another one. I'd just like to renew it, please.

W Certainly. Also, I'll send you a brochure listing all of our publications in case you change your mind.

Questions 41-43 refer to the following conversation.
| BR - AU |

W Hello, Alvin. Have you had a chance to look at the report on our theater's ticket sales for last month? The sales tend to keep falling.

M Yes, I have. We definitely need to do something about it. What do you think we should do?

W We should consider finding a new approach to reach the public. Probably, expanding our overall advertising effort can be the answer.

M Absolutely! We have a management meeting this week to talk about the budget. Let's address your idea in more detail at the meeting.

Questions 44-46 refer to the following conversation.
| US - US |

W Milton, you told me that you are taking a day off on Friday, but we need some more help.

We will be providing our catering service for a banquet at the city center. We were just informed that the attendance will be much bigger than originally scheduled.

M Hmm... A repair person is scheduled to visit my apartment on Friday to inspect my heater. She'll be there early in the afternoon.

W I don't think that's going to work out. The event will be held at noon.

M I'm sorry. However, I think Janet will be free, and she wants to work extra hours.

Questions 47-49 refer to the following conversation with three speakers.
| BR - US - AU |

W Hey, Eric. This is Rubin Williams. It's his first day here at Hampstead Hotels Corporation. He is the new chief designer in Web site development.

M1 Hi, Rubin. I'm Eric Shelton. Welcome to the company.

M2 Nice to meet you, Eric. I heard that you will be giving a presentation at the staff seminar tomorrow.

M1 Yeah, I'll be discussing how to improve our online service.

M2 That sounds wonderful. I look forward to it.

W I'm just about to give Rubin a tour. I thought we'd start at the reception area on the main floor.

M1 Okay. Rubin, I guess I'll see you at the meeting tomorrow.

Questions 50-52 refer to the following conversation.
| US - AU |

W Thank you for preparing the press release about our company's winter internship program, Lowell. But, the deadline for application is approaching, and only three candidates have applied so far. Do you have any ideas to make more people interested in the program?

M Well... Why don't we contact the business administration department at the local college and ask them to encourage their students to participate?

W That sounds like a great idea. Then I believe we can push back the application deadline for the students who would be interested.

Questions 53-55 refer to the following conversation.

| AU - BR |

M   Hi, Lillie. Could you look over the slides for the presentation we are scheduled to do at the conference?

W   Yeah, I already reviewed them early in the morning. They seem to have no errors and all the information is very well organized.

M   Perfect. Then, we're all set for the conference. I think I should go ahead and book my flight this afternoon. Would you like me to reserve yours as well?

W   Well, I should've told you earlier that you probably need to make a presentation on your own. I won't be able to leave for the conference because one of the important clients is coming to see me.

M   I heard this presentation is really important, but I've only recently started my new job.

W   You prepared most of the presentation, so there won't be any problem. I'm sure you will make it without me.

Questions 56-58 refer to the following conversation.

| US - US |

M   Hi, Ms. William, have you seen the report on the clinical tests for the new herbal medicines for digestion our company's getting ready to put on the market?

W   Oh, were there any issues?

M   Actually, there was one. We found some side effects of the medicine. Some people seem to have difficulties breathing and although they are not serious symptoms, we need to take care of the issue.

W   Hmm... that was not expected at all. You are right. We definitely need more time.

M   But the product release date is coming up soon. Why don't we adjust our timeline? So we can clarify the cause and be ready to launch it by then.

Questions 59-61 refer to the following conversation.

| US - AU |

W   Hello, this is Holly Perez from accounting and I'd like to reach Carl Porter in personnel, please.

M   Yeah, this is Carl speaking.

W   Hi, a new hire is supposed to start in our division next Monday. And, I'd like to check how many days of vacation new employees have.

M   Twenty days a year. Actually, we will talk about that at the orientation session next week. It's scheduled for Tuesday at 1 o'clock.

W   Thank you. We'll make sure Mr. Nelson will attend the session. Does he have to register in advance?

M   That's right. But I can put his name on the list right now. Just give me his full name, please.

Questions 62-64 refer to the following conversation and report.

| US - BR |

M   I have done the evaluation of our footwear company's expenses, and all reports have been compiled. Here, could you take a look?

W   Hmm... It seems like our overall expenditure has increased during the last month. We should consider cutting some shipping costs.

M   Well, the current shipping service from our contractor seems too expensive. Maybe, it's time to find a new contractor for the service.

W   Yes, let's search for possible contractors and make a list.

Questions 65-67 refer to the following conversation and elevator panel.

| BR - AU |

W   Hi, Jason. I'm so happy you got in the elevator just now.

M   Hello, Silvia. I did not expect to see you here. I am working at the reception of this building. What made you come here?

W   I'm here to see my lawyer, Mr. Jennings and I think I'm lost. Could you tell me where his office is?

M   Oh, you're on the wrong floor. This floor only has cafés and bakeries. All of the lawyers' offices are one floor down.

W   Thanks a lot. You know I was expecting to find lawyers' names on the elevator panel.

M   I was just going to that office to deliver this memo. If you want, I'll go there with you.

Questions 68-70 refer to the following conversation and schedule.

| US - US |

W Peggy Airline. How may I help you?

M Hi, I'd like to fly from Beijing to Vancouver tomorrow. I tried to book a ticket online, but I couldn't do it.

W We're sorry for the inconvenience. We accept any ticket reservation less than 24 hours before departure only over the phone. But I'm glad to help reserve tickets for you. What time do you prefer to leave?

M I don't mind any departure time as long as I can reach Vancouver before 2:00 P.M. I have an important meeting with prospective investors.

PART 4

Questions 71-73 refer to the following telephone message.

| US |

W Hello, Gordon. This is Lydia, the restaurant supervisor. I'm calling to ask you a favor. Could you come to work a bit early today? I was scheduled to be there when the shipment of our food supplies arrives, but I think I won't be able to make it in time for the delivery. I need to pick up my husband from the hospital. If you get to work early for me, you'll be allowed to have Friday evening off. Please get back to me as soon as you hear this message. Thank you.

Questions 74-76 refer to the following instruction.

| AU |

M Good morning, everyone. My name is Jim Hopkins from the personnel department. I congratulate you all on joining Pinner Publishing. We have some paperwork to complete. Oh, let me tell you this form is the most important one since it will be used to put you on the payroll. The form needs to be handed in by Thursday. Otherwise, your first paycheck will be delayed. Please go ahead and take your time to go through the rest of the papers in the information packet. Feel free to ask if you have any questions while you're filling them out.

Questions 77-79 refer to the following announcement.

| US |

M Good afternoon, everyone. Although we need to pack up so many shipments and send them out today, I still need to make this brief but important announcement before we start our work in the warehouse. A new system for handling suggestions and complaints from our employees will be introduced. We're well aware that our employees' feedback is invaluable. But, most of the employees had difficulty in giving theirs. It was uneasy and uncomfortable to talk directly to management. Starting next week, a box will be placed in the staff lounge. Every Monday morning, the management team will summarize the comments from the box to share in the weekly meeting.

Questions 80-82 refer to the following excerpt from a meeting.

| BR |

W All right, let's start this month's staff meeting. As staff members of Town Park Recreation Division, we are responsible for arranging various services to promote residents' health and safety with our informative events and classes. So, first, let's discuss how the programs we talked about for this winter are coming along. We've already proposed providing discounts on bus tickets during winter months. The director of the town's transportation authority will soon give us their decision. We still have a lot of things to do before December. So, why don't we share updates on the progress each team has made since last month? I would like to start with Clara, please.

Questions 83-85 refer to the following telephone message.

| AU |

M Hi, Betty. It's Harris. I'm on the way to the conference hall. But due to an unusual traffic jam, it looks like it will take another thirty minutes to get there. Traffic is really backed up now. I don't think I can make it on time. Please do me a favor. I'll e-mail the updated agenda to you now so that you can get the meeting started without me. Oh, don't forget we need at least twenty copies of the agenda for the conference. And as I know, Timmy, the assistant manager, is supposed to distribute all the promotional materials to guests at the entrance. I'll call Timmy and ask him to do that. If you need anything else, please text me.

Questions 86-88 refer to the following broadcast.
| US |

W   Good morning, listeners. My name is Celia Sharp, host of this radio show, *Tech, Today*. We have Devin Stone, a manager working for a local software company, with us at our studio to talk about the latest software system. Mr. Stone is working on developing commercial programs. Recently, he has introduced a new software program that helps avoid scheduling conflicts when organizing a meeting. Well, before starting today's interview, I'd like to remind you that we are always happy to welcome any ideas for new program topics from our listeners. And, if you have any questions about today's topic, please send us a text message at 3322-4431.

Questions 89-91 refer to the following telephone message.
| US |

M   Hi, Thomas. It's Douglas. Thank you for leading a training session today while I was preparing for my trip to Osaka. I just received a call from Mr. Jennings, a manager at Pearson Warehouse. He wanted us to send an invoice for his order. I'm just about to board a flight. Could you send it to him? Also I have something to remind you about. As you know, Mr. Park and his team will be visiting us tomorrow. Please be sure to make all arrangements for the meeting. You know they are one of our major clients. Just call me if anything happens. Thanks.

Questions 92-94 refer to the following news report.
| US |

W   Welcome to *Kingsbury Town News*! Yesterday, the town council announced that it's planning to change the current recycling system to a multiple stream system. So, recyclable waste would need to be separated by the type of material. Residents would not be permitted

to put all recyclable materials into the same recycling bin. Prior to the final decision, a research firm and an accounting agency have been hired to examine how much this recycling system would cost the town. It is expected to take a month to complete the examination. Once the result comes out, the council members will discuss the implementation of the new system in more detail. Channel 4 *Kingsbury Town News* would like to know our listeners' opinions. Feel free to visit our Web site and leave your comments about the change.

Questions 95-97 refer to the following telephone message and schedule.
| BR |

W   Hello. This is Donna Martin from Wapping Real Estate and I'm calling to talk about the house on Bermondsey Rd. I'd just like to inform you that before moving in this week, please stop by my office so that you can pick up the keys. Also, you told me that you will need to commute to work on Devons St. every morning. The Bermondsey Rd. train station is near your new house. I had my assistant print out a copy of the morning schedule for you. So, you can take it with you when you visit our office. See you then. Thank you.

Questions 98-100 refer to the following excerpt from a meeting and graph.
| AU |

M   Welcome to this month's board meeting for Loughton Apparel. As discussed, we are planning to acquire a clothing manufacturing firm in South America. Four manufacturers have been narrowed down and we're about to choose which one of them to purchase. But, a few factors need to be considered before making the final decision. First, the cost of acquiring Imelda Wear tends to be too high and after much debate, at this time we decided to give up expanding into the kids' clothing market. Thus, we can clearly see a very desirable option with its 28 million dollars within our budget. Now, let's hear from our president, Wendy West, about what changes this acquisition will bring to our company, especially to its leadership. Thank you.

PART 1

1
AU
(A) She's putting a box into her bag.
(B) She's choosing an item.
(C) She's bending over to pick up a bottle.
(D) She's taking some medicine.

2
US
(A) They're reviewing some materials.
(B) They're looking for documents in a cabinet.
(C) They're replacing the label of a folder.
(D) They're adjusting book shelves.

3
BR
(A) A man is replacing a broken door.
(B) A man is holding some clothes.
(C) A washing machine is being loaded into a truck.
(D) A basket has been filled with items.

4
US
(A) Menus have been provided for the diners.
(B) One of the men is serving a meal to customers.
(C) One of the women is pouring some water into a glass.
(D) A table is covered with a tablecloth.

5
AU
(A) The carpet has a circular pattern.
(B) Pillows are positioned on chairs.
(C) A light fixture is on the table.
(D) The floor is being cleaned.

6
BR
(A) Some vehicles are parked near the curbs.
(B) People are all walking in one direction.
(C) Some pedestrians are crossing a street.
(D) Some people are waiting in line to board a bus.

PART 2

7
US
AU
When did you start working for Carlson bank?
(A) I am a branch manager.
(B) The banking industry.
(C) About 20 years ago.

8
US
BR
What kind of books do you like to read?
(A) She worked for a publishing company.
(B) I enjoy reading novels.
(C) Yes, from the community library.

9
US
US
Would you like to order today's special?
(A) A discount coupon.
(B) At the counter.
(C) I was planning on a Greek salad.

10
US
BR
How did you miss your flight?
(A) My credit card.
(B) By working too late last night.
(C) At the lost and found.

11
AU
US
Do you know how to install the safety alarm?
(A) Yes, let me show you.
(B) It is not safe for children.
(C) Yes, I heard that.

12
US
US
Where is the international trade show next week?
(A) It's in Dallas, I think.
(B) Sure, I'm a mechanic.
(C) In early February.

13
US
AU
Please forward any calls and e-mails to my assistant while I am away.
(A) Sure, no problem.
(B) Yes, to my address.
(C) We need your password.

14
BR
US
Who was nominated for the Employee of the Year Award?
(A) That's mine.
(B) It was just a normal day.
(C) It still hasn't been announced.

15
BR
AU
I heard you've been working in London for a year, haven't you?
(A) It is not going well.
(B) Yes, it's been great.
(C) My one-week vacation.

16
US
US
Should I prepare ten or twenty chairs for the meeting?
(A) It was yesterday.
(B) A few hours.
(C) I think ten will be enough.

17
AU
US
How long will the summer jazz concert last?
(A) During the last weekend.
(B) It's about thirty meters.
(C) Let's check the leaflet.

18
US
BR
I'd like to exchange this microwave oven.
(A) Let me check the exchange rate first.
(B) Thanks, but I had some bread.
(C) Sure, I can help you with that.

19 Why did all the supervisors come to work early?
AU
BR
(A) I have no idea.
(B) You don't need to come in.
(C) They're working now.

20 Town Bank decided to merge with JR Investment,
US
US
didn't it?
(A) It is an emerging company.
(B) I decided against him.
(C) I'm not working at the bank anymore.

21 Will the training seminar end before 4 P.M.?
US
AU
(A) No, the late departure.
(B) I saw the advertisement.
(C) Today's schedule is in your e-mail.

22 Are there any wireless keyboards available?
BR
US
(A) These computers look expensive.
(B) Sure, we have 10 seats left.
(C) I can order them for you.

23 Should we arrive at the Peterson station at 1
BR
AU
o'clock or 2 o'clock?
(A) No, that's not necessary.
(B) Our train is at 3.
(C) Take the next left.

24 Haven't you reviewed the proposed budget
US
US
report?
(A) There are lots of good reviews online.
(B) You must report to the main office tomorrow.
(C) No, I just got back from Sydney last night.

25 This color printer is out of order again.
US
BR
(A) Should we order more?
(B) This is the third time this month.
(C) There's another color upstairs.

26 Can you find anyone to cover my shift tonight?
AU
US
(A) The shipping is free.
(B) All of us are already working overtime.
(C) He is too busy right now.

27 Who do I need to ask about assembling these
AU
BR
shelves?
(A) No, he doesn't know.
(B) Kelly agrees on it.
(C) I have the information on my desk.

28 How's the Mexican food at Kay's restaurant?
US
US
(A) Yes, it was very big.
(B) Do you think so?
(C) I would go somewhere else.

29 Would you like to join the pilot project team next
US
AU
month?
(A) I will be busy developing a new product.
(B) It was very helpful.
(C) The sales projections.

30 Where did you have your mobile phone fixed?
BR
US
(A) I updated it last month.
(B) If I were you, I wouldn't go there.
(C) That'll be $50.

31 Is your computer also unable to connect to the
BR
AU
Internet?
(A) I just called a tech support.
(B) A local Internet provider.
(C) By fixing the problem.

PART 3

Questions 32-34 refer to the following conversation.
| US - AU |

W Hello, Louis. Have you taken your lunch break, yet? I wanted to eat my lunch at the company cafeteria, but there are so few menu options available. Some of them are not really good.

M How about trying the order-in service at the Web site mealforyou.com? You can use their pickup and delivery service for almost all restaurants in the city for a nominal fee. I often use it.

W Hmm... I don't think I would pay more for pickup and delivery service. I should bring my own lunch box from home.

Questions 35-37 refer to the following conversation.
| US - BR |

M Hello, I'm calling to ask you about the Dallas IT Conference scheduled for July. Do you have any hotel accommodation near the conference center that you recommend?

W Of course. For our attendees, we offer a discount coupon that can be used at the hotels, just two blocks away from the center. And you will receive a 20% discount.

M Sounds good. However, I'm planning to stay a few more days after the conference. Is that okay?

W I'm sorry. They offer the discount only during the conference. After the event, you will need to pay the regular price.

Questions 38-40 refer to the following conversation with three speakers.

| US - BR - AU |

W1 Hello, Nora. You've already checked the note for arranging our weekly video conference, right? How's it going?

W2 It's difficult to hook up the camera. I think we should call the office manager to get some help.

W1 OK, I'll call him right now. Rudy? Nora and I are in meeting room 5. We're having difficulty installing some video equipment. We definitely need some help.

M Oh, not again! The cables in the room seem to have some problems. You should move to another room.

W1 Hmm... but the other rooms are already booked up for today.

M Well, there was a cancellation of a conference in room 3. Let's meet there and I'll help you install the equipment.

Questions 41-43 refer to the following conversation.

| US - US |

M Thank you for showing your interest in renting an office space in our complex. I'm sure you will be very happy with it.

W I believe so. Since most of our clients are quite close to this complex, our management is interested in renting an office in this area. Renting an office here would save some travel costs when meeting them. Which office is available?

M Well, right here. Let's have a look at this space. It has a nice city view from the balcony even though it is not so big.

W The size is just right for us. There are only four employees in our firm.

M Then, it seems a perfect one for you. And also, you can see on the rental agreement – it includes the shared meeting room and kitchen.

Questions 44-46 refer to the following conversation.

| BR - AU |

W Hello, would you mind me sitting here? I'm so interested in this presentation on the current market trends.

M Not at all! So am I. I'm expecting some useful information for the organization I work for. This year's conference has been really informative.

W Absolutely! What kind of work do you do at your organization?

M I'm in sales and marketing at Osterley Tech. We mainly carry products like computers, printers, and copiers.

W Oh, I work in the purchasing division at Bermondsey Accounting. Actually, we are currently considering buying new computers for our new branch office.

M Well, I'd be glad to tell you more about our computers and other products. Let me give you my business card. Please call me sometime this week at your earliest convenience.

Questions 47-49 refer to the following conversation.

| US - AU |

W We're happy to be working with you, Alan. Have you finished settling into your new apartment since you relocated to our branch?

M Yeah, thank you. Almost, but I'm still looking for some furniture, and I want to buy something affordable.

W Do you know the furniture store on Charing Avenue? You can find various used items such as furniture sets and appliances. Even though some of them have minor scratches and dents, their prices are reasonable.

M That sounds interesting. I wonder if they offer free delivery. My car is not big enough to carry much.

W Well, unfortunately, they don't. However, Curtis working in our office has a large van. He might be able to help you. Let me speak with him after work.

Questions 50-52 refer to the following conversation.

| US - BR |

M Hello, my name is Rogers, the operational manager. Thanks for coming today. Let me show you the staff lounge that we will ask your company to renovate.

W Well, you told me on the phone that you'd like to give the lounge a totally different look, right? So, we need to remove all the things in here before we install a new carpet and walls.

M Hmm... there will be a welcoming party for our new staff members sometime in the first week of March, and the party is supposed to be held in the lounge. Is it possible to complete the work by then?

W If we start work as soon as possible, there shouldn't be a problem with that. I will send you an estimate today after I go back to my office. Let me know if you want us to work on the project.

M Sure, I will decide after reviewing it.

Questions 53-55 refer to the following conversation.

| US - US |

M Hello, I want to order a special cake for my son for his birthday next Monday. His name is Gerry Dennis.

W Oh, yes. I remember you called this morning. Did you see the pictures of our cakes?

M Yes, as you suggested, I had a look at your Web site. According to your Web site, you can top the cake with a toy motorcycle or other items, right?

W That's right. How would you like your cake?

M Hum. I wanna order a cake with a toy train set on the top of the cake.

W Alright. Do you have any more requests? Your cake will go out for delivery early Monday morning.

M Well, just make sure it arrives before noon when the birthday party begins.

W Of course. We'll have it there around 9 o'clock.

Questions 56-58 refer to the following conversation with three speakers.

| BR - US - AU |

W Are there any more questions before we leave for Seoul for an annual conference?

M1 Actually, I have one. I remember that we could get reimbursed for all business-related transportation fees last quarter. Is that still applicable?

W Well... unfortunately, not this time. It resulted in making the travel expenses too high, so the company will only compensate for flight tickets.

M2 Hmm... I heard about a firm called Benny Travel that provides various package deals for transportation at no additional charge including all ground transportation. Since we make a lot of overseas trips, we should switch to them.

W Right. Lewis, you're responsible for purchasing, right? Why don't you learn more about Benny Travel?

M1 OK, I'll contact them right away to check their price range.

Questions 59-61 refer to the following conversation.

| BR - AU |

W Hello, Leon. Have you completed the drawings for Soto Telecommunication's office complex building project?

M Well, I talked with them over the phone earlier today, and they said they wanted to make a change to their plan. They are considering adding a wing to use as their research lab on the side of the main building.

W Is that so? Do we still have to complete the drawings by the beginning of next week?

M Yes, that's right. I will cancel my other appointments including a team meeting to make the drawing ready for your review by Wednesday.

Questions 62-64 refer to the following conversation and invitation.

| US - AU |

W Hi, can I talk to Paul Taylor? This is Alison Torres. He sent me an invitation for a charity fundraising banquet he is organizing. I would like to confirm that I'll be able to join the event.

M Hello, Alison. It's great to hear that you'll be attending. Well, could you tell me which meal option you prefer?

W Oh, that's right. Actually, I can't eat any meat.

M We have a couple of vegetarian options – a mushroom soup noodle and a tofu steak with honey sauce.

W Hmm... I'd like the noodle, please.

M Alright! And, don't forget there will be live entertainment at the event. I think you may be able to take a seat closer to the front stage if you arrive a bit earlier.

Questions 65-67 refer to the following conversation and shelving unit.

| US - BR |

M Lynda, can you take a look at the stockroom? A shipment of our summer clothing line is coming this afternoon, so we have to make some space for them.

W OK, I'll work on it after I put these jackets away. Well, these three boxes of jackets seem nearly empty. I think I should pack them together in a box so that some more room can be made for the shipment.

M That's a very good idea. And once you've done that, please take an additional display shelf to the entrance of the shop.

Questions 68-70 refer to the following conversation and sign.

| AU - BR |

M Cindy, don't forget the concert is this evening after work.

W Oh, right. It begins at 7:00, doesn't it? And do we need to get there a bit early?

M That's right. To secure a good seat, we should arrive when they open. People like this concert very much, but they don't provide assigned seats.

W I was told that this concert is performed by a local band. I believe that's why people like it so much.

M Yeah. I heard some of the band members live in our town.

W Would you like to have dinner before the concert?

M I know a good Chinese restaurant near the concert hall. Why don't we go there?

PART 4

Questions 71-73 refer to the following announcement.

| US |

W Okay. Before we end today's meeting, I have an important announcement to make for all our staff members here at our factory. As one of our employee benefits, our company gives every employee a free physical check-up every year. So, this year, health professionals from Dearborn General Hospital will be visiting our factory next Thursday and Friday. And, after checkups, participants will be given a free meal voucher that can be used at our cafeteria. If you're interested, you can fill out a form at the end of the meeting.

Questions 74-76 refer to the following broadcast.

| AU |

M Now, it's time for the local news. Today, the ownership of the well-known 150-year-old structure in the town center, Perivale Hotel, was officially changed. This old building has been loved by everyone. The new owner is planning to turn it into a new museum with the architectural company Megan Construction. They were chosen since they have extensive experience in renovating historic structures, and the owner is confident that they can complete this challenging project successfully. The town is expecting that the new addition will attract more tourists once the project is done.

Questions 77-79 refer to the following telephone message.

| BR |

W Hello, this is Dora. I'm calling regarding Pam's farewell party. I'm so happy to help you arrange the party. You wanted me to book the Indian restaurant downtown, but you know about fifty people will be attending. So, why don't we try Golden House – the one with the large private hall? Anyway, I think we should meet up this week to talk about all the details. Planning this event won't be as simple as we originally thought. Let me put our meeting on the schedule for Thursday. Thank you.

Questions 80-82 refer to the following excerpt from a meeting.

| US |

M Hi, everyone. Thank you for attending today's staff meeting. As some of you already know, I'd like to announce that Phyllis Russell will win the "Employee of the Year" award. Phyllis has been the head Web designer for six years. Her most recent design made our company's Web site more attractive. In fact, since our Web site was newly renovated by her, the overall traffic to access to our Web site has increased significantly, by 20% compared to last year. Also, starting next month, Phyllis will hold a training course for our employees on creating innovative visual materials. Please give a big hand to Phyllis Russell, the employee of the year.

Questions 83-85 refer to the following speech.

| US |

W I'm honored to welcome you all to the 12th annual Southern Region Real Estate conference. This year's venue is much larger than before and there are various events taking place across the site during the week-long course. I hope everyone is wearing comfortable shoes. Well... I feel bittersweet with this year. As some of you are probably aware, I myself began this event twelve years ago with the clear objective of not only selling more properties, but also inviting people to our annual event to let them share their own ideas. And fortunately, it's been very successful. That's what made it very difficult for me to decide to resign as the host of this event after over a decade of work. But, I'm sure Lynne Mann, my successor, will make the event even more successful.

Questions 86-88 refer to the following announcement.

| AU |

M Hello, passengers. Welcome aboard Flight GA47 to Berlin. Before we take off, I'd like to inform you of a new service you can enjoy. On top of music and films, we provide digital versions of a wide range of publications through the entertainment monitor on the seat back in front of you. With the touchscreen monitor, not only current but also previous issues of various magazines can be accessed. If you are interested in this new service, please just put your credit card into the slot. Thank you.

Questions 89-91 refer to the following excerpt from a meeting.

| US |

M As most of you are aware, our firm's been encountering stiff competition over the last few months. As the competitors' presence in the market has been stronger than ours, it's essential for us to improve our marketing skills that help us to gain a competitive advantage. Thus, a professional development workshop is scheduled next Thursday at 3 o'clock. Although some of you may need to attend other meetings or have other work to do at that time,

this is very important to our firm's success. After the workshop, detailed feedback should be submitted, so a form will be sent to each of you. Please make sure to fill it out properly and forward it to me within a day. Thank you.

Questions 92-94 refer to the following telephone message.

| US |

W Hello, Chris. This is Katie, floor manager. I'm calling to find out if you can work both the lunch and the dinner shifts today. Unexpectedly, two of the other dinner servers called in sick, so we need someone who can cover their shifts. If you are OK, can you come in at 10:30 A.M.? Since you'll be doing a double shift today, I'll make sure you are able to leave before 11 P.M. when the other dinner staff start to prepare closing. If you can make it, please call me and let me know as soon as possible. Thank you.

Questions 95-97 refer to the following excerpt from a meeting and product information page.

| AU |

M Thanks for coming all of you. Let me start today's meeting with reviewing the progress on the development of options of our new wearable device, K-10 Smart Watch. We've just finished all the final tests and now we're ready to introduce this year's new model with surprisingly innovative options. People can customize their own devices by selecting an option from each of the four components: cover, size, band, color. According to the recent survey, most of our customers prefer a larger selection of colors, so we've decided to offer two more color options next month. Next is something I'm very excited about. As you know, we participated in the Expo in New York last week and I heard we got several calls for orders from India and Europe.

Questions 98-100 refer to the following excerpt from a meeting and form.

| BR |

W Good afternoon, everyone. I'm Emily Barnes. As membership coordinator at the National

History Gallery, I sincerely appreciate employees from most of our departments volunteering to help with our membership campaign next month. More than half of our gallery's operating costs were covered from membership fees. So, next month's campaign is very important to us. You will be mostly responsible for greeting visitors as they enter the entrance and encouraging them to join our membership. If they'd like to, ask them to complete this form. There are four types of membership listed in the form. As some of you may notice, this season we have increased the fee for platinum level.

TEST 06 스크립트

PART 1

1
US
(A) They're cooking some food.
(B) They're exiting the building.
(C) They're walking under the umbrellas.
(D) They're seated outdoors.

2
US
(A) Some tables are being assembled.
(B) Some paper is scattered on the floor.
(C) A man is sipping from a cup.
(D) A man is holding the back of a chair.

3
AU
(A) They're putting some dirt onto a truck.
(B) They're wearing work vests.
(C) They're sweeping the road.
(D) They're using shovels to dig a hole.

4
BR
(A) Some plants are being grown in a garden.
(B) Some vegetables are on display in the store.
(C) One of the women is opening her bag.
(D) One of the women is removing items from shelves.

5
US
(A) She's walking down the aisle.
(B) She's transporting some items on a cart.
(C) She's paying for some merchandise.
(D) She's carrying her bag on her shoulder.

6
BR
(A) Trees in the garden are being trimmed.
(B) A stairway is divided by a railing.
(C) Some stairs lead up to an entrance.
(D) A stone archway is being built.

PART 2

7
US
US
What time does the seminar begin?
(A) International Education.
(B) Yes, it's been delayed.
(C) In about 30 minutes.

8
US
BR
Which conference room has been reserved?
(A) The largest one on the fourth floor.
(B) The online booking system.
(C) The last week of this month.

9
AU US

Where did you get the mug?
(A) I haven't been there yet.
(B) It's good to see you again.
(C) The gift shop next to the post office.

10
AU BR

Did anyone talk to the technical department?
(A) Please take the technology class.
(B) The printer is out of order.
(C) Yes, they will send someone in an hour.

11
US US

I will pay for your dinner today.
(A) Thank you, I'd appreciate that.
(B) Today's special please.
(C) Yes, every other day.

12
US AU

Could you help me move these chairs to the basement?
(A) The desk has a heavy base.
(B) Sure, but let me finish this report first.
(C) We have already moved to the city.

13
BR US

This is the latest model in the store, isn't it?
(A) They ordered more storage devices.
(B) It's not far from here.
(C) Yes, it just arrived a few days ago.

14
BR AU

Why was this year's exports exhibition canceled?
(A) We invited some experts in this field.
(B) At the convention hall.
(C) Because not enough companies wanted to attend.

15
US US

When will our framed pictures be delivered?
(A) At my office.
(B) Talk to Julia.
(C) I'll show you how to make it.

16
US BR

Where's the price tag for this laptop computer?
(A) The price will drop down soon.
(B) It's on the back of the product label.
(C) It is rather overpriced.

17
AU US

Who has been appointed as the new chief financial officer?
(A) Our chef is not working today.
(B) That would be Mr. Cohen.
(C) Yes, I have an appointment at 2.

18
AU BR

Should we hire a new delivery company for next year or not?
(A) It arrives at 2 P.M.
(B) At this year's inspection.
(C) Yes, we need the one with more trucks.

19
US US

This vacuum cleaner is so popular in Europe.
(A) When are you leaving?
(B) That's a nice place.
(C) I know it's selling well.

20
US AU

This dining table comes with four chairs, doesn't it?
(A) A one-year warranty.
(B) I can't come with you.
(C) Actually, they're not included in the price.

21
BR US

Where will the annual conference take place?
(A) I will check my calendar.
(B) His speech was very impressive.
(C) The weeklong conference.

22
BR AU

Are we supposed to visit the factory with the regional director?
(A) He is one of the visitors.
(B) The assembly line has been removed.
(C) It's still being renovated.

23
US US

Who should I ask for the sales report?
(A) Three copies please.
(B) It was a helpful offer for me.
(C) I have an extra copy.

24
US BR

Hasn't the board of directors approved the final budget yet?
(A) Isn't it too expensive?
(B) A proposed one.
(C) The manager received it this morning.

25
AU US

Do you think the client's flight will arrive on schedule?
(A) I will pick it up by myself.
(B) It left on time from Hong Kong.
(C) For factory tours.

26
AU BR

Would you like to take a taxi or a bus to the conference?
(A) It's about the marketing strategies.
(B) Julia will be here to pick us up.
(C) I prefer blue.

27
US US

Shouldn't we order more refreshments for the press preview?
(A) We have enough already.
(B) A problem with the screen.
(C) No, he will review it.

28 Why didn't Mr. Hale return to his office yet?
US AU
(A) We'll book your flight today.
(B) Thirty miles from here.
(C) He is attending an urgent client meeting.

29 Most customers seem to buy their clothes online.
BR US
(A) By credit card.
(B) But some still prefer trying them on in the store.
(C) All lines are busy.

30 I can't get the storage room to open.
BR AU
(A) The lock has been changed.
(B) It's close to my office.
(C) No, we need to order more.

31 Has anyone booked a meeting room for this afternoon?
AU BR
(A) The meeting is next Monday.
(B) Did you bring the equipment?
(C) I need a family room.

PART 3

Questions 32-34 refer to the following conversation.
| US - AU |

W Hi, excuse me. Could you give me some directions to the closest subway station?

M OK. Well, can you see that five-story glass building over there? When you get to the building, turn left, and then go straight about two blocks. That's where you can find the Turnham subway station.

W Does the subway head to the town center? I'm going to see a play that begins in half an hour at the King Theater.

M Yeah, but I heard the subway line is being delayed due to some railroad work. I think you should take a taxi if you are in a hurry. They are usually waiting just around the corner.

Questions 35-37 refer to the following conversation.
| BR - US |

W Ian, I heard you were not able to make it to this morning's meeting, so I'd like to let you know what we discussed. We're considering opening a new massage shop, and the location would be in Wembley.

M Oh, that's great news! Well, but the location seems too close to our current shop, right? It's just a 15 minute walk from us. Do you think there will be plenty of business for both locations?

W Yeah, I also worried about that initially, but the Wembley area is rapidly growing. Many people keep moving into the area. In addition, we have found a very affordable space. I'm going there tomorrow to check it again and to see if we made the right decision.

Questions 38-40 refer to the following conversation with three speakers.
| AU - US - BR |

M Hi, my name is Neal Wolfe calling from WG Consulting. The conference I was supposed to attend in Singapore has been canceled, so I would like to reschedule the hotel and flight reservations that your travel agency arranged for me.

W1 Certainly, but that requires additional charge.

M Hmm... That's strange. I've never paid any fee for changing my travel arrangements before.

W1 My manager is with me right here. Hold a moment please, and I will check with her. Ms. Torres, a client from WG Consulting would like to rearrange his travel reservations. Is there any charge for that?

W2 WG Consulting has a contract enabling them to make changes with no additional fee as far as a sufficient notice is given. Can you check the original reservation dates?

W1 No problem. He is on the line. I will check with him.

Questions 41-43 refer to the following conversation.
| AU - BR |

M Thank you for calling the Warwick Sports Club. How can I help you?

W Hello, I registered for the everyday morning fitness class that starts next week and I have some questions.

M Sure.

W I wonder if you offer a personal class. I do not want to participate in competitive team activities, so even if I have to pay more, I want to work out on my own or with my own group of friends. Is there such a personal class that I can take for about an hour?

M There are several private classes on demand. Let me have a look in our computer scheduling system. I can tell you which classes and instructors are available and at what time.

Questions 44-46 refer to the following conversation.
| US - US |

M Hello, my name is Omar Garza from Goodwin Bistro. I'm calling regarding my order for potatoes.

W OK, sir. How may I help you?

M The order has just arrived. And I only received 3 boxes of big potatoes, but actually I ordered 8.

W Hmm... One moment, please. I'll check your invoice on the computer. Oh, that's right. We're very sorry about that.

M Can I get those other 5 boxes as soon as possible? I really need them today.

W Well, we can deliver them to you by 4 P.M. today by express shipping. Is that OK, sir?

M That's perfect. Thank you so much.

W And, as a token of our apology for the mistake, we'll send you some free boxes of our new sweet potatoes for you to try.

Questions 47-49 refer to the following conversation.
| AU - BR |

M Darlene Jones, I phoned you to talk about the report on the sales of our firm's new fruit juice drinks.

W Hello, Lonnie. I hope you have some good news.

M Well, I'm afraid that you might be disappointed with the figures. The sports celebrity endorsement for the drinks didn't increase the sales.

W Hmm... I believe it's time to talk about other ways of advertising.

M Shouldn't we consider putting more effort into social media advertising? For instance, we could reward customers who post photos of themselves drinking our products at various places.

W Yeah, that's a good idea. That will surely work for us as most people nowadays use social media very often.

Questions 50-52 refer to the following conversation.
| US - US |

M Sarah, do you have a minute to talk about some complaints we received recently from our customers? They are not pleased with the long wait time to be connected to one of our representatives to inquire about their credit card.

W Alright. Since we started our new ad campaign, our customer service representatives have been receiving much higher volumes of calls from customers than before. So, the wait time's getting even worse.

M I see. Should we hire more staff to solve this issue?

W Yeah, I think we should. And also, processing payments tends to take too much time. Should we install a system that allows customers to make payments over the phone? Customers' payment information can be automatically processed by the system, and it would enable our representatives to handle other work.

Questions 53-55 refer to the following conversation.
| AU - US |

M OK, Ms. Foster. Here's the key for your room. It's 318 – just to the left after getting off the elevator. I hope you enjoy your stay at Ferguson Inn.

W Thank you. I'm here in the city for a convention, but it seems I can have a little free time. It's my first time visiting this city.

M Alright, I would recommend you go to the Royal History Gallery. It's well known for its large collection of 18th-century sculptures and paintings.

W That sounds interesting. I love to see historical art pieces.

M If you purchase your ticket on the Internet, you'll be able to get a 20% discount.

W That's nice. Thank you for the great information.

Questions 56-58 refer to the following conversation with three speakers.
| US - BR - US |

M Hello, Stella and Jodi. It's good to see you all again at this management seminar.

W1 Nice to see you, Julian. I think we haven't seen you since the last company-wide conference, right? How have you been?

M   I've been quite busy recently. I heard your division is working on our company's new Web site. How is it going?

W2   Well, it's almost done. We are in the final stage of the project. The new one will be a lot faster than the current one.

M   That'd be nice. I was in charge of reviewing the comments from the users this quarter. Many of them who participated in the survey indicated it tends to be too slow.

Questions 59-61 refer to the following conversation.

| AU - US |

M   Hi, Brandy. Mr. Horton phoned this afternoon. He stopped by the construction site this morning to check how our project is going, and he said everything is okay except for the exterior wall. He'd like to have the wall painted in white rather than gray.

W   Did he? That is the paint he picked out in our office last week.

M   Well, he was not happy with how it looks, so he decided to choose a new one. I placed an order, but I don't think it will be here until next week.

W   But, according to the contract, the project has to be completed no later than this week.

M   Yeah, that's right. I'm going to call him right now to extend the deadline.

Questions 62-64 refer to the following conversation and seating chart.

| BR - AU |

W   Hello, Bryant. I'm trying to book our tickets for the opera now. Do you have any seating preference?

M   Well, I normally book a seat close to the front, near the stage so I can see the performance better.

W   Yeah, there are still a few seats left in the front row, on the left side, far from the exit.

M   Perfect. Why don't we leave early to park our car?

W   Hmm, how about taking the subway? That way, we won't need to worry about finding a parking space.

Questions 65-67 refer to the following conversation and bill.

| BR - AU |

W   Hi, Mr. Kim. The pictures you asked us to frame are ready for pickup. You're here for them, right?

M   Oh, thanks. I knew it was such short notice, but I wanted to donate them to a charity auction this Saturday.

W   That sounds great. I hope the framed pictures help raise enough funds for the charity. Let me give you the bill.

M   Thank you. Hmm... I think it seems to have an error. I didn't have four pictures framed, only three. The charge for a 9 inch by 9 inch frame doesn't seem to be one of them.

W   Oh, sorry. There seems to be a mistake. I'll remove that and print a new bill for you. In the meantime, let one of my coworkers take the pictures out to your vehicle.

M   That'd be nice. Thank you.

Questions 68-70 refer to the following conversation and schedule.

| US - US |

W   It was great to speak with our company president at the staff meeting.

M   Yes, it was. Our company is growing rapidly, so the expansion plan has to be well organized for everyone.

W   Oh! I almost forgot to tell you that I reviewed your e-mail about the opening schedules for our new branch offices. The office in South Park is behind schedule, so it has to be revised.

M   Alright. What's the reason?

W   The construction work has been delayed by several storms and heavy snow. They asked us to change the schedule to sometime in late September.

M   That shouldn't be a problem, and we can have extra time to search for new employees.

Questions 71-73 refer to the following broadcast.

| US |

W Good morning everyone. You are listening to ABC radio. Today's first topic of the world business news show is about outdoor advertising. Most of us are questioning the efficiency of traditional marketing tools such as television, radio, print advertising, billboards and so on. 'Isn't that just a lot of wasting of money?' In fact, most companies are spending increasingly more of their marketing budget on online promotion. But recently, some marketing research papers found that outdoor advertising has more potential than you might imagine. Today, I'll be talking with four renowned marketing specialists to find out how your business can benefit from increased outdoor advertising.

Questions 74-76 refer to the following telephone message.

| AU |

M Hi, I'm calling from Lewis Modern Furniture. I'd like to update you on the order that you placed a few days ago. The office cabinets you requested have arrived. We planned to deliver them to your office tomorrow. But, according to our delivery schedule, it seems like none of our trucks will be available for a week. Also, we didn't receive the chairs you ordered yet. The manufacturing plant will complete them in a few days. As a token of our apology for these delays, we will give you 20% off your next order with us.

Questions 77-79 refer to the following telephone message.

| BR |

W Hi, Ms. Hicks. My name is Lynda calling from Pat Law Firm, regarding the construction project your company is planning to do in Croxley. I'm going to draw up the agreement today. But, I need detailed information on the budget for the project since the contract should include a schedule for when the payment will be made by your client during the project. Please send me the information as soon as possible. If you have any questions, please feel free to contact me. Thank you.

Questions 80-82 refer to the following talk.

| US |

M Welcome to the International Trade Fair for Innovation, and also thank you for coming by our company's booth. If you are searching for the most effective way to create unique and attractive packaging materials for your goods, we can give you the answer. Our new machines will allow you to stop spending so much money purchasing customized packaging materials from outside vendors. You can produce your own materials with our new machines. It is not only efficient but also very user-friendly. OK, now let me show you how it works.

Questions 83-85 refer to the following tour information.

| US |

W Ladies and gentlemen, welcome to the National History Museum. Our museum is hosting a special exhibition to celebrate the 100th anniversary from Feb. 2 to Feb. 12. We'll be starting our tour of the new exhibit on the history of the modern city. So if you want to join us, please come to the east wing right now. It will be a great opportunity for you and your children to learn about how cities are planned, and who does the planning. During the tour, you can ask me any questions. That's why I'm here. Before we start, please turn off your mobile phones.

Questions 86-88 refer to the following news report.

| US |

M Welcome to the Wood Green local news. This afternoon, the city council approved the renovation plans for the whole office complex buildings on Arnos Avenue. The project is scheduled to start in June and should be finished by the beginning of next year. What makes this location great is its proximity to the main subway station and bus stops in the city. Commuters won't need to walk a long distance to catch the subway and buses. If you need more information about the complex, you can see the new floor plan of the newly renovated complex buildings on the city's Web site. The spaces in the buildings can be leased in the short and long term.

Questions 89-91 refer to the following advertisement.

| AU |

M Do you need an extra battery for your mobile phone? Dalon X–20000 will meet your needs. Dalon X is easy to carry because it is small enough to easily fit into a small bag or any of your pockets. It also comes with a universal charger that works with various cell phones and other mobile devices. You should keep in mind that the extra battery can be used at any time and anywhere. Just visit our Web site and you'll find hundreds of reviews from satisfied customers.

Question 92-94 refer to the following excerpt from a meeting.

| AU |

M OK, everyone. Since we've discussed how to present a cost estimate for the installation of an air conditioner, now let's learn about good communication skills with our potential clients. When talking about the energy efficiency of our products, don't forget: many people have a limited understanding of the subject. Particularly, we should explain how much they can save by using our products compared to other companies' products. You can refer to a chart in your training packet. It should be very informative when you convince clients. Please remember each of you has a goal that is to meet a sales quota of at least 2 units per week.

Questions 95-97 refer to the following announcement and weather report.

| BR |

W Everyone, may I have your attention, please? Now, our coach is about to stop in front of the Ruislip Hotel where we're scheduled to stay tonight. We're going to be here until tomorrow afternoon and I'd like to remind you that everyone can enjoy free time until we start our group tour tomorrow. If you have a plan to go out and look around the town, please keep in mind that a 90% chance of rain is forecast today. If you need a raincoat or an umbrella, you can borrow them from the hotel at no cost. If you don't have any special plan, why don't you visit Sudbury Furniture? This famous store is located just a few blocks away.

Questions 98-100 refer to the following excerpt from a meeting and neighborhood map.

| AU |

M I'm pleased to announce that demand for recycling pick-up in the town has risen to the point we need to add more than one pick-up in some areas thanks to the outreach and public education campaigns. The route that needs a change the most is the Wednesday one. To accommodate all the increased demand for using our curbside recycling service, we'll go around the area not only on Wednesday but also on Thursday. Also, with the rapid increase in business, extra vehicles will be purchased by the end of this quarter to do our work more effectively.

🎧 TEST07.mp3

PART 1

1
BR
(A) They're looking at the computer monitor.
(B) They're cleaning the office.
(C) The man is pointing at a document.
(D) The woman is typing on a keyboard.

2
AU
(A) A man is getting into a taxi.
(B) A man is standing on the street.
(C) A tower is being built in the park.
(D) Some buses are stopped at the traffic light.

3
US
(A) Some people are standing outdoors.
(B) Some workers are leaving a laboratory.
(C) They're working at counters.
(D) A woman is moving some furniture.

4
US
(A) Some merchandise has been displayed.
(B) Some signs are leaning against a wall.
(C) Some fruits are being harvested.
(D) Some shoppers are sheltered by an umbrella.

5
AU
(A) A man is walking with his dogs.
(B) A man is resting on the deck.
(C) A man is holding a handrail.
(D) A man is taking off his hat.

6
BR
(A) Some vehicles are entering a garage.
(B) Tables have been placed next to the building.
(C) An outdoor café is deserted.
(D) People are crossing the street.

PART 2

7
BR
US
How long is the commute to downtown Seattle?
(A) An hour train ride.
(B) About 2:30.
(C) At the local branch.

8
US
US
Which flavor of popcorn do you want?
(A) I'll take caramel, please.
(B) The store over there.
(C) Yes, at the corner.

9
US
AU
Should we get delivery for dinner or do you prefer eating out?
(A) That sounds good.
(B) I like the new restaurant across the street.
(C) Chinese is my favorite.

10
BR
US
What time is the president's speech on our 10th anniversary?
(A) On Tuesday.
(B) Front seats.
(C) Right before lunch.

11
BR
AU
Michael Foods Group is hiring, right?
(A) Too late, they already filled the position.
(B) I'd like to have a fish and salad.
(C) The restaurant is on the left side of this road.

12
US
US
Where can I find more information about the refund policy?
(A) Your exchange policy.
(B) On our company Web site.
(C) Within 14 days.

13
US
US
How come Jordan left early today?
(A) Through our Web site.
(B) To pick up a client from the airport.
(C) He left it on your desk.

14
AU
US
When will the renovation work be finished?
(A) Yeah, last night.
(B) The main lobby is fantastic.
(C) Sorry, I don't work here.

15
AU
BR
Do you want me to transfer this call to you?
(A) He didn't answer the phone.
(B) Please call me, Linda.
(C) Sure, I'll take it in my office.

16
US
US
Did you have a look at our refurbished offices in Tokyo?
(A) I already tried reviewing it.
(B) Okay, I will look at the file now.
(C) Yes, it's a nice change.

17
US
AU
Who's been appointed as marketing director?
(A) Joan Carter just took that position.
(B) Sorry, I have an appointment tomorrow.
(C) It was a successful advertising campaign.

18
BR
US
Where should we post this notice?
(A) We need a boarding pass.
(B) As soon as we receive it.
(C) How about next to the main entrance?

19
BR
AU
Does your bus stop by the conference center downtown?
(A) Did you leave on Monday or Tuesday?
(B) Actually, we are going by train.
(C) A new convention hall.

20
US
US
Didn't Randi sign the contract with our new distributor?
(A) A great deal.
(B) No, not as far as I know.
(C) I haven't contacted her.

21
US
BR
You'll be leaving for London this week, right?
(A) Yes, he will.
(B) At the headquarters.
(C) The conference was delayed.

22
AU
US
I don't see any manual in this box.
(A) Some missing parts.
(B) I'll also have some.
(C) Maybe they forgot to include it.

23
AU
BR
Do you want me to give you the samples and brochures today?
(A) At the staff meeting yesterday.
(B) I'll be in my office from noon onwards.
(C) He did not ask.

24
US
US
How many of us are able to attend the conference this year?
(A) We had more participants than last year.
(B) The budget allows us to send ten representatives.
(C) I was told it will be in Boston.

25
US
AU
Do you know where I can have my mobile phone charged?
(A) I bought a charger there.
(B) One battery, please.
(C) There is a shop on Peterson Drive.

26
BR
US
Who should I speak with to open a savings account?
(A) Yes, you can save $50.
(B) When would you like to see me?
(C) I can help you with that.

27
BR
AU
What is the name of the advertising award our company won?
(A) The ceremony was in Washington.
(B) Best Television Commercial Award.
(C) The list of nominations.

28
AU
BR
Are we going to buy a new fax machine or lease one?
(A) The committee has not approved the budget yet.
(B) It comes with a printer.
(C) A larger size.

29
US
US
Maybe, I could extend the deadline for the project.
(A) Just one week would be enough.
(B) It's for Jason Insurance.
(C) At the end of this month.

30
US
BR
Mr. Howard asked all of our engineers to be here when he visits our factory.
(A) We haven't decided.
(B) Several pages long.
(C) I'm meeting a client then.

31
AU
US
We should finalize the contract before any more issues arise.
(A) I'll give you the contact number.
(B) Our legal team is still reviewing it.
(C) Issue an ID badge.

PART 3

Questions 32-34 refer to the following conversation.
| US - AU |

W Hey, Reed. You've lived in Cleveland, right? I'm thinking to visit the Cleveland City Park tomorrow. And I can't decide whether to drive or take a bus.

M Well, you know the city park is one of the most popular places. If you drive, it will be almost impossible to find parking. Especially on a weekend like tomorrow, I'd definitely take the bus to avoid the parking problems.

W OK, thanks.

M By the way, how long will you be in Cleveland?

W A couple of days.

M Well, if you need more information about hotels and public transportation, the Cleveland Tourist Site is very helpful. If you need the Web site's address, I will let you know later.

Questions 35-37 refer to the following conversation.
| BR - AU |

W Hi, Stevie. How's it going there?

M We are doing fine. It seems we can finish everything this week.

W Good to hear that. By the way, I'm calling to ask your crew to stop at the customer's house on Jackson Street, actually ah... Mr. Baker's house, and check if the paint on the wall has dried well.

M I thought Mr. Baker was going to check the work by himself.

W He found some cracks and some wet paint. And he wants someone to take care of it. Could you stop by his place when you finish installing carpets?

M Our crew is going to be here all day.

W If so, never mind. I'll check this week's schedules and see if another team can fit in a visit tomorrow.

M OK, just call me back if you need anything else.

Questions 38-40 refer to the following conversation.
| US - US |

W Hello, I saw your advertisement that your complex has apartments available for rent. I'm calling to see if any of those are studio apartments.

M Yes, we do have a few available on the third floor.

W Good, but I have a problem. I usually ride a bicycle, which is pretty heavy to carry.

M Actually, we are planning to install an elevator in the building next month because some tenants are having difficulties with the stairs.

W That's good news for me. Then, can I take a look at those apartments?

M Sure. When do you want to come by and see them?

Questions 41-43 refer to the following conversation.
| US - BR |

M Hi, Sondra. This is Vance from accounting. I'm calling to find out if the meeting room schedule for this week has been completed.

W Yes, we already posted the monthly schedule on the Web site. What's up? Does your department need to add any more meetings?

M Yes, indeed. I was just informed that one of our directors from the head office in Manchester will be here next Tuesday. She'll speak to employees about the company's new payroll system.

W Hum... I cannot say for sure but I will see what I can do for you. If you send me an e-mail with a short description of the presentation, I'll let you know if I can add it to the schedule.

Questions 44-46 refer to the following conversation.
| US - AU |

W Mr. Alton. I've reviewed the findings from the staff opinion survey. They show that many of our employees are unhappy with the new open office layout.

M Really? That's weird. I heard that employees working in an open space are more likely to be creative and have collaborative attitudes than those working in individual cubicles.

W That's right. But the findings indicate that distracting noise from work conversations in the office is the main problem.

M Why don't we post a memo about our policy? That way, people will be aware that they have to use a meeting room for their work-related conversations.

W That sounds good.

Questions 47-49 refer to the following conversation.
| AU - BR |

M Wilma, how is the preparation for your relocation to the Tokyo office coming along?

W Well, I've never expected to live abroad. I will need an apartment and to find out how I should get around while I'm there.

M Isn't there some support from the company for you to get settled?

W That's right. But the thing is I have no friends in Tokyo other than our coworkers.

M Hmm... Have you heard about the mobile app called 'New City's Life'? I think it can help connect you to a network of people who are about to start living in the city. It could be a kind of social connection for you.

W That sounds great. I should check that out.

M And, I can give you a travel guide which has a lot of useful information. I'll bring it from home for you next week.

Questions 50-52 refer to the following conversation.

| US - US |

M Hello, this is George Patterson calling from *Boston Daily*. I'm scheduled to come to interview the mayor next week. Before then, our photographer will visit your office this afternoon. So I wanted to confirm today's appointment.

W Hello, Mr. Patterson. Actually, I was going to call you. I just found out that the mayor is currently attending a staff meeting. But it seems to take longer than we expected. Could we reschedule the photo shoot early tomorrow morning?

M No problem at all. Umm, how about 9 o'clock tomorrow?

W Okay. I will let the mayor know of the new schedule.

M Oh, and one more thing. We'll need an official place such as a meeting room for the photos.

W Of course. I'll have a conference hall ready for you.

Questions 53-55 refer to the following conversation with three speakers.

| US - US - AU |

M1 Hi, Graciela. Hi, Gail. I've heard that you two finished preparing for Saturday's annual banquet for our investors. Thanks for your hard work and do you have a moment?

W Of course, Mr. Rodgers. Is there something else you'd like us to do?

M1 I just spoke with Jarvis Taylor.

M2 I know he's the financial director who is in charge of our investment, right?

M1 Yes, you are right. Well, he was originally going to be out of town this weekend, but he thinks it is a good opportunity to meet all of our investors and make a speech on behalf of our company. So he'll be coming after all.

W Sure. I'll add his name to the speaker list right away.

Questions 56-58 refer to the following conversation.

| BR - US |

W Miguel, did you find anything at last Friday's cooking fair that could be useful for our restaurant?

M Yes, I did, Clara. At the fair, there was a demonstration showing an interesting way to steam various kinds of vegetables. I think that technique can be used to cook some of our dishes effectively.

W That would be great. A lot of customers have been suggesting adding more vegetarian dishes to our menu. I think that could work well.

M Absolutely. I have some spare time now, so let's prepare some vegetable dishes by using the technique. Then, we will see how we can work this out.

Questions 59-61 refer to the following conversation with three speakers.

| BR - AU - US |

W Hi, Michael and Donald. I wanted to show you my draft design for one of our main articles in the July Issue of *Hamilton Monthly*.

M1 Thanks, Jane. Hmm... This image is good. But I can't read the writing at the bottom because the font size is too small.

M2 Yeah. It looks like just a couple of thick lines rather than some phrases. I don't think we can have it printed like this.

M1 You'd better change the size. Remember we should start printing this Thursday.

W Okay, Donald. Maybe I can enlarge the font and change the color. You'll have a new design in about an hour.

M2 Sounds great!

Questions 62-64 refer to the following conversation and product list.

| US - US |

W Hi. Are you looking for something?

M Yes. Could you tell me where the men's wear department is?

W OK. What are you looking for?

M I need a jacket, but I'm not really sure what to buy. Hmm... I have a meeting every day. So I might need something fashionable, but I can't afford a very costly one.

W Don't worry about the price. All of the goods are currently marked down by 20% and there are some really nice classic jackets. Take a look at this brochure.

M Oh, this one looks great. Do you have this one in size 46?

W I need to check if we have any in that size in stock. Why don't you sit here? I will be back shortly.

refer to the following conversation and coupon.

I US - AU I

W Hello, Marcus. Have you heard? Claire from sales has been promoted. So, she's going to be transferred to the headquarters in Milan, soon.

M Wow. That's good. It will be a great opportunity for her.

W We're going out to have dinner with her this evening at the Barrett Bistro to congratulate her. Would you like to join us?

M That sounds great. I'd be happy to. Oh, actually, I have a discount coupon for the place. We can try some of their special dishes at lowered prices.

W Really? Claire loves pasta. Let's order some pasta dishes for her, and we can also share them.

M Sounds perfect. Why don't we drive to the restaurant? I brought my car.

Questions 68-70 refer to the following conversation and trade show floor plan.

I BR - AU I

W Mark, do you have some time to discuss our trade show? It's an urgent issue. We have to choose an exhibitor space by tomorrow. There aren't many available.

M Look, there's still one large booth open, but that costs much more than our budget allows. Moreover, we need to distribute the brochures and samples with the company logo on them.

W I know. We already spent too much on promotional items.

M I think we can't afford a large booth. Let's go with the one closest to the exit. That way, attendees will see us when they walk out the door.

W I agree. We need to notify the organizer as soon as possible.

M Sure, I'll call her right now.

PART 4

Questions 71-73 refer to the following telephone message.

I US I

W Hello, Alicia. This is Ana Silva calling from Sharp House Care. I would like to inform you that I won't be able to set up your new doors tomorrow as scheduled. I mistakenly ordered some sizes that don't fit. I'm really sorry about this. I've already called the supplier and the right sizes will arrive soon. When I receive the shipment, I will tell you. Meanwhile, would you remove the furnishings for our replacement work? If you have any questions, please call me back. Thank you.

Questions 74-76 refer to the following excerpt from a meeting.

I AU I

M OK, everyone. That's all for today's planning meeting. I'm so pleased our firm is hosting the marketing conference this quarter and very happy we had our budget settled at today's meeting. I'm going to hand in the request for financial support to the accounting team later today. As soon as they give us approval, we will be able to begin making travel arrangement for the presenters we'll select. So, please be sure everyone here attends the next staff meeting. We'll talk about who should be invited for the keynote speech at the conference. Thank you.

Questions 77-79 refer to the following excerpt from a workshop.

I BR I

W Good morning, everyone. Thank you for attending the first day of your presentation skills training workshop. I'm Amanda Morgan. I've been working as a consultant and author for 10 years. By the time you complete this course, I'm sure you will feel much more comfortable during your presentation. At the end of today, you will each have an opportunity to present for yourself. So, please keep following my directions through out today's workshop. Okay, before we start, I'll give you some forms you will need to fill out. They're for your self-assessment to help you diagnose yourself.

Questions 80-82 refer to the following talk.

| US |

W Welcome to our historic Dearborn Garden. My name is Mary Watson and I'll be your guide today. We'll begin our tour with a walk through the main garden. As you may know, it was first built by James Cohen, a famous novelist, in 1849. We'll see this garden fast. After that, we'll be visiting the main building located in the center of the garden. You'll see exhibits on history of this garden. And then, we will move to the Cream House, located behind the main building where we'll have lunch. At the end of the tour, you'll have an opportunity to purchase some souvenirs for your friends and family. Okay, let's get started.

Questions 83-85 refer to the following instructions.

| US |

M Hello, everybody. Before the Saturday evening rush starts, I'd like to inform you of our new evening special. This evening special is a beef dish. The beef is grilled with garlic and sliced onions, and served with roasted potatoes. Please make sure to let our customers know about it as handing out the menus to them. If diners would like to learn more about our regular dishes, well, it's not your first day working here. And, I should tell you about the time sheets mentioned last week. The management team has moved up the deadline for handing them in. It will be Tuesday evening instead of Wednesday evening.

Questions 86-88 refer to the following announcement.

| US |

W Good morning, everyone. I have a brief announcement to make about the multi-function copiers which have been installed in our office. I'm aware that some of you were expecting new monitors, but I don't think that'll happen until next quarter. Well, the copiers tend to have a rather high level of security, but they're not difficult to use. Before making a copy, just type in your employee ID code using the keypad on the machine. If there is any problem, our technicians can help you out. But I hope you understand they're usually tied up with other work. Please tell me if you have trouble contacting them.

Questions 89-91 refer to the following excerpt from a meeting.

| BR |

W Good evening, everyone. Sorry for this last-minute meeting. We were just informed that Rick Hansen from *Global Industry Magazine* will be here on Thursday. He got a good impression of our hydrogen fueled vehicles and he'd like to hear about the way our company makes them so affordable. So, when he gets here, I'll take him around every department. Please explain to him what contribution you make as a team member to these car models. Just a brief explanation of what each of you does on the job will be enough.

Questions 92-94 refer to the following broadcast.

| US |

M Thank you for listening to my radio show, *Business Issues*. This is Andres Fletcher, and I've been running a small business myself for over fifteen years. So, today I'd like to give some simple but effective advice that can help improve your small business. Have you ever thought about participating in a trade show? I know it sounds very costly, but you would be able to introduce your products to a lot of potential customers at one time. On top of that, it can give you a great chance to not only check out the competition but also expand your business network. Alright, now let me give you some tips on how we can make our trade show experience a great one.

Questions 95-97 refer to the following advertisement and price list.

| AU |

M Becky Furnishing is holding its annual sale and currently our most popular armchairs can be purchased at a 40% discounted price. You don't need to worry about a delivery fee. Just order online and pick it up at your nearest store. A small container includes all of the components. Since it is easy to assemble at any place without spending much time, most of our customers like this armchairs. Our brief assembly instructions are accessible by logging on to our Web site. Visit us today and take advantage of this great opportunity.

Questions 98-100 refer to the following telephone message and map.

| BR |

W Hello, Mr. Martinez. It's Maggie from Western & Southern Realty. I found the perfect property for your new store. It was just updated on the sale list. It is located on Lincoln Street directly across from Joe's Cafe. This area is always packed with people, especially now that the City Hall has extended hours and holds various events open to the public on the weekends. So there has been much more foot traffic. Because a lot of other people are interested in the property, you'd better hurry if you want to see this place. I know it's a little more expensive than you expected. But once you come down here and see it in person, you might think it's worth the increased cost. Please call me and let me know what you think.

PART 1

1
BR
(A) A man is posting a sheet of paper.
(B) A man is looking for a document in a cabinet.
(C) A woman is holding a pen.
(D) A woman is examining a pair of glasses.

2
US
(A) A woman is mowing the grass.
(B) A woman is removing her hat.
(C) A woman is raking leaves in the garden.
(D) A woman is pulling a cart with some branches.

3
US
(A) A man is paying for some fruits.
(B) A man is unloading some vegetables from a cart.
(C) A man is walking into a grocery store.
(D) A man is selecting some items.

4
AU
(A) A woman is assembling a desk.
(B) A carpet is being unrolled on the floor.
(C) An armchair is unoccupied.
(D) Potted plants are lined along the wall.

5
BR
(A) The men are greeting each other.
(B) A man is handing some documents to another man.
(C) A woman is rearranging some office furniture.
(D) Each person is seated in front of a computer.

6
AU
(A) Some people are strolling along the water's edge.
(B) Some stalls have been erected near the trees.
(C) Some chairs have been arranged on a beach.
(D) Shells are scattered across the sand.

PART 2

7
AU
BR
How many chairs do we need to order for tomorrow?
(A) Arrange them in numerical order.
(B) 15 or so.
(C) Near the desk.

8
BR
AU
Why don't you come to the opera with me and James?
(A) Thanks, but I have to work overtime tonight.
(B) She is not coming today.
(C) Yes, it was sold out.

9
US US

Are we going to buy wooden or plastic tables?
(A) A bulk order.
(B) Plastic would be cheaper.
(C) A 10% discount coupon.

10
US BR

Isn't our department going to move into the headquarters?
(A) We are using a moving company.
(B) Yes, but not for another month.
(C) I guess you didn't order enough for them.

11
AU US

What will the presenter be showing us during the product demonstration?
(A) He'll attend the show.
(B) There are a few models.
(C) Mainly newly updated functions.

12
AU BR

I left the revised report on your desk this morning.
(A) First thing tomorrow.
(B) Thanks for letting me know.
(C) Leave it to my assistant.

13
US BR

Why is my mobile phone running slowly?
(A) Sure, that works.
(B) To buy a new one.
(C) I had to upgrade applications in mine.

14
US AU

Is the company planning to replace all the computers?
(A) He's out today.
(B) Yes, he will replace me.
(C) Yes, we're getting new ones this week.

15
BR US

Have all of the invitations been mailed out?
(A) Paige from the dispatching department might know.
(B) Two times this week.
(C) Thanks. I will definitely go.

16
BR AU

How long does it take you to commute to work?
(A) There was a traffic jam.
(B) About two hours ago.
(C) Less than an hour by train.

17
US US

You offer a discount on women's apparel, right?
(A) I'll do it right away.
(B) Yes, we only sell children's clothing.
(C) Yes, it's 50% off.

18
US BR

Who's supposed to attend the one day workshop on Monday?
(A) Please put that on his calendar.
(B) The training workshop is held on Fridays.
(C) I know I'm not.

19
AU US

What is your favorite at this restaurant?
(A) I recommend the Italian restaurant.
(B) She asked me a favor.
(C) This is my first time here.

20
AU BR

Where do you want me to leave this copier?
(A) I left it in the basement.
(B) Every other week.
(C) We don't have any room in our office.

21
US US

I'm working on the research project to investigate the side effects of our sleeping pill.
(A) No, it did not affect our sales.
(B) Let me know if you need any help.
(C) I'd rather not take any medicine.

22
US AU

Why has the café on the first floor been closed all this week?
(A) Yes, they are open until 9.
(B) They're doing some repairs.
(C) It is very crowded.

23
BR US

Mr. Jacobs has been in the banking industry for a long time, hasn't he?
(A) No, a financial director.
(B) It takes longer than I thought.
(C) Yes, for about forty years.

24
BR AU

Should we go over the survey results sometime tomorrow?
(A) For research and development.
(B) Customer feedback is quite positive.
(C) I'll be out of the office this week.

25
AU BR

Why did you drop our marketing proposal for next year?
(A) I forgot to bring it.
(B) It includes all the expenses.
(C) Because the funding was limited.

26
US US

Did we sign the contract already?
(A) We still need Mr. Park's approval.
(B) Just your signature.
(C) Four pages long.

27
US BR

Have you booked a flight ticket for your vacation?
(A) I'm not sure I can go.
(B) I need your passport, please.
(C) My flight was delayed.

28

AU
US

We don't have much storage space in the warehouse.

(A) I already reported that to the manager this morning.

(B) Cash on delivery.

(C) The boxes are stacked in numerical order.

29

AU
BR

How are we going to market our new sports shoes?

(A) I've been stopped at the market.

(B) Mostly with commercials.

(C) A new sports product line.

30

US
US

When is the due date to finish the annual sales report?

(A) I already submitted it.

(B) He will tell us.

(C) To human resources.

31

US
AU

Should I buy a brand new sedan or a used one?

(A) It's a customer service number.

(B) I know a good car dealer.

(C) A different department.

PART 3

Questions 32-34 refer to the following conversation.

| US - BR |

M Hi, I made a reservation for a rental car. Is it possible to pick it up now?

W OK, thank you for using Della Rental service. Before letting you take the car, we need a few more details from you to complete your rental agreement in our system.

M Sure. Hmm... I actually forgot to bring my confirmation number. Is it OK without it?

W That's totally OK. We can find it in our system right away. Please just give us your phone number and name.

Questions 35-37 refer to the following conversation.

| AU - US |

M Hello, Ms. Grant. Have you finished putting up a wooden fence around the house?

W Hello, Mr. Gordon. It's almost done. But there is a small issue we need to take care of.

M Oh, what's the matter?

W We've run out of some wooden materials for

the gate. So, I need to go to Gospel Supplies on Barnet Road now to get some more.

M Alright. Well, don't take Highway 16 since it's closed for maintenance. You should use Stanmore Road. That is probably much less crowded.

W OK, thank you for the information.

Questions 38-40 refer to the following conversation.

| BR - AU |

W Clayton, I'm very happy that our business suit clearance sale has been going so well. We have never been busy like this since we started our shop.

M Yeah, it's much better than we expected. I think featuring Howard's navy-blue suits was an excellent idea. People seem to really like the suit a lot.

W That's right. Only a few boxes are left in the storage room.

M I'm surprised that Howard creates such trendy styles. We should consider doing more business with the company.

W Indeed. Let's ask a sales person to bring some more samples of other clothes. Carrying more of their products will definitely help our business.

Questions 41-43 refer to the following conversation.

| US - US |

W Good afternoon, Philadelphia City Public Library. How can I help you?

M Yes. I'm a reporter for *Daily Australia*. I'm doing some research about French literature. I've heard your library has a collection of rare classic books such as old French novels, plays, and poetry. Would I be able to borrow those books?

W Actually, those books don't circulate. You can only use them here in the library.

M Thanks. Should I make an appointment to see the rare book section?

W Yes. I'll put your call through to the rare books desk right now.

Questions 44-46 refer to the following conversation.

| BR - AU |

W Good to see you back, Brad. How was the banking seminar you attended?

M Well, it was a great opportunity to learn more about the current banking trends.

W Oh, that sounds interesting. Please tell me more.

M OK. For one, Anthony Lee, one of the presenters, encouraged bank employees like us to take the latest online training courses to keep up with new market trends.

W That's a great idea. If we do, we can save a lot of time by avoiding leaving our office for face-to-face training sessions.

M And, the most informative thing was that he provided online training information created by Southeast Banking Association. It is definitely useful for us.

W Well, that sounds good. But, my question is whether we can afford the courses.

M Actually, that's what I need to work on next. I have to check how much they will cost and make a report for the management meeting.

Questions 47-49 refer to the following conversation.
| US - BR |

M Hello, I'm staying in room 303. The wireless Internet in my room doesn't seem to be working as of this morning.

W Oh, we're really sorry for the inconvenience. We're experiencing a minor technical issue. But our maintenance team is working on it, so the service will be available again by this evening.

M OK. Then, I'd like to know if the fee for today's access can be refunded. I think I've already been charged for the Internet service for each day while I stay here.

W Certainly. The fee will be deducted from your bill right now, and you can find the details when you check out.

Questions 50-52 refer to the following conversation.
| US - AU |

W Vince, you did a really good job. I want to thank you for preparing the presentation on time. I didn't think you could finish it before the deadline.

M Yes. These days, it's been hard to keep up with all the requests by myself. But what can I do? Our sales department is still short handed.

W Actually, I have good news for you. We have some interviews scheduled to fill the vacant

positions in your department.

M Oh, I'm glad to hear that. Also, I've been meaning to ask about my request to be considered for a managerial position in the research and development department.

W I believe a transfer is a definite possibility. Since both departments are related to each other, your experience will be a great asset to R&D as well.

Questions 53-55 refer to the following conversation.
| US - US |

M Sabrina, the winter holiday package sales were much lower than expected. I think our travel agency does not reach out to as many potential customers as our competitors do.

W Yeah, that's true. Our new advertisement will start in a week, so more sales can be expected soon.

M Well... The thing is that the holiday season is nearly over.

W That's right. By now, there should be more winter holiday bookings.

M Actually, I'm thinking about asking transportation vendors and hotels in partnership with us to arrange additional two- or three-day package tours. I believe it will bring in more people willing to take a short vacation.

W It's worth trying. I'll contact them right away and talk about it in detail.

Questions 56-58 refer to the following conversation with three speakers.
| US - AU - BR |

M1 Hello, Mr. Kim and Ms. Jackson. Thank you for meeting with me about your store renovation on such short notice.

M2 Sure, Peter. So how's it going?

M1 As I told you, we planned to finish the work by tomorrow. But there was a delivery problem. Some of the light fixtures were sent to our office instead of to the store. Although we can get those items delivered here on Friday morning, it will take a couple of days to install them.

W Oh, no. We invited the guests over for the Grand Reopening Celebration this weekend. Are you going to finish by then, Peter?

M1 I'm afraid not. One day won't be enough for the electrician to install everything.

W OK, we'd better postpone the event until next Monday. I'll call the guests right now to inform them about the change.

Questions 59-61 refer to the following conversation.
| BR - AU |

W Hi, Fred. Our restaurant was so slow last night. Normally, we don't have many patrons after eight o'clock during weekdays.

M That's true. We should consider closing early. How about suggesting changing our operation hours to the management?

W You're right. Well, tomorrow's menu still needs to be updated. I couldn't find where the chef left the note.

M Have you checked the back office? She usually leaves the next day's menu on the back office door.

W Alright, I found it. I should post tomorrow's special on the board before we close.

Questions 62-64 refer to the following conversation and table.
| US - BR |

M Finally, we've made great progress in planning our annual company picnic. The options for the picnic shelter for our lunch and entertainment have been narrowed down. We can now finalize the arrangement with the budget approved this morning.

W That's right. Choosing the shelter is the most important thing. Let's look at the list of the options.

M Well... Actually, I've been to the Hendon Green area. It was nice, but more than 60 people are coming. In case of rain, a shelter that has larger space will be required. So let's go with the largest one.

W Absolutely. Please just inform me of the exact date. Then, I'll book a shuttle bus for everyone to the park from the office.

Questions 65-67 refer to the following conversation and rental chart.
| US - AU |

W Thank you for visiting Walton Car Rental. How

may I help you?

M Hello, we're moving to a new office building soon, so we're searching for a truck to rent to take our office furniture and supplies to the new place.

W Okay. Well, you can refer to this brochure showing the types and sizes of vehicles you can rent. Could you tell me how much you are trying to transport?

M Hmm... Basically, we have two offices and a waiting lounge with three sofas and two coffee tables.

W If that's the case, I'd like to recommend the second largest vehicle we offer. It's 17 feet long and can carry three rooms of furniture.

M Well, a bit smaller one looks enough for me. Can I rent one of your 15 feet vehicles?

W Certainly. When do you need the vehicle? Let me print out the contract.

Questions 68-70 refer to the following conversation and flowchart.
| US - US |

M Hi, Ms. Ellis. Thank you for visiting Robin's Financial Solution. Please have a seat and let's talk about your current situation.

W OK, I'm running a small business that carries rare books such as old novels and textbooks.

M Right, and have you had a chance to check the chart showing the process for financial planning on our Web site?

W Yes, I have. And it was very informative. My aim is to open a few more stores in the near future.

M Great. So what would you like me to do for you?

W Hmm... Actually, I'm having difficulty in designing an action plan to accomplish my aim. That's why I am here to talk about designing a plan with you today.

Questions 71-73 refer to the following excerpt from a meeting.
| AU |

M Let's shift gears and talk about the next item on the agenda. We were supposed to start working on the smart phone application advertisement. However, the client informed us that the application will not be ready until the end of this month. So, I think it is impossible to begin the advertising campaigns as originally scheduled. They don't want to run any ads until next quarter. As this will influence our schedule for other projects, let me show you our updated timeline. Please review it carefully and tell me if there are any conflicts with your schedule for other assignments.

Questions 74-76 refer to the following talk.
| US |

W On behalf of our company, I'd like to welcome all of you to CP Tire & Rubber Company. My name is Jennifer Hawkins. I am the director of product development and I will give you a tour of our factory since it is your first day. I believe all of you already know our company has been in operation for over 200 years with a great reputation and now you are a part of this established company. Okay, we're now moving to the assembly area of the factory. Before we leave, your orientation package and safety equipment will be distributed.

Questions 77-79 refer to the following tour information.
| US |

M OK, everyone. This will be the last part of today's tour. We will have three hours to explore the village. You can take a walk around the outdoor market and also do some shopping. Don't forget that we will meet in front of the gallery where our tour bus is parked. Oh, speaking of the gallery, if you are not sure about how to spend the three hours, think about enjoying artworks in the gallery. Since our dinner reservation is at six o'clock at the Singh Bistro, please be sure to come back in time. The place is very popular, so they won't give us any time for delay.

Questions 80-82 refer to the following recorded message.
| BR |

W Good morning. Thank you for calling Alberta Legal Office. Due to the office renovation work

from July 9 to July 14, we are currently closed. We're very sorry for any inconvenience you may experience because of this closure. If you are in need of legal advice, you can contact our office administrator, Jessica Brown, by sending an e-mail to j-brown@albertalegaloffice.com. Your inquiry will be redirected by her to one of our lawyers who has relevant experience to your case. Thank you.

Questions 83-85 refer to the following broadcast.
| US |

M Now, it's time for the latest local business news. On Tuesday, Casey Appliances has announced that its main store will relocate to a bigger location on Kensington Road from the current one on Boston Avenue. The decision on this has become inevitable due to the shop's growing popularity since Brett Armstrong was hired as CEO. With Mr. Armstrong's great leadership, Casey Appliances, which is famous for its energy efficient products with modern designs, will be releasing a new line of LCD TVs next winter. The product launch will be held at the new location.

Questions 86-88 refer to the following excerpt from a meeting.
| BR |

W Okay, everyone is here. As you know, we are planning our tourism industry conference next month. And I asked you to submit presentation proposals at last month's staff meeting. However, I've only received 20 proposals so far. Now, this is a bit disappointing because it is good to have more proposals to choose from. But, we have another week until the deadline. In the meantime, we need some volunteers to make a survey for participants, which will be used at the end of the conference. If you'd like to be a part of the team, please drop by my office after the meeting.

Questions 89-91 refer to the following talk.
| US |

W Welcome to the Small and Home Business Club. My name is Margaret Lawrence and I've been teaching how to build up and foster a successful partnership, relationships and social network at Ontario University. The topic of today's workshop is "Making A Better Business Network". Statistics have shown that a local business network can help small companies increase sales. We'll specifically talk about how to establish a network with other small companies in the same field and how to support each other. And if you have any questions, you can interrupt me during my talk.

Questions 92-94 refer to the following announcement.

| AU |

M Before starting your shift on the assembly line, I'd like to give you a brief reminder. Although you are under pressure to complete your work quickly due to the heavy workload, we have to be more attentive when doing welding work. It's important not to neglect to grind the edge of each beam before you start on the next one. The beams with rough edges are not acceptable. Many clients have recently talked about this issue. As the quality control manager, I need to ensure materials are processed smoothly and efficiently with no compromise in quality. As of next week, in order to ensure this important step in the process is done properly, each beam will be inspected by our newly organized team.

Questions 95-97 refer to the following telephone message and floor plan.

| BR |

W Hello, my name is Mae Beck, one of the organizers for the annual trade fair. I'm calling to let you know that I've just e-mailed you a revised floor plan for the exhibit hall. As last year, a display shelf has been provided to you. So, you can display your newest digital cameras in the middle. And also, according to your request, a separate space in the back has been added for meeting with customers privately. If you have any questions, please call me back at 443-7733. Thank you.

Questions 98-100 refer to the following telephone message and weather report.

| US |

W Hello, this is Lola. I'm calling regarding the three-mile charity marathon that is being organized to raise funds for the new public park. Actually, we are facing a problem. Did you check the weather report? It is expected to rain heavily on the day we scheduled the event. Although we can hand out some raincoats to participants, I think no one will really want to run under such weather conditions. So, why don't we get together early tomorrow and talk about rescheduling it to an alternative day if possible? If it can be done, we will need to make a lot of adjustments to our plan. Thank you.

TEST 09 스크립트

🎧 TEST09.mp3

PART 1

1
US
(A) She's moving a scale.
(B) She's checking some equipment.
(C) She's writing with a pen.
(D) She's taking an item down from a shelf.

2
AU
(A) She's trying on a shoe.
(B) She's checking a price tag.
(C) She's talking to a sales clerk.
(D) She's holding an item.

3
BR
(A) They're seated at workstations side by side.
(B) They're looking at a monitor hanging from a ceiling.
(C) One of the chairs is situated near the window.
(D) An office is separated by a partition.

4
US
(A) Some hikers are crossing over a stream.
(B) Some people are resting on the bridge.
(C) Mountains can be seen from an outdoor pool.
(D) Some tourists are pointing at some mountains.

5
US
(A) A man is chaining a bicycle to a post.
(B) Some trees are casting shadows on the ground.
(C) Bicycles have been parked outdoors.
(D) A sign post is being installed.

6
BR
(A) Some people are resting on the stone fence.
(B) A group of tourists are posing for a photograph.
(C) An outdoor area is crowded with people.
(D) A walkway is lined with trees.

PART 2

7
US
US
When are you going on vacation?
(A) There is a vacancy.
(B) My flight leaves on Sunday.
(C) For this summer.

8
US
BR
Who has been appointed as the vice president?
(A) I will meet the doctor this afternoon.
(B) It's Ms. Erickson.
(C) No, the director will present himself.

9
AU
US
Should I book the train ticket soon?
(A) You are right, I really enjoyed the trip.
(B) Yes, you'd better do it now.
(C) With a receipt.

10
AU
BR
Where are we supposed to meet the clients in London?
(A) Our director, Griffin.
(B) A direct flight.
(C) At a hotel downtown.

11
US
US
Are you looking for something in particular?
(A) No thanks, I'm just looking around.
(B) I care about it.
(C) In the next aisle.

12
US
AU
When do you want me to schedule your next appointment?
(A) Sorry, it is not on the list.
(B) I am available this Friday afternoon.
(C) I met Dr. Carroll.

13
BR
US
We haven't received the invoice yet, have we?
(A) A voice mail message.
(B) The company account.
(C) No, not yet.

14
BR
AU
Does this bus go to Manchester?
(A) He will be here shortly.
(B) Only two stops.
(C) That's what the driver told me.

15
US
US
Are there more candidates to interview tomorrow?
(A) Yes, we have a fantastic view.
(B) That was more than we expected.
(C) No, we don't have anything scheduled this week.

16
US
BR
How much will it cost to fix the laptop computer?
(A) It will be ready in two days.
(B) About 250 dollars.
(C) Post it on our Web site.

17
AU
US
Why don't you bring it back to the store while I am cleaning the room?
(A) He already bought one.
(B) Sure, I will.
(C) A list of clearance items.

18 Have you decided on the dates for interviewing
AU
BR applicants?
(A) Yes, I'll e-mail you about it.
(B) A job advertisement.
(C) More than thousands of applications.

19 Where's the waiting room?
US
US (A) She's in her office.
(B) I'll show you.
(C) In about 10 minutes.

20 Do you know where I can get office supplies?
US
AU (A) Yes, to the supply room.
(B) He is one of our suppliers.
(C) What do you need?

21 Who can I talk to about a guided tour here?
BR
US (A) No, it's a very famous gallery in town.
(B) Let me take you to the reception desk.
(C) Three times a day.

22 How do I access my account on my mobile
BR
AU phone?
(A) On the screen of the phone.
(B) Download the application from our Web site.
(C) The account is not available now.

23 All of our storage spaces are filled with goods.
US
US (A) There is more space in the basement.
(B) She will file them.
(C) No, just store the boxes.

24 What brand of cosmetics do you recommend?
US
BR (A) I will put on makeup later.
(B) I forgot what it's called.
(C) It is a new costume designed by Ms. Kim.

25 Didn't you call the agency to send more flyers?
AU
US (A) They haven't delivered them yet.
(B) In numerical order.
(C) Check the contact information.

26 Can you make a copy of the customer survey
AU
BR results for me?
(A) Sure, let me finish this first.
(B) A focus group interview.
(C) There are a few negative responses.

27 Tim, this project is due in a week.
US
US (A) It will expire soon.
(B) Yes, he will do.
(C) I'll get started right away.

28 Do you want me to schedule your presentation
US
AU first or second?
(A) Yes, it was my first time.
(B) I wish to have some extra time before my
turn.
(C) See if you have your own materials.

29 I think all of us should work overtime tonight,
BR
US shouldn't we?
(A) It's about 6 o'clock now.
(B) No, the project deadline was extended.
(C) The timesheet was posted last week.

30 Who's going to give a presentation on Monday?
BR
AU (A) He can not make it.
(B) At the press release.
(C) It was cancelled.

31 Why are we reviewing all the proposals today?
AU
BR (A) The proposed budget.
(B) Elma will be out of the office tomorrow.
(C) Most of them look good though.

PART 3

Questions 32-34 refer to the following conversation with
three speakers.
| US - US - BR |

W1 Excuse me, can I talk with the manager here?
M   Yes, I'm the manager, ma'am. How may I help
you?
W1 I ordered the beef dish. One of your servers,
Lola, told me it wouldn't take long, but the
dish hasn't come out yet.
M   Oh, sorry. How long have you been waiting
for it?
W1 More than half an hour, so far.
M   Hmm... It can't be... Why don't I find out
what's happening? Lola, the lady here hasn't
received her meal for over 30 minutes.
W2 Oh, I beg your pardon. It seems like our
kitchen is backed up with so many orders
now. I've already asked them several times.
M   OK, I will talk to the chef and bring your food
right away.

Questions 35-37 refer to the following conversation.

| AU - BR |

M   Hello, thanks for calling Italiano Garden.

W   Hi. I'm planning an anniversary celebration. Your restaurant's been recommended, but I'd like to know how many people you can accommodate at once.

M   Our restaurant has a seating capacity of 200 people inside and we also have more than 10 tables on the patio.

W   And how much does a full course meal cost per person?

M   Our full course dinner is 150 dollars.

W   Hmm... The Queen's Café charges 120 dollars.

M   Well, if you leave me your phone number, I'll call you back right after I speak to the manager. It won't take long.

W   Thanks. I'd appreciate that.

Questions 38-40 refer to the following conversation.

| US - BR |

M   Good afternoon, Sara. How's designing new jogging shoes going? Don't forget that the general manager is expecting the final version of the design later this week.

W   The entire division is solely focusing on the work at the moment. Except the color scheme, we're almost ready for the basic model. We're a little bit worried about the deadline.

M   I believe that won't be a problem. Your team's work has always been great. Just remember to e-mail me the progress report on Thursday.

W   OK, I will. Thank you.

Questions 41-43 refer to the following conversation.

| AU - US |

M   Oh, hello, Juana. It's good to see you here. What are you doing?

W   Hi, Edgar. Actually, I've been writing a novel. I have a dream of becoming a published author.

M   That's wonderful. You know a friend of mine works for a publishing company. He is working as an editor, so he reviews a lot of manuscripts from new writers every day. Do you want me to tell him about your work?

W   Really? That'd be a great help! Well, but I think I should contact him myself. Can you give his e-mail address to me?

M   Of course, let me write it down here for you.

Questions 44-46 refer to the following conversation with three speakers.

| AU - BR - US |

M   Lucy, I didn't expect to see you still working in the office. You are supposed to leave at 5:00, aren't you?

W1 Yes, but I couldn't come to work until 10:30 this morning because my car broke down. It's in the service center right now.

M   Oh, that sometimes happens. Anyway, how will you get home, then?

W1 Hilda will be here soon. Her apartment is close to my place, so she offered to drive me home. Oh, here she is now.

W2 Hello, Lucy. Are you ready to leave now? Since the fuel is very low, we need to stop by the gas station on the way.

W1 Oh, that's OK. Well, actually, I'd like to pay for it to express my appreciation for giving me a ride.

Questions 47-49 refer to the following conversation.

| US - US |

M   Tracy, can I talk to you for a minute? I want to tell you that I've found some new cleaning goods, called "Fresh and Bright." It will definitely be a good addition for our supermarket to sell.

W   Well, that sounds interesting. I want to know more about it.

M   Because of its environmentally friendly ingredients, our customers will like to use it.

W   Hmm... If that is so, let's call the supplier and order some samples to see how our customers will like it before making a large quantity order. So, we can see whether it would sell well or not.

Questions 50-52 refer to the following conversation.

| US - US |

W   Hi, Ed. Where are you heading to?

M   I need to make a presentation at the surgeons' meeting today.

W   Oh, I thought Vicky is going to do that. Is she doing something else?

M   Vicky is tied up with some other reports.

W   I see. So, what will we be talking about today?

M   The agenda will be all about the renovation plan for the medical offices starting next year. As the renovation work will be carried out floor by floor, some of us will need to see patients at different offices for several months.

Questions 53-55 refer to the following conversation.

| BR - US |

W I believe it's time to consider increasing production of our Natural Fresh refrigerator. It's been so popular since last summer that the product is often sold out at many of our chain stores.

M Oh! What good news! Well, but you know, it may be difficult to do so since we're now short-handed. Currently, many of our employees are already staying late to meet the recent demand.

W Why don't you come with me to talk to Ms. Cortez in Personnel? I've already scheduled a meeting with her for Thursday.

M Why not? I think I can do that.

W I'd like to talk about hiring extra staff promptly for our assembly line so that we can keep up with the demand.

Questions 56-58 refer to the following conversation.

| AU - US |

M South Town music store. How may I help you?

W Hello, I'm running a fairly small recording studio and I have some broken speakers. Do you have a repair service for this kind of equipment?

M Certainly, we can fix that equipment. Just drop them off before 5 P.M. today, and we'll have them ready by Friday.

W Hmm... Well, I'll be out of town for a conference in London on Friday, so it'll be difficult for me to pick them up then. But I think I can come by on Saturday. Is that OK?

M Sure. Then, we'll have more time to work on them then.

W Your location is 549 South Avenue, isn't it?

M Exactly! You can leave your vehicle in front of our building when you arrive here. We have a designated parking lot for our customers.

Questions 59-61 refer to the following conversation.

| AU - BR |

M Hi, I'm calling from WQ High Tech. You sent us an e-mail requesting information about our TM 400 Watcher.

W Yes, thank you for such a quick response. I'm running my own farm, and I think your TM 400 can be used to measure soil moisture, right? I

need some kind of equipment that helps me figure out when my fields should be watered.

M TM 400 is exactly what you're looking for. Its automated sensors will detect the levels of moisture in your fields, so it can inform you which parts require water.

W That's perfect. Hmm... But, I'm worried about the price.

M Our payment plan, $125 per month, will cover everything.

W Well, can I call you back after checking my budget? Your number is 3321-4444, right?

Questions 62-64 refer to the following conversation and request form.

| US - US |

W Mr. Chandler, I just talked with the conference center on the phone.

M Was it about the conference next month?

W Yeah. They asked us to provide a revised list of the supplies and equipment needed for the event. I reviewed the original request form. And I think we should ask for more folding chairs.

M That's right. 72 participants have signed up. So, call the center back and inform them about it, please. By the way, has Mr. Collins, our keynote speaker, sent a draft of his speech?

W Yes, we just received it by e-mail, and I was about to print it out. Let me do it right now and then leave the speech in your office.

Questions 65-67 refer to the following conversation and GPS map.

| US - AU |

W Thank you for giving me a ride home this evening, Stevens. I was so worried about how to get home since my car is in the service center.

M Your apartment is close to mine, so it's not a problem. But because of the Jazz Concert being held this evening, the route I usually use to go home is closed.

W Yeah, I heard that, too. My mobile phone's GPS map indicates that three other roads are available for us to use. One of them will take us only 15 minutes.

M That's good. We should take that one.

Questions 68-70 refer to the following conversation and list.

| AU - BR |

M Ms. Oliver. I heard there will be a workshop which will give me a great chance to learn more about marketing in social media. I just wonder if our firm could pay for it. It'll be very informative for me to be aware of various ways to reach many potential customers through social media.

W I think that's a great idea. We always want to know how to bring in more customers. What's the registration fee for it?

M I have a list showing how much it will be. Well, basically, it's too late to get a discount for advance registration.

W Hmm... Alright! Just go ahead and register for it. I also want to know what kind of topics they will address at the workshop.

M I will forward you all the details about it including topics and schedules by e-mail.

PART 4

Questions 71-73 refer to the following broadcast.

| US |

W Good morning, listeners. Thank you for listening to *QRC Alice*, our town's favorite radio show. I'd like to mention a few updates on the community event calendar. There will be a cancellation of an event. The outdoor music concert at Canons Park will not take place this Friday. This must cause a huge disappointment to most of you, but a large storm is expected to hit our region. Once a different date for the concert has been set, we'll inform you. Let's turn over to Roxanne Moss. She will give us local business news right after the commercial break.

Questions 74-76 refer to the following telephone message.

| BR |

W Hi, my name is Heidi Austin. I live in apartment 401. I'm calling to make a complaint about the residents next door to me. They've often parked their vehicle in the parking space assigned to me. A few days ago, I tried to speak to them, but they behaved in an uncooperative manner.

I don't want to look for a place to park every night. It's very inconvenient. I think this issue needs to be discussed in person. So, I'd like to come by your office on Monday afternoon. Please call me and let me know if you're available. Thank you.

Questions 77-79 refer to the following excerpt from a meeting.

| US |

M Good morning, everyone. And thank you for coming to this meeting on such short notice. I know you are all busy today here at the factory. But it will only take a couple of minutes. As you know, last Friday a group of inspectors from our headquarters came in and checked all our working conditions. And we've received excellent ratings in most of the sections. But they did identify just one thing that we could improve on. Our efficiency will be increased if we revise some of our work flow. So I've invited Jeff Clark, the chief inspector, back this afternoon to share what we can do better. He'll provide some tips for improving work efficiency.

Questions 80-82 refer to the following broadcast.

| AU |

M Good morning, I'm Peter Cohen from ENG local news. I'm here at the newly renovated Fremantle City Community Center. It's the first day to open to the public. There are many things to see as well as enjoyable family activities. As one of the most impressive features in the center, once you enter the main hall, you can see a variety of paintings on the wall which were donated from local artists. They are also available for sale. If you want, you can consult with a receptionist on site. For more information about the paintings, you can call the center directly or visit the Web site at www.fremantlecommuntiycenter.com.

Questions 83-85 refer to the following telephone message.

| US |

W Hello, Isabel. This is Bannie. I'm calling to talk about the new smart phone model. At the moment, the first round of consumer focus groups is being prepared to conduct a review. I'm aware that you're very concerned about letting people review a new model which is still being developed. But, only the appearance of the phone will be examined by the reviewers at this time. Just continue to focus on the remaining details of its interior. Then, the second round of groups will meet after a sample model is completed by your team. Meanwhile, please inform me of the date the preparation for the first round can be done.

Questions 86-88 refer to the following advertisement.

| BR |

M Do you want to be more educated and smarter? There's no need to go to private institutes in person every day. Think about all the time and effort you have to spend. Now all you need is our online distance learning program that allows you to get a high quality university education from anywhere in the world. In today's increasingly busy society, the most important thing is that our program allows people to gain a new qualification while maintaining their current jobs. You will be surprised at how flexibly you can combine courses and times. Find out which program matches you by taking a free test on our Web site.

Questions 89-91 refer to the following instructions.

| US |

M Before we move onto the next agenda, let's talk about the result of the surveys we sent to customers who made a purchase of a car from our dealership last quarter. As you may remember, the surveys were created to figure out whether the customers were happy with the service we provided. We sent out the surveys four weeks ago and I'm so glad that we've received back more than 50% of them. Honestly, this is a much higher rate than expected. I believe this is probably because a coupon for a free car wash is provided when the customers have sent back a completed survey. So, I think the incentive can be applied when we do other promotional events.

Questions 92-94 refer to the following speech.

| US |

W Thank you all for coming here to celebrate Julia Sharon's retirement. On behalf of our office, I'd like to say a few words. When I first joined General Apparel, Julia was the first person I met and I've learned a lot from her. As many of you know, she is one of the legendary business women in the fashion industry. Well, like many of her staff members, I always stopped by her office and asked questions. I don't know what I'm going to do now. I think after 30 years of working here, she deserves a break. And we'd like to present you with a small token of our appreciation. All of us here contributed to buy a gift. Julia, could you please come up here?

Questions 95-97 refer to the following telephone message and identification badge.

| AU |

M Hello, Mr. Ford. My name is Barry Garza and I'm calling about my employee ID badge and parking permit. You issued them to me when I visited your security office earlier, since it was my first day here at Clapham Inc. But as soon as I came back to my office, I found that the extension number on the badge is wrong. Except that, other details on it look just fine. Please call me back when you have time. My phone number is 322-4431. Thank you.

Questions 98-100 refer to the following excerpt from a meeting and pie chart.

| AU |

M It is our last agenda for today's meeting. I'd like to tell you about the result of the survey conducted last month. First, as head of the product development, I'd like to thank the sales and marketing team for conducting the survey. As you all know, it's about what kind of salad dressing we will add to our current items. As you see, we have a tie for first place. So we have to make a decision. Our main goal is to enter into the Asian market. Therefore, we'd better introduce the dressing which they are familiar with. Although the Garlic and Herb would be as popular in all of our markets, we're not going to produce that one now. Instead, we're going to make the other dressing that tied for first place. Moreover, the sales and marketing agreed with us. Any question so far?

PART 1

1
US
(A) She's repairing a vehicle.
(B) She's wearing glasses.
(C) She's washing a car with a piece of cloth.
(D) She's mounting some equipment on the wall.

2
BR
(A) A woman is holding the machine lid open.
(B) A woman is carrying a basket.
(C) A woman is loading some clothes into a machine.
(D) A woman is kneeling on the tile floor.

3
AU
(A) He's resting his hand on the desk.
(B) He's looking at his watch.
(C) He's folding a paper.
(D) He's working on wooden stairs.

4
US
(A) A woman is looking through a handbag.
(B) A woman is walking along the corridor.
(C) A woman is adjusting some art works.
(D) A woman is mopping the floor.

5
US
(A) There is a display stand filled with items.
(B) People are moving potted plants.
(C) One of the men is stacking some tables.
(D) A line is being painted on the road.

6
BR
(A) A fence around the building is being installed.
(B) An apartment is under construction.
(C) Some workers are using tools.
(D) Heavy machinery has been left on the ground.

PART 2

7
US
US
Why were you late for the meeting this morning?
(A) I thought she was in the meeting.
(B) Because I got stuck in traffic.
(C) Later tomorrow.

8
US
BR
Where did you buy those folders?
(A) A few days ago.
(B) At a stationery store.
(C) Our office supplies.

9
AU
US
Which computer is yours?
(A) No, that's not mine.
(B) The one next to Mr. Leonard's desk.
(C) It was very useful, wasn't it?

10
AU
BR
Who's in charge of the new product development?
(A) Mr. Miles is.
(B) Our company account.
(C) Yes, that's really successful.

11
US
US
Where's the photo copier I can use here?
(A) I thought he knew that.
(B) Ours is broken.
(C) 20 copies.

12
US
AU
When will the replacements and other parts be delivered?
(A) By air mail, please.
(B) In a day.
(C) A manufacturing plant.

13
BR
US
Thomas was promoted to the position of sales manager, right?
(A) More positions than I thought.
(B) We have to recommend him.
(C) No, it was Ben Henderson.

14
BR
AU
How did you enjoy your dinner?
(A) We had a good time, thanks.
(B) I can make a reservation.
(C) He was our server.

15
US
US
Who portrayed the main role of Sophia in the movie?
(A) In order to play an important role.
(B) An unknown actress, Kimberley Larson.
(C) I did meet the film director.

16
US
BR
Why don't you ask Chrystal to help you to install it?
(A) A new system controller.
(B) I'll ask her later.
(C) We need to order more.

17
AU
US
Would you be willing to make a speech at the banquet?
(A) It would be a successful event.
(B) Yes, I'd be happy to.
(C) Sorry, I was not there.

18 AU BR I can bring some snacks to the meeting room, right?
(A) Just throw them away.
(B) No, that's not allowed.
(C) It's somewhere in the lobby.

19 US US Could you show me where I can try these shirts on?
(A) The size 6.
(B) Sure, follow me.
(C) You should try it again.

20 US AU What's this coat made of?
(A) Yes, it's pure wool.
(B) In China, I think.
(C) Let me check the label.

21 BR US Do you want to go somewhere to discuss the budget?
(A) I delivered them in time.
(B) It is a bit noisy in here.
(C) In the list.

22 BR AU Which table do you like better, the brown one or the black one?
(A) The brown one looks good to me.
(B) You should make a reservation now.
(C) It's an annual banquet.

23 US US I am thinking to expand my garden next month.
(A) Around the wooden fence.
(B) Gardening is my favorite, too.
(C) Is that going to be expensive?

24 US BR I want to make a reservation for 5 people for tonight at 6 o'clock.
(A) Yes, we do have vegetarian dishes.
(B) We're fully booked today.
(C) There are no specials today.

25 AU US Why don't we leave early for our dinner with the clients?
(A) I still have a lot to do.
(B) A Japanese restaurant.
(C) Yes, I have called him.

26 AU BR When are you going to buy a new warehouse?
(A) We don't have a real estate agent yet.
(B) A maximum capacity.
(C) Yes, we will renew the contract.

27 US US It's hard to tell how many people will attend tomorrow's event.
(A) It was well attended.
(B) You're right. It depends on the weather.
(C) Sometime next month.

28 US AU How often does Rachel want to attend these training programs?
(A) At the last staff meeting.
(B) What has she done in the past?
(C) She missed her train.

29 BR US Do we have some extra chairs in the storage?
(A) We're using them for tomorrow's meeting.
(B) Yes, you can close it.
(C) Maria just ordered more paper.

30 BR AU Where are the expense folders?
(A) That's not the one.
(B) Cheaper than the previous model.
(C) Did you check the cabinet?

31 AU BR Should we change vendors for office supplies?
(A) You can find the vending machine at the corner.
(B) The contract expires at the end of next month.
(C) Some staplers and printing paper.

PART 3

Questions 32-34 refer to the following conversation.
| US - AU |

W Hi, Kris. I don't know how to deal with so many questions about our company's restructuring. Recently many of our employees have contacted us here in the Human Resources Department to ask about the restructuring plan.

M Yes, I know. There seems to be a lot of confusion about how it will go. Do you have any suggestions for what we can do?

W I think we should hold an information session about our restructuring strategies.

M That's a good idea. We can hold a session to clear things up and let them know no one will be let go.

W That's true. There will be only integration between departments.

M Okay. If you want me to schedule a session, I can do that right now.

Questions 35-37 refer to the following conversation.

| US - US |

W I saw a TV commercial for your fitness center, and I'd like to become a member. But, before joining the membership, could I get more information about it?

M Certainly. If you become a member of Stanmore Gym, you'll be eligible to use the most advanced equipment at any of our fitness facilities in the region. What makes our facilities the most convenient is that we provide our service 24 hours a day through the year, which few of our competitors do.

W That's excellent. Actually, I'm planning to participate in a marathon race that's taking place in October. So, it'd be great for me to have access to your indoor athletics track until late night.

Questions 38-40 refer to the following conversation.

| BR - US |

W Hi, you have reached City Concert Hall. How can I help you?

M Hi, I already have two tickets to the jazz concert for tomorrow and I'm wondering if I can buy one more ticket.

W I'm very sorry, but tomorrow's show is completely sold out. How about the day after tomorrow? That would be Saturday. We do have some tickets still available on that night.

M That will work. Would it be possible for me to exchange the tickets I already have for tomorrow for the Saturday performance? That way, my friends and I can go all together.

W Okay. Let me book your seats first. If you can come early on Saturday, the actors will be signing posters before the show that night.

M Great. Thanks for the information.

Questions 41-43 refer to the following conversation.

| AU - BR |

M Hello, I've signed up to attend this year's international convention for the whole four days. But, I think I misplaced my entry badge somewhere. Is it possible to get in the convention without it?

W I'm sorry to tell you that no one can enter the hall without it. I think you have to get a new one.

M Yeah, I thought so. Where can I get a new one? How much will it be?

W You don't need to pay any fee for it. And actually if you'd like, I can take care of it for you.

M Oh, thank you very much.

W Well, I need to verify your registration, so show me your photo ID please.

Questions 44-46 refer to the following conversation.

| US - US |

W Hi, Mason. Did you hear that we've got to make the decision about choosing the contractor for our cleaning service? I think the local office cleaning's service is too limited. They offer the service only three times a week. I think that Holland Cleaning is much better for our needs.

M I agree with you about Holland. But the problem is it costs almost double, which means we have to cut down on other expenses. Otherwise, we will go over this year's budget.

W We are aware of the concern, of course. But we've got increasingly more complaints about the store's cleanliness. I think we can convince our financial manager that it'll contribute to our sales.

M That's right. Then, let's write a proposal together and submit it to the management.

Questions 47-49 refer to the following conversation with three speakers.

| AU - BR - US |

M OK, everyone. This is almost the end of the tour of our headquarters. Our next stop is the personnel office where you will fill out your new employee paperwork. Are there any questions?

W1 Yes, I have one. Could you tell me where we can get a pass to access the employee fitness center?

M Well, you don't need to get any particular pass for the facility. Employees can use it until 9 P.M. during weekdays. You can access it with your employee ID card. Are there any other questions?

W2 Hmm... I would like to know when we'll be heading to the sales department. I'm really looking forward to seeing our coworkers.

M Then, let's go there first. They are also eager to meet you all.

Questions 50-52 refer to the following conversation.

| US - BR |

M   Judy, what happened to our delivery timetable for the furniture? I was told that about 20 orders were shipped later than originally scheduled.

W   The problem was found in the online ordering system we have been using. The confirmation e-mail sent to customers indicated the incorrect shipping date.

M   Hmm.. Then, has the problem been fixed?

W   Yeah, but I think we should set up another step in the process. Let's send text messages to our customers before shipping products so that each customer can expect when they'll receive their order.

M   That's a good idea. Let's inform our employees of this change at the staff meeting today.

W   Sure, it will definitely make our process more efficient.

Questions 53-55 refer to the following conversation.

| US - AU |

W   Hello, my name is Inez Vazquez. I'm calling about the application I submitted for the web designer position 2 weeks ago. Is it possible to know when my interview will be held?

M   Hi, Ms. Vazquez. Sorry, we haven't reviewed the application yet, but may I ask you to tell me about yourself right now?

W   Well, my major at university was computer programming and I completed my degree about a month ago.

M   That's great. Congratulation! Hmm... But the position requires some previous work experience.

W   Actually, I used to develop the Web site for my brother's online trading company while studying at university.

M   That's very impressive. May I have the link to the Web site? I would like to have a look at your work.

W   Certainly. I'll e-mail it to you right now.

Questions 56-58 refer to the following conversation with three speakers.

| US - US - BR |

M   Hi, I'm Evan Gregory, a reporter from *Contemporary Fashion Magazine*. I have an appointment with Ms. Griffin. I'm scheduled to have an interview with her at 3 o'clock.

W1   OK, she's expecting you. I'll tell her you're here. Meanwhile, please sign in. We need to record all visitors' names here.

M   Of course, I will.

W1   Ms. Griffin will be down here in a minute. Oh, here she is. Ms. Griffin, this is Evan Gregory. He is here for your 3 o'clock appointment.

W2   Nice to meet you, Mr. Gregory. Thank you for coming. I'm very sorry, but could you wait for a moment before we start? I have an urgent matter to take care of right now.

Questions 59-61 refer to the following conversation.

| AU - BR |

M   Welcome to the Oriental Noodle House. Did you make a reservation?

W   No, I didn't know I should.

M   That's not a problem. How many in your party?

W   There are four of us. Do we have to wait for a table? We only have an hour for lunch.

M   I am afraid all the tables are reserved inside. But we do have a balcony table upstairs.

W   Actually, it is a kind of business meeting so it's too noisy outside for us.

M   OK, then why don't I put you on our wait list?

W   Hum. We'd better try somewhere else. However, I will make a reservation next time.

Questions 62-64 refer to the following conversation and schedule.

| US - US |

M   Hello, Carla. This is Holt. Did you arrive at the train station yet? I think it will take me about 20 more minutes to get there. I'm stuck in a traffic jam. I hope I'll be there before our train leaves. The next one is 4 hours later.

W   That's ok. I got here a few minutes ago and found that our train's been delayed about half an hour. I'm sure you won't miss it.

M   Oh, what a relief! But, could you call Mr. Park? I think we should tell him that we won't be able to make it on time to the reception party this evening.

Questions 65-67 refer to the following conversation and chart.

| AU - US |

M   Hi, this is Levi and I'm calling about the apricot trees I'd like to purchase from your nursery. I'm planning to have some trees planted around my house. I believe they are going to make my house look much better. I'm browsing your online store now.

W   Certainly, can you find the tree measurement chart?

M   Yes. Hmm... Could you tell me how different these smaller sizes are?

W   Size 4 trees can be planted in pots on terraces or balconies while size 3 trees should be planted in the ground, but they tend to produce much more fruit.

M   Well, I don't think I will plant them in pots. There're plenty of spaces for them around my house. Could you deliver them to my house?

W   Of course, sir. And also, our work crew can plant the trees at no additional charge.

Questions 68-70 refer to the following conversation and building directory.

| BR - AU |

W   Welcome to the Harman International building. How can I help you?

M   Yes. Actually Sally Beauty Holdings is expecting me. Could you tell me where they're located?

W   They are on the second floor. They've been waiting for you for a while now. If you want, I can give you a copy of our building directory.

M   That would be very helpful. Thanks.

W   By the way, I think you'd better hurry. Their office manager called down here several times to see if you'd arrived yet.

M   Well, the manager called too late yesterday. So we could not make an appointment this morning. However, I came here as soon as possible.

W   OK. I will call the office and let them know you are coming up.

PART 4

Questions 71-73 refer to the following announcement.

| BR |

W   Attention, shoppers! Thank you for shopping at RCO Supermarket. I'd like to remind you again to come by aisle 8 where customers can sample our new line of bakery goods. Some fresh bread's just been baked. Our bakery goods are much healthier than the other competitors' since we only use organic ingredients. In addition, all the bakery goods can be purchased at discounted prices only during this month. Thank you.

Questions 74-76 refer to the following recorded message.

| AU |

M   You have reached the Transportation Department of Newark City. We're sorry to inform you that all work regarding issuing a driver's license will now take seven business days, which is longer than before. Due to a new policy starting next year, all applications must be sent to Newtonville for review. If you want to check the status of your license, be sure to have your registration number ready and one of our representatives will be with you shortly.

Questions 77-79 refer to the following excerpt from a meeting.

| US |

M   Thanks for attending this planning meeting. From next week we will conduct the customer satisfaction survey but we don't have enough questionnaires yet. So we need to develop a series of questions to find out their opinions and purchasing behaviour. I'll give each of you a list of previous questions. I know most of you haven't done this work before, but we do not have any guidelines or templates. To be honest, I don't have much experience with this. But Frederick, our marketing expert, has done a lot of surveys. Frederick, could you help me?

Question 80-82 refer to the following talk.

| US |

W Okay. Thank you for attending our monthly staff meeting. Before we start the meeting, I have an important announcement. We will have new ID cards that you can use on all our factory floors. Currently, all staff members get their plastic ID badges when they first join our company. But starting next week, all ID badges will be replaced with new ID cards embedded with chips. The chip will allow you to enter all laboratories and even the cafeteria. By doing this, we can further strengthen security. So please don't forget to replace your ID badge with a new one at the security office by the end of the month.

Questions 83-85 refer to the following excerpt from a meeting.

| AU |

M I'd like to start today's marketing department meeting with preparations for our upcoming summer season here at the Springfield Hotel. As you all know, during the last summer season we offered a variety of new water activities for our guests. It was well received by our guests. So, we decided to offer some of the activities this season, too. But, I want you to do some brainstorming for this season's new additions. As a reference, I'll pass out a list of activities we've provided so far. So, let's talk about what we can add to our services.

Questions 86-88 refer to the following introduction.

| US |

W Good to see you again at today's seminar, everyone. First of all, I heard that many of you had a problem finding this room. I'm sorry that I thought the room was the same as the one we used last week. Okay, today I'm very excited to introduce our first speaker, William Wiseman. Mr. Wiseman is one of the established financial experts at Karlson Communication Group. His lectures focus on how to create a realistic budget proposal effectively and efficiently. As a consultant, since he has advised many local businesses, he will figure out what your needs are and help you develop your own proposals. Let's give a warm welcome to Mr. Wiseman.

Questions 89-91 refer to the following telephone message.

| BR |

W Hi, Susan. This is Molly. How are you doing? Listen, you know Kevin got a promotion, right? I think we should throw a party to celebrate it. So, let's meet up to make a plan in detail. We'll definitely need to talk about finding the right place with good foods. I think you remember how the last party was. This time, I don't want to miss seeing Kevin surprised. Well, I'm going to have dinner with a friend of mine at the newly opened restaurant on 51st Avenue tomorrow night. I'll tell you about how the space and food are. Probably, we can hold the party there if everything is OK. See you soon.

Questions 92-94 refer to the following broadcast.

| US |

W Thank you for tuning in to our program. Let's continue talking about cost-effective marketing methods for small business. During the commercial break, a business owner called in and told us that his new business is reliant on word-of-mouth advertising and it seems very successful. However, Jodi Horton from Willesden Business College is here with us to talk more about various ways to reach a wider audience. He'll start by talking with us about sponsored advertisements on different social media. Now, Jodi, many people may already know this approach is very effective, but could you tell us more about how much it would cost?

Questions 95-97 refer to the following announcement and chart.

| AU |

M I'd like to welcome all of you to this year's Agricultural Trade Fair here at Agriculture and Marine Product Market. Today, we have scheduled several informative talks throughout the day such as "How to be a farmer" which will start shortly. A famous agriculturalist, Michael Lee, will share his expertise with us. If you are interested in the building of our distribution center, you'll see me again. I'm leading a talk this afternoon. It's about where and when we will build an Agricultural and Marine Products Distribution Center. Okay, then, please take advantage of the refreshments we have set out for you on the table next to the entrance.

Questions 98-100 refer to the following excerpt from a meeting and graph.

| US |

W Okay, did you get the sales report for our office supplies stores? Look at the sales records on the second page. It shows that the highest sales figure hit 500 thousand dollars, which has climbed for the third month in a row. So, I'd like to talk about a way to boost the sales of that store even more. As you know, we have almost the same space for each location. I suggest we could try to make more space for our highest sales record location. I'll ask the manager to do some market research about what they need.

eng.conects.com

ANSWER SHEETS
TEST

✂ 자르는 선

수험번호								응시일자	20 · ·
성명	한글							맞은 개수	/ 100
	영자							환산 점수	/ 495

Listening Comprehension (PART I ~ PART IV)

Reading Comprehension (PART V ~ PART VII)

eng.conects.com

✂ 자르는 선

ANSWER SHEETS
TEST ____________

수험번호								
성명	한글							
	영자							

응시일자	20 . . .
맞은 개수	/ 100
환산 점수	/ 495

Listening Comprehension (PART I ~ PART IV)

1	a b c d	26	a b c	51	a b c d	76	a b c d
2	a b c d	27	a b c	52	a b c d	77	a b c d
3	a b c d	28	a b c	53	a b c d	78	a b c d
4	a b c d	29	a b c	54	a b c d	79	a b c d
5	a b c d	30	a b c	55	a b c d	80	a b c d
6	a b c d	31	a b c	56	a b c d	81	a b c d
7	a b c	32	a b c d	57	a b c d	82	a b c d
8	a b c	33	a b c d	58	a b c d	83	a b c d
9	a b c	34	a b c d	59	a b c d	84	a b c d
10	a b c	35	a b c d	60	a b c d	85	a b c d
11	a b c	36	a b c d	61	a b c d	86	a b c d
12	a b c	37	a b c d	62	a b c d	87	a b c d
13	a b c	38	a b c d	63	a b c d	88	a b c d
14	a b c	39	a b c d	64	a b c d	89	a b c d
15	a b c	40	a b c d	65	a b c d	90	a b c d
16	a b c	41	a b c d	66	a b c d	91	a b c d
17	a b c	42	a b c d	67	a b c d	92	a b c d
18	a b c	43	a b c d	68	a b c d	93	a b c d
19	a b c	44	a b c d	69	a b c d	94	a b c d
20	a b c	45	a b c d	70	a b c d	95	a b c d
21	a b c	46	a b c d	71	a b c d	96	a b c d
22	a b c	47	a b c d	72	a b c d	97	a b c d
23	a b c	48	a b c d	73	a b c d	98	a b c d
24	a b c	49	a b c d	74	a b c d	99	a b c d
25	a b c	50	a b c d	75	a b c d	100	a b c d

Reading Comprehension (PART V ~ PART VII)

101	a b c d	126	a b c d	151	a b c d	176	a b c d
102	a b c d	127	a b c d	152	a b c d	177	a b c d
103	a b c d	128	a b c d	153	a b c d	178	a b c d
104	a b c d	129	a b c d	154	a b c d	179	a b c d
105	a b c d	130	a b c d	155	a b c d	180	a b c d
106	a b c d	131	a b c d	156	a b c d	181	a b c d
107	a b c d	132	a b c d	157	a b c d	182	a b c d
108	a b c d	133	a b c d	158	a b c d	183	a b c d
109	a b c d	134	a b c d	159	a b c d	184	a b c d
110	a b c d	135	a b c d	160	a b c d	185	a b c d
111	a b c d	136	a b c d	161	a b c d	186	a b c d
112	a b c d	137	a b c d	162	a b c d	187	a b c d
113	a b c d	138	a b c d	163	a b c d	188	a b c d
114	a b c d	139	a b c d	164	a b c d	189	a b c d
115	a b c d	140	a b c d	165	a b c d	190	a b c d
116	a b c d	141	a b c d	166	a b c d	191	a b c d
117	a b c d	142	a b c d	167	a b c d	192	a b c d
118	a b c d	143	a b c d	168	a b c d	193	a b c d
119	a b c d	144	a b c d	169	a b c d	194	a b c d
120	a b c d	145	a b c d	170	a b c d	195	a b c d
121	a b c d	146	a b c d	171	a b c d	196	a b c d
122	a b c d	147	a b c d	172	a b c d	197	a b c d
123	a b c d	148	a b c d	173	a b c d	198	a b c d
124	a b c d	149	a b c d	174	a b c d	199	a b c d
125	a b c d	150	a b c d	175	a b c d	200	a b c d

✂ 자르는 선

ANSWER SHEETS
TEST ____________

수험번호								
성명	한글							
	영자							

응시일자	20 . . .
맞은 개수	/ 100
환산 점수	/ 495

Listening Comprehension (PART I ~ PART IV)							
1	a b c d	26	a b c	51	a b c d	76	a b c d
2	a b c d	27	a b c	52	a b c d	77	a b c d
3	a b c d	28	a b c	53	a b c d	78	a b c d
4	a b c d	29	a b c	54	a b c d	79	a b c d
5	a b c d	30	a b c	55	a b c d	80	a b c d
6	a b c d	31	a b c	56	a b c d	81	a b c d
7	a b c	32	a b c d	57	a b c d	82	a b c d
8	a b c	33	a b c d	58	a b c d	83	a b c d
9	a b c	34	a b c d	59	a b c d	84	a b c d
10	a b c	35	a b c d	60	a b c d	85	a b c d
11	a b c	36	a b c d	61	a b c d	86	a b c d
12	a b c	37	a b c d	62	a b c d	87	a b c d
13	a b c	38	a b c d	63	a b c d	88	a b c d
14	a b c	39	a b c d	64	a b c d	89	a b c d
15	a b c	40	a b c d	65	a b c d	90	a b c d
16	a b c	41	a b c d	66	a b c d	91	a b c d
17	a b c	42	a b c d	67	a b c d	92	a b c d
18	a b c	43	a b c d	68	a b c d	93	a b c d
19	a b c	44	a b c d	69	a b c d	94	a b c d
20	a b c	45	a b c d	70	a b c d	95	a b c d
21	a b c	46	a b c d	71	a b c d	96	a b c d
22	a b c	47	a b c d	72	a b c d	97	a b c d
23	a b c	48	a b c d	73	a b c d	98	a b c d
24	a b c	49	a b c d	74	a b c d	99	a b c d
25	a b c	50	a b c d	75	a b c d	100	a b c d

Reading Comprehension (PART V ~ PART VII)							
101	a b c d	126	a b c d	151	a b c d	176	a b c d
102	a b c d	127	a b c d	152	a b c d	177	a b c d
103	a b c d	128	a b c d	153	a b c d	178	a b c d
104	a b c d	129	a b c d	154	a b c d	179	a b c d
105	a b c d	130	a b c d	155	a b c d	180	a b c d
106	a b c d	131	a b c d	156	a b c d	181	a b c d
107	a b c d	132	a b c d	157	a b c d	182	a b c d
108	a b c d	133	a b c d	158	a b c d	183	a b c d
109	a b c d	134	a b c d	159	a b c d	184	a b c d
110	a b c d	135	a b c d	160	a b c d	185	a b c d
111	a b c d	136	a b c d	161	a b c d	186	a b c d
112	a b c d	137	a b c d	162	a b c d	187	a b c d
113	a b c d	138	a b c d	163	a b c d	188	a b c d
114	a b c d	139	a b c d	164	a b c d	189	a b c d
115	a b c d	140	a b c d	165	a b c d	190	a b c d
116	a b c d	141	a b c d	166	a b c d	191	a b c d
117	a b c d	142	a b c d	167	a b c d	192	a b c d
118	a b c d	143	a b c d	168	a b c d	193	a b c d
119	a b c d	144	a b c d	169	a b c d	194	a b c d
120	a b c d	145	a b c d	170	a b c d	195	a b c d
121	a b c d	146	a b c d	171	a b c d	196	a b c d
122	a b c d	147	a b c d	172	a b c d	197	a b c d
123	a b c d	148	a b c d	173	a b c d	198	a b c d
124	a b c d	149	a b c d	174	a b c d	199	a b c d
125	a b c d	150	a b c d	175	a b c d	200	a b c d

ANSWER SHEETS
TEST ____

성명	수험번호				
	한글				
	영자				

	20 . .
응시일자	
맞은 개수	/ 100
환산 점수	/ 495

Listening Comprehension (PART I ~ PART IV)

1	ⓐ ⓑ ⓒ ⓓ	26	ⓐ ⓑ ⓒ	51	ⓐ ⓑ ⓒ ⓓ	76	ⓐ ⓑ ⓒ ⓓ
2	ⓐ ⓑ ⓒ ⓓ	27	ⓐ ⓑ ⓒ	52	ⓐ ⓑ ⓒ ⓓ	77	ⓐ ⓑ ⓒ ⓓ
3	ⓐ ⓑ ⓒ ⓓ	28	ⓐ ⓑ ⓒ	53	ⓐ ⓑ ⓒ ⓓ	78	ⓐ ⓑ ⓒ ⓓ
4	ⓐ ⓑ ⓒ ⓓ	29	ⓐ ⓑ ⓒ	54	ⓐ ⓑ ⓒ ⓓ	79	ⓐ ⓑ ⓒ ⓓ
5	ⓐ ⓑ ⓒ ⓓ	30	ⓐ ⓑ ⓒ	55	ⓐ ⓑ ⓒ ⓓ	80	ⓐ ⓑ ⓒ ⓓ
6	ⓐ ⓑ ⓒ ⓓ	31	ⓐ ⓑ ⓒ	56	ⓐ ⓑ ⓒ ⓓ	81	ⓐ ⓑ ⓒ ⓓ
7	ⓐ ⓑ ⓒ	32	ⓐ ⓑ ⓒ ⓓ	57	ⓐ ⓑ ⓒ ⓓ	82	ⓐ ⓑ ⓒ ⓓ
8	ⓐ ⓑ ⓒ	33	ⓐ ⓑ ⓒ ⓓ	58	ⓐ ⓑ ⓒ ⓓ	83	ⓐ ⓑ ⓒ ⓓ
9	ⓐ ⓑ ⓒ	34	ⓐ ⓑ ⓒ ⓓ	59	ⓐ ⓑ ⓒ ⓓ	84	ⓐ ⓑ ⓒ ⓓ
10	ⓐ ⓑ ⓒ	35	ⓐ ⓑ ⓒ ⓓ	60	ⓐ ⓑ ⓒ ⓓ	85	ⓐ ⓑ ⓒ ⓓ
11	ⓐ ⓑ ⓒ	36	ⓐ ⓑ ⓒ ⓓ	61	ⓐ ⓑ ⓒ ⓓ	86	ⓐ ⓑ ⓒ ⓓ
12	ⓐ ⓑ ⓒ	37	ⓐ ⓑ ⓒ ⓓ	62	ⓐ ⓑ ⓒ ⓓ	87	ⓐ ⓑ ⓒ ⓓ
13	ⓐ ⓑ ⓒ	38	ⓐ ⓑ ⓒ ⓓ	63	ⓐ ⓑ ⓒ ⓓ	88	ⓐ ⓑ ⓒ ⓓ
14	ⓐ ⓑ ⓒ	39	ⓐ ⓑ ⓒ ⓓ	64	ⓐ ⓑ ⓒ ⓓ	89	ⓐ ⓑ ⓒ ⓓ
15	ⓐ ⓑ ⓒ	40	ⓐ ⓑ ⓒ ⓓ	65	ⓐ ⓑ ⓒ ⓓ	90	ⓐ ⓑ ⓒ ⓓ
16	ⓐ ⓑ ⓒ	41	ⓐ ⓑ ⓒ ⓓ	66	ⓐ ⓑ ⓒ ⓓ	91	ⓐ ⓑ ⓒ ⓓ
17	ⓐ ⓑ ⓒ	42	ⓐ ⓑ ⓒ ⓓ	67	ⓐ ⓑ ⓒ ⓓ	92	ⓐ ⓑ ⓒ ⓓ
18	ⓐ ⓑ ⓒ	43	ⓐ ⓑ ⓒ ⓓ	68	ⓐ ⓑ ⓒ ⓓ	93	ⓐ ⓑ ⓒ ⓓ
19	ⓐ ⓑ ⓒ	44	ⓐ ⓑ ⓒ ⓓ	69	ⓐ ⓑ ⓒ ⓓ	94	ⓐ ⓑ ⓒ ⓓ
20	ⓐ ⓑ ⓒ	45	ⓐ ⓑ ⓒ ⓓ	70	ⓐ ⓑ ⓒ ⓓ	95	ⓐ ⓑ ⓒ ⓓ
21	ⓐ ⓑ ⓒ	46	ⓐ ⓑ ⓒ ⓓ	71	ⓐ ⓑ ⓒ ⓓ	96	ⓐ ⓑ ⓒ ⓓ
22	ⓐ ⓑ ⓒ	47	ⓐ ⓑ ⓒ ⓓ	72	ⓐ ⓑ ⓒ ⓓ	97	ⓐ ⓑ ⓒ ⓓ
23	ⓐ ⓑ ⓒ	48	ⓐ ⓑ ⓒ ⓓ	73	ⓐ ⓑ ⓒ ⓓ	98	ⓐ ⓑ ⓒ ⓓ
24	ⓐ ⓑ ⓒ	49	ⓐ ⓑ ⓒ ⓓ	74	ⓐ ⓑ ⓒ ⓓ	99	ⓐ ⓑ ⓒ ⓓ
25	ⓐ ⓑ ⓒ	50	ⓐ ⓑ ⓒ ⓓ	75	ⓐ ⓑ ⓒ ⓓ	100	ⓐ ⓑ ⓒ ⓓ

Reading Comprehension (PART V ~ PART VII)

101	ⓐ ⓑ ⓒ ⓓ	126	ⓐ ⓑ ⓒ ⓓ	151	ⓐ ⓑ ⓒ ⓓ	176	ⓐ ⓑ ⓒ ⓓ
102	ⓐ ⓑ ⓒ ⓓ	127	ⓐ ⓑ ⓒ ⓓ	152	ⓐ ⓑ ⓒ ⓓ	177	ⓐ ⓑ ⓒ ⓓ
103	ⓐ ⓑ ⓒ ⓓ	128	ⓐ ⓑ ⓒ ⓓ	153	ⓐ ⓑ ⓒ ⓓ	178	ⓐ ⓑ ⓒ ⓓ
104	ⓐ ⓑ ⓒ ⓓ	129	ⓐ ⓑ ⓒ ⓓ	154	ⓐ ⓑ ⓒ ⓓ	179	ⓐ ⓑ ⓒ ⓓ
105	ⓐ ⓑ ⓒ ⓓ	130	ⓐ ⓑ ⓒ ⓓ	155	ⓐ ⓑ ⓒ ⓓ	180	ⓐ ⓑ ⓒ ⓓ
106	ⓐ ⓑ ⓒ ⓓ	131	ⓐ ⓑ ⓒ ⓓ	156	ⓐ ⓑ ⓒ ⓓ	181	ⓐ ⓑ ⓒ ⓓ
107	ⓐ ⓑ ⓒ ⓓ	132	ⓐ ⓑ ⓒ ⓓ	157	ⓐ ⓑ ⓒ ⓓ	182	ⓐ ⓑ ⓒ ⓓ
108	ⓐ ⓑ ⓒ ⓓ	133	ⓐ ⓑ ⓒ ⓓ	158	ⓐ ⓑ ⓒ ⓓ	183	ⓐ ⓑ ⓒ ⓓ
109	ⓐ ⓑ ⓒ ⓓ	134	ⓐ ⓑ ⓒ ⓓ	159	ⓐ ⓑ ⓒ ⓓ	184	ⓐ ⓑ ⓒ ⓓ
110	ⓐ ⓑ ⓒ ⓓ	135	ⓐ ⓑ ⓒ ⓓ	160	ⓐ ⓑ ⓒ ⓓ	185	ⓐ ⓑ ⓒ ⓓ
111	ⓐ ⓑ ⓒ ⓓ	136	ⓐ ⓑ ⓒ ⓓ	161	ⓐ ⓑ ⓒ ⓓ	186	ⓐ ⓑ ⓒ ⓓ
112	ⓐ ⓑ ⓒ ⓓ	137	ⓐ ⓑ ⓒ ⓓ	162	ⓐ ⓑ ⓒ ⓓ	187	ⓐ ⓑ ⓒ ⓓ
113	ⓐ ⓑ ⓒ ⓓ	138	ⓐ ⓑ ⓒ ⓓ	163	ⓐ ⓑ ⓒ ⓓ	188	ⓐ ⓑ ⓒ ⓓ
114	ⓐ ⓑ ⓒ ⓓ	139	ⓐ ⓑ ⓒ ⓓ	164	ⓐ ⓑ ⓒ ⓓ	189	ⓐ ⓑ ⓒ ⓓ
115	ⓐ ⓑ ⓒ ⓓ	140	ⓐ ⓑ ⓒ ⓓ	165	ⓐ ⓑ ⓒ ⓓ	190	ⓐ ⓑ ⓒ ⓓ
116	ⓐ ⓑ ⓒ ⓓ	141	ⓐ ⓑ ⓒ ⓓ	166	ⓐ ⓑ ⓒ ⓓ	191	ⓐ ⓑ ⓒ ⓓ
117	ⓐ ⓑ ⓒ ⓓ	142	ⓐ ⓑ ⓒ ⓓ	167	ⓐ ⓑ ⓒ ⓓ	192	ⓐ ⓑ ⓒ ⓓ
118	ⓐ ⓑ ⓒ ⓓ	143	ⓐ ⓑ ⓒ ⓓ	168	ⓐ ⓑ ⓒ ⓓ	193	ⓐ ⓑ ⓒ ⓓ
119	ⓐ ⓑ ⓒ ⓓ	144	ⓐ ⓑ ⓒ ⓓ	169	ⓐ ⓑ ⓒ ⓓ	194	ⓐ ⓑ ⓒ ⓓ
120	ⓐ ⓑ ⓒ ⓓ	145	ⓐ ⓑ ⓒ ⓓ	170	ⓐ ⓑ ⓒ ⓓ	195	ⓐ ⓑ ⓒ ⓓ
121	ⓐ ⓑ ⓒ ⓓ	146	ⓐ ⓑ ⓒ ⓓ	171	ⓐ ⓑ ⓒ ⓓ	196	ⓐ ⓑ ⓒ ⓓ
122	ⓐ ⓑ ⓒ ⓓ	147	ⓐ ⓑ ⓒ ⓓ	172	ⓐ ⓑ ⓒ ⓓ	197	ⓐ ⓑ ⓒ ⓓ
123	ⓐ ⓑ ⓒ ⓓ	148	ⓐ ⓑ ⓒ ⓓ	173	ⓐ ⓑ ⓒ ⓓ	198	ⓐ ⓑ ⓒ ⓓ
124	ⓐ ⓑ ⓒ ⓓ	149	ⓐ ⓑ ⓒ ⓓ	174	ⓐ ⓑ ⓒ ⓓ	199	ⓐ ⓑ ⓒ ⓓ
125	ⓐ ⓑ ⓒ ⓓ	150	ⓐ ⓑ ⓒ ⓓ	175	ⓐ ⓑ ⓒ ⓓ	200	ⓐ ⓑ ⓒ ⓓ

✂ 자르는 선

ANSWER SHEETS
TEST ______________

수험번호		
성명	한글	
	영자	

응시일자	20 . . .
맞은 개수	/ 100
환산 점수	/ 495

Listening Comprehension (PART I ~ PART IV)

1	ⓐ ⓑ ⓒ ⓓ	26	ⓐ ⓑ ⓒ	51	ⓐ ⓑ ⓒ ⓓ	76	ⓐ ⓑ ⓒ ⓓ
2	ⓐ ⓑ ⓒ ⓓ	27	ⓐ ⓑ ⓒ	52	ⓐ ⓑ ⓒ ⓓ	77	ⓐ ⓑ ⓒ ⓓ
3	ⓐ ⓑ ⓒ ⓓ	28	ⓐ ⓑ ⓒ	53	ⓐ ⓑ ⓒ ⓓ	78	ⓐ ⓑ ⓒ ⓓ
4	ⓐ ⓑ ⓒ ⓓ	29	ⓐ ⓑ ⓒ	54	ⓐ ⓑ ⓒ ⓓ	79	ⓐ ⓑ ⓒ ⓓ
5	ⓐ ⓑ ⓒ ⓓ	30	ⓐ ⓑ ⓒ	55	ⓐ ⓑ ⓒ ⓓ	80	ⓐ ⓑ ⓒ ⓓ
6	ⓐ ⓑ ⓒ ⓓ	31	ⓐ ⓑ ⓒ	56	ⓐ ⓑ ⓒ ⓓ	81	ⓐ ⓑ ⓒ ⓓ
7	ⓐ ⓑ ⓒ	32	ⓐ ⓑ ⓒ ⓓ	57	ⓐ ⓑ ⓒ ⓓ	82	ⓐ ⓑ ⓒ ⓓ
8	ⓐ ⓑ ⓒ	33	ⓐ ⓑ ⓒ ⓓ	58	ⓐ ⓑ ⓒ ⓓ	83	ⓐ ⓑ ⓒ ⓓ
9	ⓐ ⓑ ⓒ	34	ⓐ ⓑ ⓒ ⓓ	59	ⓐ ⓑ ⓒ ⓓ	84	ⓐ ⓑ ⓒ ⓓ
10	ⓐ ⓑ ⓒ	35	ⓐ ⓑ ⓒ ⓓ	60	ⓐ ⓑ ⓒ ⓓ	85	ⓐ ⓑ ⓒ ⓓ
11	ⓐ ⓑ ⓒ	36	ⓐ ⓑ ⓒ ⓓ	61	ⓐ ⓑ ⓒ ⓓ	86	ⓐ ⓑ ⓒ ⓓ
12	ⓐ ⓑ ⓒ	37	ⓐ ⓑ ⓒ ⓓ	62	ⓐ ⓑ ⓒ ⓓ	87	ⓐ ⓑ ⓒ ⓓ
13	ⓐ ⓑ ⓒ	38	ⓐ ⓑ ⓒ ⓓ	63	ⓐ ⓑ ⓒ ⓓ	88	ⓐ ⓑ ⓒ ⓓ
14	ⓐ ⓑ ⓒ	39	ⓐ ⓑ ⓒ ⓓ	64	ⓐ ⓑ ⓒ ⓓ	89	ⓐ ⓑ ⓒ ⓓ
15	ⓐ ⓑ ⓒ	40	ⓐ ⓑ ⓒ ⓓ	65	ⓐ ⓑ ⓒ ⓓ	90	ⓐ ⓑ ⓒ ⓓ
16	ⓐ ⓑ ⓒ	41	ⓐ ⓑ ⓒ ⓓ	66	ⓐ ⓑ ⓒ ⓓ	91	ⓐ ⓑ ⓒ ⓓ
17	ⓐ ⓑ ⓒ	42	ⓐ ⓑ ⓒ ⓓ	67	ⓐ ⓑ ⓒ ⓓ	92	ⓐ ⓑ ⓒ ⓓ
18	ⓐ ⓑ ⓒ	43	ⓐ ⓑ ⓒ ⓓ	68	ⓐ ⓑ ⓒ ⓓ	93	ⓐ ⓑ ⓒ ⓓ
19	ⓐ ⓑ ⓒ	44	ⓐ ⓑ ⓒ ⓓ	69	ⓐ ⓑ ⓒ ⓓ	94	ⓐ ⓑ ⓒ ⓓ
20	ⓐ ⓑ ⓒ	45	ⓐ ⓑ ⓒ ⓓ	70	ⓐ ⓑ ⓒ ⓓ	95	ⓐ ⓑ ⓒ ⓓ
21	ⓐ ⓑ ⓒ	46	ⓐ ⓑ ⓒ ⓓ	71	ⓐ ⓑ ⓒ ⓓ	96	ⓐ ⓑ ⓒ ⓓ
22	ⓐ ⓑ ⓒ	47	ⓐ ⓑ ⓒ ⓓ	72	ⓐ ⓑ ⓒ ⓓ	97	ⓐ ⓑ ⓒ ⓓ
23	ⓐ ⓑ ⓒ	48	ⓐ ⓑ ⓒ ⓓ	73	ⓐ ⓑ ⓒ ⓓ	98	ⓐ ⓑ ⓒ ⓓ
24	ⓐ ⓑ ⓒ	49	ⓐ ⓑ ⓒ ⓓ	74	ⓐ ⓑ ⓒ ⓓ	99	ⓐ ⓑ ⓒ ⓓ
25	ⓐ ⓑ ⓒ	50	ⓐ ⓑ ⓒ ⓓ	75	ⓐ ⓑ ⓒ ⓓ	100	ⓐ ⓑ ⓒ ⓓ

Reading Comprehension (PART V ~ PART VII)

101	ⓐ ⓑ ⓒ ⓓ	126	ⓐ ⓑ ⓒ ⓓ	151	ⓐ ⓑ ⓒ ⓓ	176	ⓐ ⓑ ⓒ ⓓ
102	ⓐ ⓑ ⓒ ⓓ	127	ⓐ ⓑ ⓒ ⓓ	152	ⓐ ⓑ ⓒ ⓓ	177	ⓐ ⓑ ⓒ ⓓ
103	ⓐ ⓑ ⓒ ⓓ	128	ⓐ ⓑ ⓒ ⓓ	153	ⓐ ⓑ ⓒ ⓓ	178	ⓐ ⓑ ⓒ ⓓ
104	ⓐ ⓑ ⓒ ⓓ	129	ⓐ ⓑ ⓒ ⓓ	154	ⓐ ⓑ ⓒ ⓓ	179	ⓐ ⓑ ⓒ ⓓ
105	ⓐ ⓑ ⓒ ⓓ	130	ⓐ ⓑ ⓒ ⓓ	155	ⓐ ⓑ ⓒ ⓓ	180	ⓐ ⓑ ⓒ ⓓ
106	ⓐ ⓑ ⓒ ⓓ	131	ⓐ ⓑ ⓒ ⓓ	156	ⓐ ⓑ ⓒ ⓓ	181	ⓐ ⓑ ⓒ ⓓ
107	ⓐ ⓑ ⓒ ⓓ	132	ⓐ ⓑ ⓒ ⓓ	157	ⓐ ⓑ ⓒ ⓓ	182	ⓐ ⓑ ⓒ ⓓ
108	ⓐ ⓑ ⓒ ⓓ	133	ⓐ ⓑ ⓒ ⓓ	158	ⓐ ⓑ ⓒ ⓓ	183	ⓐ ⓑ ⓒ ⓓ
109	ⓐ ⓑ ⓒ ⓓ	134	ⓐ ⓑ ⓒ ⓓ	159	ⓐ ⓑ ⓒ ⓓ	184	ⓐ ⓑ ⓒ ⓓ
110	ⓐ ⓑ ⓒ ⓓ	135	ⓐ ⓑ ⓒ ⓓ	160	ⓐ ⓑ ⓒ ⓓ	185	ⓐ ⓑ ⓒ ⓓ
111	ⓐ ⓑ ⓒ ⓓ	136	ⓐ ⓑ ⓒ ⓓ	161	ⓐ ⓑ ⓒ ⓓ	186	ⓐ ⓑ ⓒ ⓓ
112	ⓐ ⓑ ⓒ ⓓ	137	ⓐ ⓑ ⓒ ⓓ	162	ⓐ ⓑ ⓒ ⓓ	187	ⓐ ⓑ ⓒ ⓓ
113	ⓐ ⓑ ⓒ ⓓ	138	ⓐ ⓑ ⓒ ⓓ	163	ⓐ ⓑ ⓒ ⓓ	188	ⓐ ⓑ ⓒ ⓓ
114	ⓐ ⓑ ⓒ ⓓ	139	ⓐ ⓑ ⓒ ⓓ	164	ⓐ ⓑ ⓒ ⓓ	189	ⓐ ⓑ ⓒ ⓓ
115	ⓐ ⓑ ⓒ ⓓ	140	ⓐ ⓑ ⓒ ⓓ	165	ⓐ ⓑ ⓒ ⓓ	190	ⓐ ⓑ ⓒ ⓓ
116	ⓐ ⓑ ⓒ ⓓ	141	ⓐ ⓑ ⓒ ⓓ	166	ⓐ ⓑ ⓒ ⓓ	191	ⓐ ⓑ ⓒ ⓓ
117	ⓐ ⓑ ⓒ ⓓ	142	ⓐ ⓑ ⓒ ⓓ	167	ⓐ ⓑ ⓒ ⓓ	192	ⓐ ⓑ ⓒ ⓓ
118	ⓐ ⓑ ⓒ ⓓ	143	ⓐ ⓑ ⓒ ⓓ	168	ⓐ ⓑ ⓒ ⓓ	193	ⓐ ⓑ ⓒ ⓓ
119	ⓐ ⓑ ⓒ ⓓ	144	ⓐ ⓑ ⓒ ⓓ	169	ⓐ ⓑ ⓒ ⓓ	194	ⓐ ⓑ ⓒ ⓓ
120	ⓐ ⓑ ⓒ ⓓ	145	ⓐ ⓑ ⓒ ⓓ	170	ⓐ ⓑ ⓒ ⓓ	195	ⓐ ⓑ ⓒ ⓓ
121	ⓐ ⓑ ⓒ ⓓ	146	ⓐ ⓑ ⓒ ⓓ	171	ⓐ ⓑ ⓒ ⓓ	196	ⓐ ⓑ ⓒ ⓓ
122	ⓐ ⓑ ⓒ ⓓ	147	ⓐ ⓑ ⓒ ⓓ	172	ⓐ ⓑ ⓒ ⓓ	197	ⓐ ⓑ ⓒ ⓓ
123	ⓐ ⓑ ⓒ ⓓ	148	ⓐ ⓑ ⓒ ⓓ	173	ⓐ ⓑ ⓒ ⓓ	198	ⓐ ⓑ ⓒ ⓓ
124	ⓐ ⓑ ⓒ ⓓ	149	ⓐ ⓑ ⓒ ⓓ	174	ⓐ ⓑ ⓒ ⓓ	199	ⓐ ⓑ ⓒ ⓓ
125	ⓐ ⓑ ⓒ ⓓ	150	ⓐ ⓑ ⓒ ⓓ	175	ⓐ ⓑ ⓒ ⓓ	200	ⓐ ⓑ ⓒ ⓓ

ANSWER SHEETS

TEST _____

✂ 자르는 선

수험번호								응시일자	20 · ·
성명	한글							맞은 개수	/ 100
	영자							환산 점수	/ 495

Listening Comprehension (PART I ~ PART IV)

Reading Comprehension (PART V ~ PART VII)

eng.conects.com

✂ 자르는 선

ANSWER SHEETS
TEST

수험번호						
성명	한글					
	영자					

응시일자	20 . .
맞은 개수	/ 100
환산 점수	/ 495

Listening Comprehension (PART I ~ PART IV)

1	ⓐ ⓑ ⓒ ⓓ	26	ⓐ ⓑ ⓒ ⓓ	51	ⓐ ⓑ ⓒ ⓓ	76	ⓐ ⓑ ⓒ ⓓ
2	ⓐ ⓑ ⓒ ⓓ	27	ⓐ ⓑ ⓒ ⓓ	52	ⓐ ⓑ ⓒ ⓓ	77	ⓐ ⓑ ⓒ ⓓ
3	ⓐ ⓑ ⓒ ⓓ	28	ⓐ ⓑ ⓒ ⓓ	53	ⓐ ⓑ ⓒ ⓓ	78	ⓐ ⓑ ⓒ ⓓ
4	ⓐ ⓑ ⓒ ⓓ	29	ⓐ ⓑ ⓒ ⓓ	54	ⓐ ⓑ ⓒ ⓓ	79	ⓐ ⓑ ⓒ ⓓ
5	ⓐ ⓑ ⓒ ⓓ	30	ⓐ ⓑ ⓒ ⓓ	55	ⓐ ⓑ ⓒ ⓓ	80	ⓐ ⓑ ⓒ ⓓ
6	ⓐ ⓑ ⓒ ⓓ	31	ⓐ ⓑ ⓒ ⓓ	56	ⓐ ⓑ ⓒ ⓓ	81	ⓐ ⓑ ⓒ ⓓ
7	ⓐ ⓑ ⓒ	32	ⓐ ⓑ ⓒ ⓓ	57	ⓐ ⓑ ⓒ ⓓ	82	ⓐ ⓑ ⓒ ⓓ
8	ⓐ ⓑ ⓒ	33	ⓐ ⓑ ⓒ ⓓ	58	ⓐ ⓑ ⓒ ⓓ	83	ⓐ ⓑ ⓒ ⓓ
9	ⓐ ⓑ ⓒ	34	ⓐ ⓑ ⓒ ⓓ	59	ⓐ ⓑ ⓒ ⓓ	84	ⓐ ⓑ ⓒ ⓓ
10	ⓐ ⓑ ⓒ	35	ⓐ ⓑ ⓒ ⓓ	60	ⓐ ⓑ ⓒ ⓓ	85	ⓐ ⓑ ⓒ ⓓ
11	ⓐ ⓑ ⓒ	36	ⓐ ⓑ ⓒ ⓓ	61	ⓐ ⓑ ⓒ ⓓ	86	ⓐ ⓑ ⓒ ⓓ
12	ⓐ ⓑ ⓒ ⓓ	37	ⓐ ⓑ ⓒ ⓓ	62	ⓐ ⓑ ⓒ ⓓ	87	ⓐ ⓑ ⓒ ⓓ
13	ⓐ ⓑ ⓒ ⓓ	38	ⓐ ⓑ ⓒ ⓓ	63	ⓐ ⓑ ⓒ ⓓ	88	ⓐ ⓑ ⓒ ⓓ
14	ⓐ ⓑ ⓒ	39	ⓐ ⓑ ⓒ ⓓ	64	ⓐ ⓑ ⓒ ⓓ	89	ⓐ ⓑ ⓒ ⓓ
15	ⓐ ⓑ ⓒ	40	ⓐ ⓑ ⓒ ⓓ	65	ⓐ ⓑ ⓒ ⓓ	90	ⓐ ⓑ ⓒ ⓓ
16	ⓐ ⓑ ⓒ	41	ⓐ ⓑ ⓒ ⓓ	66	ⓐ ⓑ ⓒ ⓓ	91	ⓐ ⓑ ⓒ ⓓ
17	ⓐ ⓑ ⓒ	42	ⓐ ⓑ ⓒ ⓓ	67	ⓐ ⓑ ⓒ ⓓ	92	ⓐ ⓑ ⓒ ⓓ
18	ⓐ ⓑ ⓒ	43	ⓐ ⓑ ⓒ ⓓ	68	ⓐ ⓑ ⓒ ⓓ	93	ⓐ ⓑ ⓒ ⓓ
19	ⓐ ⓑ ⓒ	44	ⓐ ⓑ ⓒ ⓓ	69	ⓐ ⓑ ⓒ ⓓ	94	ⓐ ⓑ ⓒ ⓓ
20	ⓐ ⓑ ⓒ	45	ⓐ ⓑ ⓒ ⓓ	70	ⓐ ⓑ ⓒ ⓓ	95	ⓐ ⓑ ⓒ ⓓ
21	ⓐ ⓑ ⓒ	46	ⓐ ⓑ ⓒ ⓓ	71	ⓐ ⓑ ⓒ ⓓ	96	ⓐ ⓑ ⓒ ⓓ
22	ⓐ ⓑ ⓒ	47	ⓐ ⓑ ⓒ ⓓ	72	ⓐ ⓑ ⓒ ⓓ	97	ⓐ ⓑ ⓒ ⓓ
23	ⓐ ⓑ ⓒ	48	ⓐ ⓑ ⓒ ⓓ	73	ⓐ ⓑ ⓒ ⓓ	98	ⓐ ⓑ ⓒ ⓓ
24	ⓐ ⓑ ⓒ	49	ⓐ ⓑ ⓒ ⓓ	74	ⓐ ⓑ ⓒ ⓓ	99	ⓐ ⓑ ⓒ ⓓ
25	ⓐ ⓑ ⓒ	50	ⓐ ⓑ ⓒ ⓓ	75	ⓐ ⓑ ⓒ ⓓ	100	ⓐ ⓑ ⓒ ⓓ

Reading Comprehension (PART V ~ PART VII)

101	ⓐ ⓑ ⓒ ⓓ	126	ⓐ ⓑ ⓒ ⓓ	151	ⓐ ⓑ ⓒ ⓓ	176	ⓐ ⓑ ⓒ ⓓ
102	ⓐ ⓑ ⓒ ⓓ	127	ⓐ ⓑ ⓒ ⓓ	152	ⓐ ⓑ ⓒ ⓓ	177	ⓐ ⓑ ⓒ ⓓ
103	ⓐ ⓑ ⓒ ⓓ	128	ⓐ ⓑ ⓒ ⓓ	153	ⓐ ⓑ ⓒ ⓓ	178	ⓐ ⓑ ⓒ ⓓ
104	ⓐ ⓑ ⓒ ⓓ	129	ⓐ ⓑ ⓒ ⓓ	154	ⓐ ⓑ ⓒ ⓓ	179	ⓐ ⓑ ⓒ ⓓ
105	ⓐ ⓑ ⓒ ⓓ	130	ⓐ ⓑ ⓒ ⓓ	155	ⓐ ⓑ ⓒ ⓓ	180	ⓐ ⓑ ⓒ ⓓ
106	ⓐ ⓑ ⓒ ⓓ	131	ⓐ ⓑ ⓒ ⓓ	156	ⓐ ⓑ ⓒ ⓓ	181	ⓐ ⓑ ⓒ ⓓ
107	ⓐ ⓑ ⓒ ⓓ	132	ⓐ ⓑ ⓒ ⓓ	157	ⓐ ⓑ ⓒ ⓓ	182	ⓐ ⓑ ⓒ ⓓ
108	ⓐ ⓑ ⓒ ⓓ	133	ⓐ ⓑ ⓒ ⓓ	158	ⓐ ⓑ ⓒ ⓓ	183	ⓐ ⓑ ⓒ ⓓ
109	ⓐ ⓑ ⓒ ⓓ	134	ⓐ ⓑ ⓒ ⓓ	159	ⓐ ⓑ ⓒ ⓓ	184	ⓐ ⓑ ⓒ ⓓ
110	ⓐ ⓑ ⓒ ⓓ	135	ⓐ ⓑ ⓒ ⓓ	160	ⓐ ⓑ ⓒ ⓓ	185	ⓐ ⓑ ⓒ ⓓ
111	ⓐ ⓑ ⓒ ⓓ	136	ⓐ ⓑ ⓒ ⓓ	161	ⓐ ⓑ ⓒ ⓓ	186	ⓐ ⓑ ⓒ ⓓ
112	ⓐ ⓑ ⓒ ⓓ	137	ⓐ ⓑ ⓒ ⓓ	162	ⓐ ⓑ ⓒ ⓓ	187	ⓐ ⓑ ⓒ ⓓ
113	ⓐ ⓑ ⓒ ⓓ	138	ⓐ ⓑ ⓒ ⓓ	163	ⓐ ⓑ ⓒ ⓓ	188	ⓐ ⓑ ⓒ ⓓ
114	ⓐ ⓑ ⓒ ⓓ	139	ⓐ ⓑ ⓒ ⓓ	164	ⓐ ⓑ ⓒ ⓓ	189	ⓐ ⓑ ⓒ ⓓ
115	ⓐ ⓑ ⓒ ⓓ	140	ⓐ ⓑ ⓒ ⓓ	165	ⓐ ⓑ ⓒ ⓓ	190	ⓐ ⓑ ⓒ ⓓ
116	ⓐ ⓑ ⓒ ⓓ	141	ⓐ ⓑ ⓒ ⓓ	166	ⓐ ⓑ ⓒ ⓓ	191	ⓐ ⓑ ⓒ ⓓ
117	ⓐ ⓑ ⓒ ⓓ	142	ⓐ ⓑ ⓒ ⓓ	167	ⓐ ⓑ ⓒ ⓓ	192	ⓐ ⓑ ⓒ ⓓ
118	ⓐ ⓑ ⓒ ⓓ	143	ⓐ ⓑ ⓒ ⓓ	168	ⓐ ⓑ ⓒ ⓓ	193	ⓐ ⓑ ⓒ ⓓ
119	ⓐ ⓑ ⓒ ⓓ	144	ⓐ ⓑ ⓒ ⓓ	169	ⓐ ⓑ ⓒ ⓓ	194	ⓐ ⓑ ⓒ ⓓ
120	ⓐ ⓑ ⓒ ⓓ	145	ⓐ ⓑ ⓒ ⓓ	170	ⓐ ⓑ ⓒ ⓓ	195	ⓐ ⓑ ⓒ ⓓ
121	ⓐ ⓑ ⓒ ⓓ	146	ⓐ ⓑ ⓒ ⓓ	171	ⓐ ⓑ ⓒ ⓓ	196	ⓐ ⓑ ⓒ ⓓ
122	ⓐ ⓑ ⓒ ⓓ	147	ⓐ ⓑ ⓒ ⓓ	172	ⓐ ⓑ ⓒ ⓓ	197	ⓐ ⓑ ⓒ ⓓ
123	ⓐ ⓑ ⓒ ⓓ	148	ⓐ ⓑ ⓒ ⓓ	173	ⓐ ⓑ ⓒ ⓓ	198	ⓐ ⓑ ⓒ ⓓ
124	ⓐ ⓑ ⓒ ⓓ	149	ⓐ ⓑ ⓒ ⓓ	174	ⓐ ⓑ ⓒ ⓓ	199	ⓐ ⓑ ⓒ ⓓ
125	ⓐ ⓑ ⓒ ⓓ	150	ⓐ ⓑ ⓒ ⓓ	175	ⓐ ⓑ ⓒ ⓓ	200	ⓐ ⓑ ⓒ ⓓ

eng.conects.com

ANSWER SHEETS
TEST ____

eng.conects.com

수험번호								응시일자	20 . .
성명	한글							맞은 개수	/ 100
	영자							환산 점수	/ 495

Listening Comprehension (PART I ~ PART IV)

1	ⓐ ⓑ ⓒ ⓓ	26	ⓐ ⓑ ⓒ ⓓ	51	ⓐ ⓑ ⓒ ⓓ	76	ⓐ ⓑ ⓒ ⓓ
2	ⓐ ⓑ ⓒ ⓓ	27	ⓐ ⓑ ⓒ ⓓ	52	ⓐ ⓑ ⓒ ⓓ	77	ⓐ ⓑ ⓒ ⓓ
3	ⓐ ⓑ ⓒ ⓓ	28	ⓐ ⓑ ⓒ ⓓ	53	ⓐ ⓑ ⓒ ⓓ	78	ⓐ ⓑ ⓒ ⓓ
4	ⓐ ⓑ ⓒ ⓓ	29	ⓐ ⓑ ⓒ ⓓ	54	ⓐ ⓑ ⓒ ⓓ	79	ⓐ ⓑ ⓒ ⓓ
5	ⓐ ⓑ ⓒ ⓓ	30	ⓐ ⓑ ⓒ ⓓ	55	ⓐ ⓑ ⓒ ⓓ	80	ⓐ ⓑ ⓒ ⓓ
6	ⓐ ⓑ ⓒ ⓓ	31	ⓐ ⓑ ⓒ ⓓ	56	ⓐ ⓑ ⓒ ⓓ	81	ⓐ ⓑ ⓒ ⓓ
7	ⓐ ⓑ ⓒ	32	ⓐ ⓑ ⓒ ⓓ	57	ⓐ ⓑ ⓒ ⓓ	82	ⓐ ⓑ ⓒ ⓓ
8	ⓐ ⓑ ⓒ ⓓ	33	ⓐ ⓑ ⓒ ⓓ	58	ⓐ ⓑ ⓒ ⓓ	83	ⓐ ⓑ ⓒ ⓓ
9	ⓐ ⓑ ⓒ ⓓ	34	ⓐ ⓑ ⓒ ⓓ	59	ⓐ ⓑ ⓒ ⓓ	84	ⓐ ⓑ ⓒ ⓓ
10	ⓐ ⓑ ⓒ ⓓ	35	ⓐ ⓑ ⓒ ⓓ	60	ⓐ ⓑ ⓒ ⓓ	85	ⓐ ⓑ ⓒ ⓓ
11	ⓐ ⓑ ⓒ ⓓ	36	ⓐ ⓑ ⓒ ⓓ	61	ⓐ ⓑ ⓒ ⓓ	86	ⓐ ⓑ ⓒ ⓓ
12	ⓐ ⓑ ⓒ ⓓ	37	ⓐ ⓑ ⓒ ⓓ	62	ⓐ ⓑ ⓒ ⓓ	87	ⓐ ⓑ ⓒ ⓓ
13	ⓐ ⓑ ⓒ ⓓ	38	ⓐ ⓑ ⓒ ⓓ	63	ⓐ ⓑ ⓒ ⓓ	88	ⓐ ⓑ ⓒ ⓓ
14	ⓐ ⓑ ⓒ	39	ⓐ ⓑ ⓒ ⓓ	64	ⓐ ⓑ ⓒ ⓓ	89	ⓐ ⓑ ⓒ ⓓ
15	ⓐ ⓑ ⓒ ⓓ	40	ⓐ ⓑ ⓒ ⓓ	65	ⓐ ⓑ ⓒ ⓓ	90	ⓐ ⓑ ⓒ ⓓ
16	ⓐ ⓑ ⓒ ⓓ	41	ⓐ ⓑ ⓒ ⓓ	66	ⓐ ⓑ ⓒ ⓓ	91	ⓐ ⓑ ⓒ ⓓ
17	ⓐ ⓑ ⓒ ⓓ	42	ⓐ ⓑ ⓒ ⓓ	67	ⓐ ⓑ ⓒ ⓓ	92	ⓐ ⓑ ⓒ ⓓ
18	ⓐ ⓑ ⓒ ⓓ	43	ⓐ ⓑ ⓒ ⓓ	68	ⓐ ⓑ ⓒ ⓓ	93	ⓐ ⓑ ⓒ ⓓ
19	ⓐ ⓑ ⓒ ⓓ	44	ⓐ ⓑ ⓒ ⓓ	69	ⓐ ⓑ ⓒ ⓓ	94	ⓐ ⓑ ⓒ ⓓ
20	ⓐ ⓑ ⓒ ⓓ	45	ⓐ ⓑ ⓒ ⓓ	70	ⓐ ⓑ ⓒ ⓓ	95	ⓐ ⓑ ⓒ ⓓ
21	ⓐ ⓑ ⓒ ⓓ	46	ⓐ ⓑ ⓒ ⓓ	71	ⓐ ⓑ ⓒ ⓓ	96	ⓐ ⓑ ⓒ ⓓ
22	ⓐ ⓑ ⓒ ⓓ	47	ⓐ ⓑ ⓒ ⓓ	72	ⓐ ⓑ ⓒ ⓓ	97	ⓐ ⓑ ⓒ ⓓ
23	ⓐ ⓑ ⓒ ⓓ	48	ⓐ ⓑ ⓒ ⓓ	73	ⓐ ⓑ ⓒ ⓓ	98	ⓐ ⓑ ⓒ ⓓ
24	ⓐ ⓑ ⓒ ⓓ	49	ⓐ ⓑ ⓒ ⓓ	74	ⓐ ⓑ ⓒ ⓓ	99	ⓐ ⓑ ⓒ ⓓ
25	ⓐ ⓑ ⓒ ⓓ	50	ⓐ ⓑ ⓒ ⓓ	75	ⓐ ⓑ ⓒ ⓓ	100	ⓐ ⓑ ⓒ ⓓ

Reading Comprehension (PART V ~ PART VII)

101	ⓐ ⓑ ⓒ ⓓ	126	ⓐ ⓑ ⓒ ⓓ	151	ⓐ ⓑ ⓒ ⓓ	176	ⓐ ⓑ ⓒ ⓓ
102	ⓐ ⓑ ⓒ ⓓ	127	ⓐ ⓑ ⓒ ⓓ	152	ⓐ ⓑ ⓒ ⓓ	177	ⓐ ⓑ ⓒ ⓓ
103	ⓐ ⓑ ⓒ ⓓ	128	ⓐ ⓑ ⓒ ⓓ	153	ⓐ ⓑ ⓒ ⓓ	178	ⓐ ⓑ ⓒ ⓓ
104	ⓐ ⓑ ⓒ ⓓ	129	ⓐ ⓑ ⓒ ⓓ	154	ⓐ ⓑ ⓒ ⓓ	179	ⓐ ⓑ ⓒ ⓓ
105	ⓐ ⓑ ⓒ ⓓ	130	ⓐ ⓑ ⓒ ⓓ	155	ⓐ ⓑ ⓒ ⓓ	180	ⓐ ⓑ ⓒ ⓓ
106	ⓐ ⓑ ⓒ ⓓ	131	ⓐ ⓑ ⓒ ⓓ	156	ⓐ ⓑ ⓒ ⓓ	181	ⓐ ⓑ ⓒ ⓓ
107	ⓐ ⓑ ⓒ ⓓ	132	ⓐ ⓑ ⓒ ⓓ	157	ⓐ ⓑ ⓒ ⓓ	182	ⓐ ⓑ ⓒ ⓓ
108	ⓐ ⓑ ⓒ ⓓ	133	ⓐ ⓑ ⓒ ⓓ	158	ⓐ ⓑ ⓒ ⓓ	183	ⓐ ⓑ ⓒ ⓓ
109	ⓐ ⓑ ⓒ ⓓ	134	ⓐ ⓑ ⓒ ⓓ	159	ⓐ ⓑ ⓒ ⓓ	184	ⓐ ⓑ ⓒ ⓓ
110	ⓐ ⓑ ⓒ ⓓ	135	ⓐ ⓑ ⓒ ⓓ	160	ⓐ ⓑ ⓒ ⓓ	185	ⓐ ⓑ ⓒ ⓓ
111	ⓐ ⓑ ⓒ ⓓ	136	ⓐ ⓑ ⓒ ⓓ	161	ⓐ ⓑ ⓒ ⓓ	186	ⓐ ⓑ ⓒ ⓓ
112	ⓐ ⓑ ⓒ ⓓ	137	ⓐ ⓑ ⓒ ⓓ	162	ⓐ ⓑ ⓒ ⓓ	187	ⓐ ⓑ ⓒ ⓓ
113	ⓐ ⓑ ⓒ ⓓ	138	ⓐ ⓑ ⓒ ⓓ	163	ⓐ ⓑ ⓒ ⓓ	188	ⓐ ⓑ ⓒ ⓓ
114	ⓐ ⓑ ⓒ ⓓ	139	ⓐ ⓑ ⓒ ⓓ	164	ⓐ ⓑ ⓒ ⓓ	189	ⓐ ⓑ ⓒ ⓓ
115	ⓐ ⓑ ⓒ ⓓ	140	ⓐ ⓑ ⓒ ⓓ	165	ⓐ ⓑ ⓒ ⓓ	190	ⓐ ⓑ ⓒ ⓓ
116	ⓐ ⓑ ⓒ ⓓ	141	ⓐ ⓑ ⓒ ⓓ	166	ⓐ ⓑ ⓒ ⓓ	191	ⓐ ⓑ ⓒ ⓓ
117	ⓐ ⓑ ⓒ ⓓ	142	ⓐ ⓑ ⓒ ⓓ	167	ⓐ ⓑ ⓒ ⓓ	192	ⓐ ⓑ ⓒ ⓓ
118	ⓐ ⓑ ⓒ ⓓ	143	ⓐ ⓑ ⓒ ⓓ	168	ⓐ ⓑ ⓒ ⓓ	193	ⓐ ⓑ ⓒ ⓓ
119	ⓐ ⓑ ⓒ ⓓ	144	ⓐ ⓑ ⓒ ⓓ	169	ⓐ ⓑ ⓒ ⓓ	194	ⓐ ⓑ ⓒ ⓓ
120	ⓐ ⓑ ⓒ ⓓ	145	ⓐ ⓑ ⓒ ⓓ	170	ⓐ ⓑ ⓒ ⓓ	195	ⓐ ⓑ ⓒ ⓓ
121	ⓐ ⓑ ⓒ ⓓ	146	ⓐ ⓑ ⓒ ⓓ	171	ⓐ ⓑ ⓒ ⓓ	196	ⓐ ⓑ ⓒ ⓓ
122	ⓐ ⓑ ⓒ ⓓ	147	ⓐ ⓑ ⓒ ⓓ	172	ⓐ ⓑ ⓒ ⓓ	197	ⓐ ⓑ ⓒ ⓓ
123	ⓐ ⓑ ⓒ ⓓ	148	ⓐ ⓑ ⓒ ⓓ	173	ⓐ ⓑ ⓒ ⓓ	198	ⓐ ⓑ ⓒ ⓓ
124	ⓐ ⓑ ⓒ ⓓ	149	ⓐ ⓑ ⓒ ⓓ	174	ⓐ ⓑ ⓒ ⓓ	199	ⓐ ⓑ ⓒ ⓓ
125	ⓐ ⓑ ⓒ ⓓ	150	ⓐ ⓑ ⓒ ⓓ	175	ⓐ ⓑ ⓒ ⓓ	200	ⓐ ⓑ ⓒ ⓓ

자르는 선

자르는 선

ANSWER SHEETS
TEST _____

수험번호							

성명	한글	
	영자	

응시일자	20 . . .
맞은 개수	/ 100
환산 점수	/ 495

Listening Comprehension (PART I ~ PART IV)

	a b c d		a b c d		a b c d
1	ⓐ ⓑ ⓒ ⓓ	26	ⓐ ⓑ ⓒ ⓓ	51	ⓐ ⓑ ⓒ ⓓ
2	ⓐ ⓑ ⓒ ⓓ	27	ⓐ ⓑ ⓒ ⓓ	52	ⓐ ⓑ ⓒ ⓓ
3	ⓐ ⓑ ⓒ ⓓ	28	ⓐ ⓑ ⓒ ⓓ	53	ⓐ ⓑ ⓒ ⓓ
4	ⓐ ⓑ ⓒ ⓓ	29	ⓐ ⓑ ⓒ ⓓ	54	ⓐ ⓑ ⓒ ⓓ
5	ⓐ ⓑ ⓒ ⓓ	30	ⓐ ⓑ ⓒ ⓓ	55	ⓐ ⓑ ⓒ ⓓ
6	ⓐ ⓑ ⓒ ⓓ	31	ⓐ ⓑ ⓒ ⓓ	56	ⓐ ⓑ ⓒ ⓓ
7	ⓐ ⓑ ⓒ	32	ⓐ ⓑ ⓒ ⓓ	57	ⓐ ⓑ ⓒ ⓓ
8	ⓐ ⓑ ⓒ	33	ⓐ ⓑ ⓒ ⓓ	58	ⓐ ⓑ ⓒ ⓓ
9	ⓐ ⓑ ⓒ	34	ⓐ ⓑ ⓒ ⓓ	59	ⓐ ⓑ ⓒ ⓓ
10	ⓐ ⓑ ⓒ	35	ⓐ ⓑ ⓒ ⓓ	60	ⓐ ⓑ ⓒ ⓓ
11	ⓐ ⓑ ⓒ	36	ⓐ ⓑ ⓒ ⓓ	61	ⓐ ⓑ ⓒ ⓓ
12	ⓐ ⓑ ⓒ	37	ⓐ ⓑ ⓒ ⓓ	62	ⓐ ⓑ ⓒ ⓓ
13	ⓐ ⓑ ⓒ	38	ⓐ ⓑ ⓒ ⓓ	63	ⓐ ⓑ ⓒ ⓓ
14	ⓐ ⓑ ⓒ	39	ⓐ ⓑ ⓒ ⓓ	64	ⓐ ⓑ ⓒ ⓓ
15	ⓐ ⓑ ⓒ	40	ⓐ ⓑ ⓒ ⓓ	65	ⓐ ⓑ ⓒ ⓓ
16	ⓐ ⓑ ⓒ	41	ⓐ ⓑ ⓒ ⓓ	66	ⓐ ⓑ ⓒ ⓓ
17	ⓐ ⓑ ⓒ	42	ⓐ ⓑ ⓒ ⓓ	67	ⓐ ⓑ ⓒ ⓓ
18	ⓐ ⓑ ⓒ	43	ⓐ ⓑ ⓒ ⓓ	68	ⓐ ⓑ ⓒ ⓓ
19	ⓐ ⓑ ⓒ	44	ⓐ ⓑ ⓒ ⓓ	69	ⓐ ⓑ ⓒ ⓓ
20	ⓐ ⓑ ⓒ	45	ⓐ ⓑ ⓒ ⓓ	70	ⓐ ⓑ ⓒ ⓓ
21	ⓐ ⓑ ⓒ	46	ⓐ ⓑ ⓒ ⓓ	71	ⓐ ⓑ ⓒ ⓓ
22	ⓐ ⓑ ⓒ	47	ⓐ ⓑ ⓒ ⓓ	72	ⓐ ⓑ ⓒ ⓓ
23	ⓐ ⓑ ⓒ	48	ⓐ ⓑ ⓒ ⓓ	73	ⓐ ⓑ ⓒ ⓓ
24	ⓐ ⓑ ⓒ	49	ⓐ ⓑ ⓒ ⓓ	74	ⓐ ⓑ ⓒ ⓓ
25	ⓐ ⓑ ⓒ	50	ⓐ ⓑ ⓒ ⓓ	75	ⓐ ⓑ ⓒ ⓓ
		76	ⓐ ⓑ ⓒ ⓓ		
		77	ⓐ ⓑ ⓒ ⓓ		
		78	ⓐ ⓑ ⓒ ⓓ		
		79	ⓐ ⓑ ⓒ ⓓ		
		80	ⓐ ⓑ ⓒ ⓓ		
		81	ⓐ ⓑ ⓒ ⓓ		
		82	ⓐ ⓑ ⓒ ⓓ		
		83	ⓐ ⓑ ⓒ ⓓ		
		84	ⓐ ⓑ ⓒ ⓓ		
		85	ⓐ ⓑ ⓒ ⓓ		
		86	ⓐ ⓑ ⓒ ⓓ		
		87	ⓐ ⓑ ⓒ ⓓ		
		88	ⓐ ⓑ ⓒ ⓓ		
		89	ⓐ ⓑ ⓒ ⓓ		
		90	ⓐ ⓑ ⓒ ⓓ		
		91	ⓐ ⓑ ⓒ ⓓ		
		92	ⓐ ⓑ ⓒ ⓓ		
		93	ⓐ ⓑ ⓒ ⓓ		
		94	ⓐ ⓑ ⓒ ⓓ		
		95	ⓐ ⓑ ⓒ ⓓ		
		96	ⓐ ⓑ ⓒ ⓓ		
		97	ⓐ ⓑ ⓒ ⓓ		
		98	ⓐ ⓑ ⓒ ⓓ		
		99	ⓐ ⓑ ⓒ ⓓ		
		100	ⓐ ⓑ ⓒ ⓓ		

Reading Comprehension (PART V ~ PART VII)

	a b c d		a b c d		a b c d
101	ⓐ ⓑ ⓒ ⓓ	126	ⓐ ⓑ ⓒ ⓓ	151	ⓐ ⓑ ⓒ ⓓ	176	ⓐ ⓑ ⓒ ⓓ
102	ⓐ ⓑ ⓒ ⓓ	127	ⓐ ⓑ ⓒ ⓓ	152	ⓐ ⓑ ⓒ ⓓ	177	ⓐ ⓑ ⓒ ⓓ
103	ⓐ ⓑ ⓒ ⓓ	128	ⓐ ⓑ ⓒ ⓓ	153	ⓐ ⓑ ⓒ ⓓ	178	ⓐ ⓑ ⓒ ⓓ
104	ⓐ ⓑ ⓒ ⓓ	129	ⓐ ⓑ ⓒ ⓓ	154	ⓐ ⓑ ⓒ ⓓ	179	ⓐ ⓑ ⓒ ⓓ
105	ⓐ ⓑ ⓒ ⓓ	130	ⓐ ⓑ ⓒ ⓓ	155	ⓐ ⓑ ⓒ ⓓ	180	ⓐ ⓑ ⓒ ⓓ
106	ⓐ ⓑ ⓒ ⓓ	131	ⓐ ⓑ ⓒ ⓓ	156	ⓐ ⓑ ⓒ ⓓ	181	ⓐ ⓑ ⓒ ⓓ
107	ⓐ ⓑ ⓒ ⓓ	132	ⓐ ⓑ ⓒ ⓓ	157	ⓐ ⓑ ⓒ ⓓ	182	ⓐ ⓑ ⓒ ⓓ
108	ⓐ ⓑ ⓒ ⓓ	133	ⓐ ⓑ ⓒ ⓓ	158	ⓐ ⓑ ⓒ ⓓ	183	ⓐ ⓑ ⓒ ⓓ
109	ⓐ ⓑ ⓒ ⓓ	134	ⓐ ⓑ ⓒ ⓓ	159	ⓐ ⓑ ⓒ ⓓ	184	ⓐ ⓑ ⓒ ⓓ
110	ⓐ ⓑ ⓒ ⓓ	135	ⓐ ⓑ ⓒ ⓓ	160	ⓐ ⓑ ⓒ ⓓ	185	ⓐ ⓑ ⓒ ⓓ
111	ⓐ ⓑ ⓒ ⓓ	136	ⓐ ⓑ ⓒ ⓓ	161	ⓐ ⓑ ⓒ ⓓ	186	ⓐ ⓑ ⓒ ⓓ
112	ⓐ ⓑ ⓒ ⓓ	137	ⓐ ⓑ ⓒ ⓓ	162	ⓐ ⓑ ⓒ ⓓ	187	ⓐ ⓑ ⓒ ⓓ
113	ⓐ ⓑ ⓒ ⓓ	138	ⓐ ⓑ ⓒ ⓓ	163	ⓐ ⓑ ⓒ ⓓ	188	ⓐ ⓑ ⓒ ⓓ
114	ⓐ ⓑ ⓒ ⓓ	139	ⓐ ⓑ ⓒ ⓓ	164	ⓐ ⓑ ⓒ ⓓ	189	ⓐ ⓑ ⓒ ⓓ
115	ⓐ ⓑ ⓒ ⓓ	140	ⓐ ⓑ ⓒ ⓓ	165	ⓐ ⓑ ⓒ ⓓ	190	ⓐ ⓑ ⓒ ⓓ
116	ⓐ ⓑ ⓒ ⓓ	141	ⓐ ⓑ ⓒ ⓓ	166	ⓐ ⓑ ⓒ ⓓ	191	ⓐ ⓑ ⓒ ⓓ
117	ⓐ ⓑ ⓒ ⓓ	142	ⓐ ⓑ ⓒ ⓓ	167	ⓐ ⓑ ⓒ ⓓ	192	ⓐ ⓑ ⓒ ⓓ
118	ⓐ ⓑ ⓒ ⓓ	143	ⓐ ⓑ ⓒ ⓓ	168	ⓐ ⓑ ⓒ ⓓ	193	ⓐ ⓑ ⓒ ⓓ
119	ⓐ ⓑ ⓒ ⓓ	144	ⓐ ⓑ ⓒ ⓓ	169	ⓐ ⓑ ⓒ ⓓ	194	ⓐ ⓑ ⓒ ⓓ
120	ⓐ ⓑ ⓒ ⓓ	145	ⓐ ⓑ ⓒ ⓓ	170	ⓐ ⓑ ⓒ ⓓ	195	ⓐ ⓑ ⓒ ⓓ
121	ⓐ ⓑ ⓒ ⓓ	146	ⓐ ⓑ ⓒ ⓓ	171	ⓐ ⓑ ⓒ ⓓ	196	ⓐ ⓑ ⓒ ⓓ
122	ⓐ ⓑ ⓒ ⓓ	147	ⓐ ⓑ ⓒ ⓓ	172	ⓐ ⓑ ⓒ ⓓ	197	ⓐ ⓑ ⓒ ⓓ
123	ⓐ ⓑ ⓒ ⓓ	148	ⓐ ⓑ ⓒ ⓓ	173	ⓐ ⓑ ⓒ ⓓ	198	ⓐ ⓑ ⓒ ⓓ
124	ⓐ ⓑ ⓒ ⓓ	149	ⓐ ⓑ ⓒ ⓓ	174	ⓐ ⓑ ⓒ ⓓ	199	ⓐ ⓑ ⓒ ⓓ
125	ⓐ ⓑ ⓒ ⓓ	150	ⓐ ⓑ ⓒ ⓓ	175	ⓐ ⓑ ⓒ ⓓ	200	ⓐ ⓑ ⓒ ⓓ

ANSWER SHEETS
TEST _____

수험번호							
성명	한글						
	영자						

응시일자	20 . .
맞은 개수	/ 100
환산 점수	/ 495

Listening Comprehension (PART I ~ PART IV)

#	a b c d	#	a b c d
1	ⓐ ⓑ ⓒ	26	ⓐ ⓑ ⓒ ⓓ
2	ⓐ ⓑ ⓒ	27	ⓐ ⓑ ⓒ ⓓ
3	ⓐ ⓑ ⓒ	28	ⓐ ⓑ ⓒ ⓓ
4	ⓐ ⓑ ⓒ	29	ⓐ ⓑ ⓒ ⓓ
5	ⓐ ⓑ ⓒ	30	ⓐ ⓑ ⓒ ⓓ
6	ⓐ ⓑ ⓒ	31	ⓐ ⓑ ⓒ ⓓ
7	ⓐ ⓑ ⓒ	32	ⓐ ⓑ ⓒ ⓓ
8	ⓐ ⓑ ⓒ	33	ⓐ ⓑ ⓒ ⓓ
9	ⓐ ⓑ ⓒ	34	ⓐ ⓑ ⓒ ⓓ
10	ⓐ ⓑ ⓒ	35	ⓐ ⓑ ⓒ ⓓ
11	ⓐ ⓑ ⓒ	36	ⓐ ⓑ ⓒ ⓓ
12	ⓐ ⓑ ⓒ	37	ⓐ ⓑ ⓒ ⓓ
13	ⓐ ⓑ ⓒ	38	ⓐ ⓑ ⓒ ⓓ
14	ⓐ ⓑ ⓒ	39	ⓐ ⓑ ⓒ ⓓ
15	ⓐ ⓑ ⓒ	40	ⓐ ⓑ ⓒ ⓓ
16	ⓐ ⓑ ⓒ	41	ⓐ ⓑ ⓒ ⓓ
17	ⓐ ⓑ ⓒ	42	ⓐ ⓑ ⓒ ⓓ
18	ⓐ ⓑ ⓒ	43	ⓐ ⓑ ⓒ ⓓ
19	ⓐ ⓑ ⓒ	44	ⓐ ⓑ ⓒ ⓓ
20	ⓐ ⓑ ⓒ	45	ⓐ ⓑ ⓒ ⓓ
21	ⓐ ⓑ ⓒ	46	ⓐ ⓑ ⓒ ⓓ
22	ⓐ ⓑ ⓒ	47	ⓐ ⓑ ⓒ ⓓ
23	ⓐ ⓑ ⓒ	48	ⓐ ⓑ ⓒ ⓓ
24	ⓐ ⓑ ⓒ	49	ⓐ ⓑ ⓒ ⓓ
25	ⓐ ⓑ ⓒ	50	ⓐ ⓑ ⓒ ⓓ
51	ⓐ ⓑ ⓒ ⓓ	76	ⓐ ⓑ ⓒ ⓓ
52	ⓐ ⓑ ⓒ ⓓ	77	ⓐ ⓑ ⓒ ⓓ
53	ⓐ ⓑ ⓒ ⓓ	78	ⓐ ⓑ ⓒ ⓓ
54	ⓐ ⓑ ⓒ ⓓ	79	ⓐ ⓑ ⓒ ⓓ
55	ⓐ ⓑ ⓒ ⓓ	80	ⓐ ⓑ ⓒ ⓓ
56	ⓐ ⓑ ⓒ ⓓ	81	ⓐ ⓑ ⓒ ⓓ
57	ⓐ ⓑ ⓒ ⓓ	82	ⓐ ⓑ ⓒ ⓓ
58	ⓐ ⓑ ⓒ ⓓ	83	ⓐ ⓑ ⓒ ⓓ
59	ⓐ ⓑ ⓒ ⓓ	84	ⓐ ⓑ ⓒ ⓓ
60	ⓐ ⓑ ⓒ ⓓ	85	ⓐ ⓑ ⓒ ⓓ
61	ⓐ ⓑ ⓒ ⓓ	86	ⓐ ⓑ ⓒ ⓓ
62	ⓐ ⓑ ⓒ ⓓ	87	ⓐ ⓑ ⓒ ⓓ
63	ⓐ ⓑ ⓒ ⓓ	88	ⓐ ⓑ ⓒ ⓓ
64	ⓐ ⓑ ⓒ ⓓ	89	ⓐ ⓑ ⓒ ⓓ
65	ⓐ ⓑ ⓒ ⓓ	90	ⓐ ⓑ ⓒ ⓓ
66	ⓐ ⓑ ⓒ ⓓ	91	ⓐ ⓑ ⓒ ⓓ
67	ⓐ ⓑ ⓒ ⓓ	92	ⓐ ⓑ ⓒ ⓓ
68	ⓐ ⓑ ⓒ ⓓ	93	ⓐ ⓑ ⓒ ⓓ
69	ⓐ ⓑ ⓒ ⓓ	94	ⓐ ⓑ ⓒ ⓓ
70	ⓐ ⓑ ⓒ ⓓ	95	ⓐ ⓑ ⓒ ⓓ
71	ⓐ ⓑ ⓒ ⓓ	96	ⓐ ⓑ ⓒ ⓓ
72	ⓐ ⓑ ⓒ ⓓ	97	ⓐ ⓑ ⓒ ⓓ
73	ⓐ ⓑ ⓒ ⓓ	98	ⓐ ⓑ ⓒ ⓓ
74	ⓐ ⓑ ⓒ ⓓ	99	ⓐ ⓑ ⓒ ⓓ
75	ⓐ ⓑ ⓒ ⓓ	100	ⓐ ⓑ ⓒ ⓓ

Reading Comprehension (PART V ~ PART VII)

#	a b c d	#	a b c d	#	a b c d
101	ⓐ ⓑ ⓒ ⓓ	126	ⓐ ⓑ ⓒ ⓓ	151	ⓐ ⓑ ⓒ ⓓ
102	ⓐ ⓑ ⓒ ⓓ	127	ⓐ ⓑ ⓒ ⓓ	152	ⓐ ⓑ ⓒ ⓓ
103	ⓐ ⓑ ⓒ ⓓ	128	ⓐ ⓑ ⓒ ⓓ	153	ⓐ ⓑ ⓒ ⓓ
104	ⓐ ⓑ ⓒ ⓓ	129	ⓐ ⓑ ⓒ ⓓ	154	ⓐ ⓑ ⓒ ⓓ
105	ⓐ ⓑ ⓒ ⓓ	130	ⓐ ⓑ ⓒ ⓓ	155	ⓐ ⓑ ⓒ ⓓ
106	ⓐ ⓑ ⓒ ⓓ	131	ⓐ ⓑ ⓒ ⓓ	156	ⓐ ⓑ ⓒ ⓓ
107	ⓐ ⓑ ⓒ ⓓ	132	ⓐ ⓑ ⓒ ⓓ	157	ⓐ ⓑ ⓒ ⓓ
108	ⓐ ⓑ ⓒ ⓓ	133	ⓐ ⓑ ⓒ ⓓ	158	ⓐ ⓑ ⓒ ⓓ
109	ⓐ ⓑ ⓒ ⓓ	134	ⓐ ⓑ ⓒ ⓓ	159	ⓐ ⓑ ⓒ ⓓ
110	ⓐ ⓑ ⓒ ⓓ	135	ⓐ ⓑ ⓒ ⓓ	160	ⓐ ⓑ ⓒ ⓓ
111	ⓐ ⓑ ⓒ ⓓ	136	ⓐ ⓑ ⓒ ⓓ	161	ⓐ ⓑ ⓒ ⓓ
112	ⓐ ⓑ ⓒ ⓓ	137	ⓐ ⓑ ⓒ ⓓ	162	ⓐ ⓑ ⓒ ⓓ
113	ⓐ ⓑ ⓒ ⓓ	138	ⓐ ⓑ ⓒ ⓓ	163	ⓐ ⓑ ⓒ ⓓ
114	ⓐ ⓑ ⓒ ⓓ	139	ⓐ ⓑ ⓒ ⓓ	164	ⓐ ⓑ ⓒ ⓓ
115	ⓐ ⓑ ⓒ ⓓ	140	ⓐ ⓑ ⓒ ⓓ	165	ⓐ ⓑ ⓒ ⓓ
116	ⓐ ⓑ ⓒ ⓓ	141	ⓐ ⓑ ⓒ ⓓ	166	ⓐ ⓑ ⓒ ⓓ
117	ⓐ ⓑ ⓒ ⓓ	142	ⓐ ⓑ ⓒ ⓓ	167	ⓐ ⓑ ⓒ ⓓ
118	ⓐ ⓑ ⓒ ⓓ	143	ⓐ ⓑ ⓒ ⓓ	168	ⓐ ⓑ ⓒ ⓓ
119	ⓐ ⓑ ⓒ ⓓ	144	ⓐ ⓑ ⓒ ⓓ	169	ⓐ ⓑ ⓒ ⓓ
120	ⓐ ⓑ ⓒ ⓓ	145	ⓐ ⓑ ⓒ ⓓ	170	ⓐ ⓑ ⓒ ⓓ
121	ⓐ ⓑ ⓒ ⓓ	146	ⓐ ⓑ ⓒ ⓓ	171	ⓐ ⓑ ⓒ ⓓ
122	ⓐ ⓑ ⓒ ⓓ	147	ⓐ ⓑ ⓒ ⓓ	172	ⓐ ⓑ ⓒ ⓓ
123	ⓐ ⓑ ⓒ ⓓ	148	ⓐ ⓑ ⓒ ⓓ	173	ⓐ ⓑ ⓒ ⓓ
124	ⓐ ⓑ ⓒ ⓓ	149	ⓐ ⓑ ⓒ ⓓ	174	ⓐ ⓑ ⓒ ⓓ
125	ⓐ ⓑ ⓒ ⓓ	150	ⓐ ⓑ ⓒ ⓓ	175	ⓐ ⓑ ⓒ ⓓ
				176	ⓐ ⓑ ⓒ ⓓ
				177	ⓐ ⓑ ⓒ ⓓ
				178	ⓐ ⓑ ⓒ ⓓ
				179	ⓐ ⓑ ⓒ ⓓ
				180	ⓐ ⓑ ⓒ ⓓ
				181	ⓐ ⓑ ⓒ ⓓ
				182	ⓐ ⓑ ⓒ ⓓ
				183	ⓐ ⓑ ⓒ ⓓ
				184	ⓐ ⓑ ⓒ ⓓ
				185	ⓐ ⓑ ⓒ ⓓ
				186	ⓐ ⓑ ⓒ ⓓ
				187	ⓐ ⓑ ⓒ ⓓ
				188	ⓐ ⓑ ⓒ ⓓ
				189	ⓐ ⓑ ⓒ ⓓ
				190	ⓐ ⓑ ⓒ ⓓ
				191	ⓐ ⓑ ⓒ ⓓ
				192	ⓐ ⓑ ⓒ ⓓ
				193	ⓐ ⓑ ⓒ ⓓ
				194	ⓐ ⓑ ⓒ ⓓ
				195	ⓐ ⓑ ⓒ ⓓ
				196	ⓐ ⓑ ⓒ ⓓ
				197	ⓐ ⓑ ⓒ ⓓ
				198	ⓐ ⓑ ⓒ ⓓ
				199	ⓐ ⓑ ⓒ ⓓ
				200	ⓐ ⓑ ⓒ ⓓ

ANSWER SHEETS

TEST _____

자르는 선 ✂

수험번호							
성명	한글						
	영자						

응시일자	20 . . .
맞은 개수	/ 100
환산 점수	/ 495

eng.conects.com

Listening Comprehension (PART I ~ PART IV)

(OMR answer grid, questions 1–100, options ⓐ ⓑ ⓒ ⓓ)

Questions 1–6 contain four options (ⓐ ⓑ ⓒ ⓓ); questions 7–100 contain fewer.

Reading Comprehension (PART V ~ PART VII)

(OMR answer grid, questions 101–200, options ⓐ ⓑ ⓒ ⓓ)

ANSWER SHEETS
TEST

✂ 자르는 선

eng.conects.com

수험번호				응시일자	20 . .
성명	한글			맞은 개수	/ 100
	영자			환산 점수	/ 495

Listening Comprehension (PART I ~ PART IV)

(answer bubbles a, b, c, d for questions 1–100)

Reading Comprehension (PART V ~ PART VII)

(answer bubbles a, b, c, d for questions 101–200)